First published August 2021

© Copyright 2021 Robert Tearle

www.roberttearle.com

All rights reserved. This book may not be reproduced in any form, in whole or in part, without written permission from the author.

The headhunter's story

by Robert Tearle

Preface

Before I get started on telling my story, I'd like to share some thoughts with you.

It was so unfair! The first in our age group to die.

Once you progress beyond the age of 10, most people kind of know what death is, before that perhaps you're a little too young to understand.

Most likely, aged under 10, perhaps someone died in the street where you lived. In your second or third decade, your grandparents may have died.

Our experience of death is that it happens to older people, not younger ones. People who have lived their lives, lived them largely to the full. Life expectancy is what? Late 70s, 80s?

As our lives unfold, we live in communities shaped by family, friends and people we work with. Our closest friends are those in our own age group. I've sometimes heard of people in their late 70s having bets on "Who's going to die first"? They chuckle in their humour and with grace.

It was so unfair.

In my age group, she was the first to die. We were all late 40s, not 60s or 70s. Her illness came as a shock to everyone. No one is immortal. You can always earn more money, but you can never buy your life back.

This book is as much about her as it is about me. We were like two peas in a pod, and when her life fell apart, so did mine.

All will be revealed.

I'm going to take you through my journey in life, how my childhood influenced my adulthood and shaped my personality.

How I seized my chances, how my marriage unfolded, how I set up my own business, enjoyed spectacular success with holidays to the sort of places you dream of, flying on Concorde and enjoying a glamorous lifestyle.

Life is never straightforward. It crashed down around me.

Let me tell you more!

Contents

Introduction 1

No ordinary childhood 3

On the way up... 31

Hitting the big time 84

The turning point 118

The aftermath 156

The pursuit of happiness 190

Covid 238

Appendices

Underneath the iceberg 265

Chronic stress 282

Counselling 287

The underlying financial cost 290

My magic bullet 296

What I've done to recover 302

Great expectations 312

Introduction

This book is about the ups and downs of life. It's my story.

From modest beginnings in the industrial North of England, my father was posted abroad, and I was sent to boarding school aged 7.

How I then eventually hit the big time in recruitment, living in an 11-bedroomed house, playing polo and enjoying a millionaire lifestyle.

We all dream of making lots of money, driving fast cars, living in a big house and flying first class to faraway places.

In my story, I share with you my journey to making it and how my life then unravelled.

It's about how I wasn't happy, proceeded to encounter one crisis after another, experiencing emotional trauma, tremendous highs and lows. I would never have imagined my life would be such a spectacular and unpredictable journey.

Men don't open up about abuse and feelings. I do.

Whilst many books are about people who made a fortune, and how they made it, this book's about how I made a fortune and lost it.

About a man, the complex feelings of a man talking about things men don't want to open up about – things I don't want to open up about.

Hero to zero is a phenomenon.

This is real life story outlining the crises I've experienced in my life, including finding love, making millions, encountering setbacks of a titanic nature, separation and freedom following despair.

Being crushed by what had happened.

It's about handling crises, anxiety, chronic stress and grief; what I've done to recover and how I ultimately found happiness.

There are anecdotes in this book about my experiences as a headhunter. Some people will be curious about what I've got to say about the nature of my work, so I've included some snippets and insights.

If these anecdotes are not for you, I hope you'll simply skip through them and enjoy the read.

How admiring someone can turn into despising them.

You never know what goes on behind closed doors. However, I'm going to share with you some of the realities of life about marriage, alcoholism, grief and emotional breakdown.

And how I confused money with happiness.

The break-up of a marriage.

Falling into honey traps.

And how I came to discover our real pursuit should be the one of happiness.

We all think that we have a long lifetime in which to live, work and love, most likely to give us a 70–80-year journey.

However, it is not guaranteed, and we must appreciate and take advantage of every day, week, month, year….

Life's not a dress rehearsal. You live it just once. You cannot go back in time and have another go.

We must seize our chances in life.

❉ ❉ ❉

Chapter 1

No ordinary childhood

From modest beginnings to the polo fields.

What you are about to read is my story. One about the ups and downs of life, in the form of a story. Because I've spent so much of my time as a recruitment consultant and head-hunter, I have learned things and made observations about careers, what makes or break success, so I've included some of my insights because they may resonate well with you, help you, or help someone you care about.

In this book I have shared some of my experiences of stress, anxiety and depression, again in the hope they may help you or someone you know.

You'll see that frequently I have been repetitious. This has been in an effort to re-enforce some of the challenges I have faced, how I truly felt and how powerful emotions can be.

OK, so let's get started, here's my story.

I was born in Leeds, in the North of England.

My mother's mother was a seamstress, her father a warehouseman. I remember visiting them when I was perhaps 4, 5 or 6 years old. Their house was in a cobbled street, a poor street with proud people. No central heating back then, in the winter it was really cold inside the house, I remember in the coldest winter months the windows would freeze on the inside. A tin bath, and the toilets were outside down the street.

When I reflect back on it, and it is humbling to think about, it would not have been an easy life nor glamourous life in a post war era. Leeds forming part of the industrial north, houses including my mother's parents' one, were in a street in which all the stone houses were heavily blackened by the coal used in furnaces and homes, pushing out smoke with tons of soot in it. It was a back-to-back terrace house, two storeys and an attic.

My father's parents were wealthier. In their time they ran various businesses, the last one running a pub. My Dad is bright, works hard, applies himself well and

No ordinary childhood

he got into grammar school. Post war he studied Russian and listened to and translated Russian military movements on the radio.

By the time I was born, my father worked for Goodyear (a US tyre manufacturer) as a salesman. I was the youngest of 3 boys. My father was supporting a household of 5. He wanted to earn more money and got an amazing opportunity, a posting to Finland.

So aged 4, I was moved to Finland, and went to kindergarten there.

To put this into perspective, this was in an era in which in the UK approximately 40% of the population holidayed within the UK, 40% holidayed in Spain and 20% stayed at home, they didn't have a holiday at all.

Going somewhere like Finland to live was very much like an adventure.

Finland borders the Arctic circle and Russia. At times it's been occupied by Russia and in its capital Helsinki the style of the buildings is really similar to much of what you'd expect to see in Russia, ranging from beautiful churches to more austere 5 or 6 storey apartment blocks with little or no character. In parts of Helsinki it felt very much like the Soviet Union.

The Finnish language sounds a bit like a mix of Swedish and Russian, so the feeling it gave me as a 4-year-old boy was somewhat intimidating, although the Finns are a quiet, introverted but kind type of people.

Finland, the land of a thousand lakes.

We first arrived in Finland in the winter, when there was an abundance of snow everywhere, long nights, short days… just 6 hours, imagine that's like it being light from 9.30 to 3.30.

I remember for the first few weeks we stayed in a bed and breakfast type hotel, what the French would call a pension, it was perhaps 5 floors high, a town house, looking onto a park, We arrived one evening and the owner of the place had bought my two brothers and I sledges.

It was cold, it was exciting.

The Finnish summers in contrast, seemingly endless days, daylight runs for as much as 19 hours.

It was c. 1970 and at the time of "the cold war".

No ordinary childhood

Mum and Dad's first home in Finland was an apartment just across the courtyard from the Russian embassy. Was this a co-incidence or was there something more to this?

It was a magnificent apartment in a mansion block, I remember it well, its exterior was painted predominantly yellow and with the main wooden structural parts in white, on the corners of the first floor where our apartment was, it had a round alcove, the floors in the apartment were wooden, it had fireplaces, was stunning to look at and a really nice place to live.

I remember it was in a fabulous location, close to the centre of Helsinki which meant my older brothers and I could walk out and play in the local park. It was also close to the harbour.

One of the things I liked most was seeing the ships and cruise liners come in to harbour. I'd be thinking what was the cargo, where had the people come from, who were they, what were they doing?

When we first moved to Finland, we flew there. However, on some of our other trips back and forth between Finland and England we journeyed through Sweden, and got the ship across the North Sea, which was always rocky and exciting.

My memories are of the winter being snow filled ones. I'd go sledging with my brothers in the park, often we'd go down the ice slide in our sledges… dangerous but fun.

We'd bomb down the ice slides, our sledges rattling on the ice, bumping into the side walls, our knuckles would get knocked. It was both exhilarating and scary.

Mum and Dad would regularly take us out to the forests in the surrounding countryside to Helsinki and we'd go cross-country skiing which is like running on skis which we often did going through the forests, it was great but tiring. If we were lucky, we got hot chocolate afterwards.

Finland is heavily forested, which means there's lots of wood, the population is small in comparison to the size of the country, so there's lots of countryside, and there are lots of beautiful wooden houses… most Finns who live in a town or city also have a country house.

No ordinary childhood

In the summer, we enjoyed several holidays in the lakes staying in wooden summer houses. In the morning we'd take a bar of soap and wash in the lake. It was really cold water which sharpened us up in the morning, there was no pollution back then.

I remember there was a time when the school I attended in Finland must have told my Mum and Dad that they had worries about me. I believe they may have drawn the conclusion that I was disruptive.

They arranged for a specialist to see me and assess me. I had to do a variety of tests, some written, some puzzles and things like that. My understanding is that the conclusion was that I was an excitable personality type and hopefully I'd settle down.

I'm pretty sure that today this is what is known as ADHD. Here's how the UK Health Service describes it:

"Attention deficit hyperactivity disorder (ADHD) is a group of behavioural symptoms that include inattentiveness, hyperactivity and impulsiveness. Symptoms of ADHD tend to be noticed at an early age and may become more noticeable when a child's circumstances change, such as when they start school."

Sums me up pretty well!

And I was soon to return to England and go to another school.

My parents no doubt had ambition. In fact, my father is a great example of people who make a lot of themselves.

I'm sure they wanted to create a good life for the family comprising mum and dad and my two elder brothers.

Today we live in a global world and one in which opportunity is wide open to most people. Back then this was not the case, most people living their entire lives in the town in which they were born. Most people from modest, working class backgrounds, would have had limited opportunity.

In those days life was not prosperous for the majority, it was only prosperous for a very small minority.

My mother and father seized their opportunity for advancement which benefited the entire family. However, this was not without cost. They spent

No ordinary childhood

much of their time abroad whilst my brothers and I were at boarding school.

Aged 7, I was sent away to boarding school at "Bronte House". My father's employer company "Goodyear" paid for this.

"Bone et Fidelis"

I joined the school mid-year; I was the new boy in an established class. I remember the first night I stayed there. I had seen the film King Kong during the day and had a related nightmare that night. I cried out loud in my sleep, waking myself up and the entire dorm. The word dormitory (aka dorm) means a bedroom in an institution such as a boarding school and in this dorm, there were perhaps a dozen boys.

To this day I can recall one or more of them saying "It´s the new boy."

I remember it being daunting, I had joined a class group of boys who had pre-established mates and so I felt like the outsider!

In the morning, I woke up in unfamiliar territory, strange surroundings. Who were these boys, where were my mum and dad, and where was I?

This was a very young age to be at boarding school and away from your parents. I was there aged 7-11, the place was austere, school uniform comprised dark grey shorts, white shirts, green blazer and tie. It was formal, very disciplined and regimented.

The school motto was "Bone et Fidelis". Latin translated into English "Good and Faithful". If you stepped out of line you'd be punished and normally beaten with a stick or cane.

To start off with I felt like an outsider, which meant I was seeking to fit in with the classmates and establish friends. I was seeking approval of both the school kids in my year and the masters and teachers.

I have memories of my time at Bronte House, some good, some not so good.

One memory is of the annual school Christmas Carol services. The school had a substantial hall, which had a large ground floor area, a staircase which rose around two sides and on the first floor, a balcony surrounding all sides.

Candles were placed throughout the hallway and lit shortly before the service commenced, and all of us boys would be upstairs, out of sight, waiting for the start of the event.

No ordinary childhood

The parents would arrive and take to their seats in the hallway, and then the service would commence with a pianist starting to play the first carol. Slowly us boys would walk in a procession from the bedrooms upstairs onto the balcony and down to the bottom of the stairs, where those first in the queue would stop, with the remainder backed up behind them, up the staircase.

We´d sing the carols, prayers would be read and then afterwards there would be tea, coffee and cake for the parents and the kids.

With few exceptions, all the boys' parents would be there. I was, of course, one of the exceptions. There was an aspect of this which to me felt pointless – why do this if your parents weren't there? The other boys' parents were there like a family unit, I felt detached in comparison. I felt part of it but not part of it, the odd one out, the lonely one all by himself.

I´d like to have been one of those kids chosen for key parts in plays and whose parents were there at the Christmas carols. I was never first nor best at anything and there were times when I felt like the rejected one.

The school was set in an amazing location. The grounds were extensive and the main school building, which was built in the Victorian era, was expansive, had huge rooms, big windows and lots of ornate period features including the plasterwork ceiling cornices and centre piece features, magnificent mid to dark wood panelling and large fireplaces.

The place was simultaneously austere and amazing, as was the disciplined environment and routine. We all had a number; can you believe it? We were all given numbers, mine was a 3 digit one.

It was a Methodist school, all very structured, strict on timekeeping, lots of activities and tasks in a fixed routine. From getting up in the morning immediately the bell went off, to having a glass of milk before going to bed.

Much of it made sense. Why every once in a while, we'd all be forced into having cold baths I do not know. We were little boys not older ones with testosterone. In hindsight this was very peculiar, they would run cold baths i.e., fill up the bath from empty to near full using the cold water tap.

And then, we'd get in the bath one by one!

One of the things I enjoyed whilst at boarding school was the expeditions.

No ordinary childhood

Perhaps once in every two or three months there would be a day trip or overnight stay away. These were ordinarily walking and sightseeing based ones.

There would be a group of us little boys, perhaps 10 to 25 and we'd jump in mini-buses and off we'd go. Even better, sometimes if it was a small group, we'd go in the school Land Rover – you know, one of the original types. All packed in together with rucksacks on the roof, it was exciting.

We'd head off in the Land Rover and up into the depths of the countryside. Arriving late afternoon or early evening, we'd stay at a hostel. Supper would be soup and bread.

I remember one trip in particular, a walking one, to some of the high peaks and it being really windy and cold. Having arrived at night, we'd set off the following morning on our trek. It became apparent I´d got flu and would have to return by myself to the hostel in which we were staying, whilst everyone else went on ahead.

So, they all headed up the hills, some more like mountains, and I went the other way by myself, down the hill. I'd been told to go to the nearest main road, find a bus stop and get the bus to take me back to the hostel.

A farmer kindly picked me up in his Land Rover Defender, it was lovely and warm in his car, and he bought me fish and chips. At boarding school, the food was meagre and the menu monotonous, this was a real treat, and then returned me to the hostel, the kindness of a stranger, this was my favourite part of the trip.

I have good and bad memories of boarding school. After playing sports in the winter, we'd all get showered in the sports changing rooms. It could be cold in the winter, freezing, sometimes we'd be playing football in the snow and afterwards having these hot showers, was truly uplifting.

In the summer we'd mainly play cricket and for me the highlight was tea, sandwiches and cakes. It's not that I'm a heavy eater, but most of the time at school you'd be hungry. Not always great food, and often not too much of it.

I wasn´t the brightest boy nor the most stupid. What I really enjoyed was playing sports. I was good at most sports but not exceptional at any of them, albeit in several I was a contender for the best in class.

No ordinary childhood

One of the games at which I excelled was table tennis, others being swimming and cricket. Whilst I did well in the table tennis league games, when it came to more competitive ones, those with spectators, I failed to reach my full potential.

Whenever it came to playing in competitive tournaments, I would be nervous and self-conscious which would compromise my performance.

This is something which has impacted my entire life. I am not as confident as I should be, I am frequently nervous in front of people, even in areas in which I am strong and should have little or no reason to be anxious.

Why should I be nervous at something if I'm good at it?

I am still nervous to this day although much of the time I´m able to hide it.

If you were to meet me, you might not realise I am nervous and shy. However, I am. Although I am often the person who will talk to strangers, get people talking and mingling together.

Your early years shape your personality and they influenced mine. My early years were at boarding school.

In the absence of family support whenever faced with challenges or problems, you must persist by yourself. With no-one to talk to, you've got to get on with things yourself and this builds a certain resolve.

Emotionally you can't open up to anyone about your worries, problems or difficulties. So, you bottle up your thoughts and emotions, and keep them to yourself.

That's what I did.

I am very persistent, which is a good trait, and keep things to myself, which is potentially a very negative one.

For me, I had no ordinary childhood.

Aged 8/9 Mum and Dad moved to Lebanon. I used to see them three times a year in the holidays, flying out in the Spring, Summer and Winter.

Dad was a Regional Sales Manager (salesperson) representing Goodyear (a massive US tyre manufacturer) across much of the Middle East. The region was quite unsettled then (still is today) and he would travel to Afghanistan, Iran, Iraq, Jordan, Saudi, Yemen… on business.

No ordinary childhood

The capital of Lebanon is Beirut, where the summers are warm, muggy and arid, extremely hot unless you're in the mountains. The winters in contrast were wet, cool and at times cold.

We were lucky. Goodyear paid for their housing, and they paid for me and my two brothers to fly out to Lebanon three times a year during school vacations. The first place where Mum and Dad lived was the upper floor flat of a two-storey building.

It was outside of Beirut in the hills and had fabulous balconies looking down towards the sea. I remember it to this day including the setting, one with quite extreme heat, a lot of dryness and these undulating hills covered with green shrubs and trees, descending towards the sea. I remember the sound of crickets, chirping in the background, mainly heard not seen, added to the strange beauty of the place.

In the summer evenings, we would often sit on the balcony looking down towards in the sea, you´d be able to see the lights of the houses below, the ships and boats.

Immediately below us there was a block of flats which was being built, we looked on most nights observing their progress, it had three levels including the ground floor, and I recall the builders working on it day after day.

At night the builders would sleep in the warm open air on the second floor, they´d light a small fire and I remember on one occasion they sacrificed a lamb and cooked it on the open fire.

A very different culture from our own.

In Lebanon there are certain times of the year when you can ski in the mountains in the morning and swim in the sea in the afternoon.

I have fond memories of Lebanon. It has a superb climate, is a beautiful country and one with great diversity, heavily mixed with very rich and very poor, Muslims and Christians co-exist!

When I came to Lebanon it was the first time I'd seen slums and shanty towns in which people were living in huts, primarily constructed from used tin cans, bits of wood, no sanitation, no running water or drainage. Many were living in just one room and they looked dirty, perhaps with just one set of clothes,

No ordinary childhood

children without shoes.

No colourful clothes, just bland colours, black, khaki, tatty clothes.

These houses, or perhaps best described as make-shift accommodation were not on streets as we know them, simply located on ground, rock and soil.

I have a distant memory of seeing these shanty towns and the people who lived in them. What hope did these people have of any meaningful life? In comparison, I was getting a good education and in the fullness of time would have tremendous opportunities presented to me. I remember seeing dirty beggars on the sides of the streets in the poorer neighbourhoods, many missing limbs, unable to work.

These shanty towns were adjacent to some of the best neighbourhoods.

The poorest living next door to the richest.

We should never forget how fortunate we are!

A call to prayer.

Lebanon, like all other Arabic countries, has considerable mystique about it. I remember hearing "Allahu Akbar" being wailed from minarets (towers) at mosques, neither a threatening sound nor warm one. To me it all sounded very foreign.

I felt in unfamiliar territory like an outsider.

The sound being projected from these minarets was the Islamic call to prayer and is something that's existed for some 1,500 years.

These calls to prayer would be made several times each day, sometime as early as 4.00am.

Muslims use the term "Allahu Akbar" to remind themselves that God is greater than the beauty and ugliness of this world.

For me, hearing these calls to prayer was a cultural awakening and I found the whole place fascinating. It's culture and climate were extreme, hot and dry in comparison to our own, a very alien environment.

On our trips, we'd do some of the regular family stuff but also some privileged activities as well. I remember swimming at the golf and country club, and on one occasion seeing Concorde flying overhead on its test flight.

No ordinary childhood

Little did I know that in years to come, I would have the good fortune to travel on Concorde myself!

In the early 20th Century Lebanon was governed by France. Lebanon kind of blended the French style with Arabic one, the middle-class Lebanese are a very stylish nationality which contrasts with the working class.

In Beirut in the space of 1 minute you could drive from slums to streets with the most elegant French style town houses. You'd see beggars and boutiques. I remember once driving down a buzzy road, and a poor man was crossing it with crutches. He must have had one of his legs removed and had a patch over one of his eyes, perhaps he'd lost an eye too. Similarly, you'd see street dogs at the roadside, some with a missing leg.

The extremes were remarkable, at its best, the playground for the rich and famous.

Film stars and rich Arabs would spend holidays or weekends in Beirut, it has an impressive waterfront "The Corniche". For me Beirut has the glamour you'd associate with Monte Carlo.

I was impressed with the chic style of the place, of the rich people and their way of life, this was the lifestyle that I wanted to live when I grew up.

Prior to visiting Lebanon I'd only lived in England and Finland; I'd not been to hot countries like Lebanon where you could swim in the warm sea. It was both off the beaten track, yet cosmopolitan. I remember going to restaurants and the food was great, they had wonderful displays of sweet dishes, puddings etc.

Central Beirut and notably the seafront area was vibrant, with upmarket hotels with French names like the Saint George and Le Commodore. Most with swimming pools adjacent to the sea, people sunbathing and drinking cocktails, similarly upmarket Beirut Sporting Club… a young boy c. 10 years old at the time, boy oh boy was I impressed, I hoped when I grew up, I'd be able to enjoy such a lifestyle.

In Beirut, there were lots of rich people living next door to poor ones, and the further you travelled out of it, generally you'd see poorer areas with poorer people.

Years later I would read a book by Jeffrey Archer, in which he said, the only

No ordinary childhood

difference between two people being "the cot they were born into".

Some of us are far luckier in life than others. We lived in a four-bedroom flat, in a great area, there were families of 5 or more living in a single room dwelling in Beirut.

During the school vacations, my brothers and I would travel out to Lebanon and were fortunate to visit places of historic interest such as Byblos on the Mediterranean Sea and Baalbek which is inland, both ancient cities with human habitation going back 8,000 years.

On our winter trips, we were fortunate to go skiing on several occasions.

In the summer we had some spectacular holidays. The one which stands out most in my mind, was the one to visit "The lost city of Petra" in Jordan, this is one of the wonders the world.

We travelled through Syria to Petra in southern Jordan.

Petra dates back to the 4th Century BC, with buildings and homes carved out of red rock, and with amazing waterways. The site remained unknown to the Western world until 1812, when it was discovered by a Swiss explorer, a remarkable place to visit.

We went on from Petra to holiday in Jordan's Red Sea coast of Aqaba and finished off the trip with a visit to the Dead Sea.

In so many ways I had a privileged upbringing.

The other holiday which still resonates with me today was one to Turkey. We travelled by car from Lebanon, through Syria and to Turkey, this was long before Turkey was a recognised, popular international holiday destination.

I remember our destination was a place called Bodrum, now a major tourist destination. However, back then for us it was Bodrum Castle to which we were headed. This medieval fortress is one of the Seven Wonders of the Ancient World, completed in the 4th century BC.

Being young I was fascinated by the castles in Turkey and to an extent the rich history of the whole region which in times gone by had been ruled by different powers: Hittites, Trojans, Persians, Macedonians, Romans, Byzantines, Seljuks and Ottomans.

I was fortunate to visit many countries, places of natural beauty and historic

No ordinary childhood

interest before they were subject to mass tourism.

No tourist hotels back then, no motorways, no signposted tourist attractions. However, the coastline was extraordinarily beautiful, perhaps a bit like the South of France and I remember us driving along the windy coast listening to the popular track of the time… Seasons in the Sun (initially sung by Terry Jacks and later Westlife):

"We had joy, we had fun. We had seasons in the sun. But the wine and the song, like the seasons, have all gone."

It's a man's world, or at least it was back then.

I distinctly remember the contrast of the then traditional Turkish people against a backdrop of beach areas, crystal turquoise seas and a handful of tourists.

The Turkish men covered shoulder to toe wearing white robes and white headgear, obviously a colour which would keep them cool in the baking heat of the summer, and women likewise covered in black robes and headgear obviously retaining the heat more.

At cafés in the streets, you'd see men smoking from hookahs (bubble pipes) – you know those contraptions, hot water bubbling away at the bottom, heating up Turkish tobacco, the vapour carried through rubber pipes to the smoker's mouth.

To have visited these countries at that time, says a lot about my mother and father, really quite brave and adventurous, this was before these countries had become international in their perspective and before mass tourism compromised some of the authenticity of really quite majestic places, with a deep history like Turkey.

Aged 8-11, I was privileged to enjoy special things like skiing, visiting the lost City of Petra, Babylon, The Dead Sea…

Mum and Dad subsequently moved into Central Beirut, "the Paris of the Middle East."

This was in contrast to living in the hills on the outside of Beirut. In the capital itself we were able to walk around the city, it was one in transition with a blend of the old and the new, the climate was perfect, and I remember several evenings when we walked to, and home from the cinema, walking through the

No ordinary childhood

city in the heat of the night.

It was around this time that my father was promoted to manager of Goodyear's Middle East business, which meant that he started managing people and no doubt got a significant salary increase.

Lebanon is an impressive country, Beirut magnificent.

I was very fortunate to spend so much time in such a beautiful country.

However, towards the end of our time there, troubles started to emerge. With disagreements between different factions of society, fighting among one another, I remember as a family walking home one night from the cinema, gunfire could be heard, and you could see people around the corner with guns.

A civil war was unfolding.

The upsides of my life at that time were travelling to these fascinating faraway places. However, the downsides were that it compromised having a close family life.

Most of the time I was at boarding school, term time represented 37 weeks of the year, 24 hours a day, 7 days a week. So I was away from my Mum and Dad the majority of the time, and we would exchange letters weekly. No mobile phones or internet back then.

Communication was by post, typically arriving upwards of 5 days after it was sent.

Which meant I felt isolated and quite alone. I had to keep my feelings to myself. I can't say that I was bullied significantly, nor could I say I was in the in-crowd. I was firmly in the upper half of the ability levels in sports, and in the lower half in studies.

There were times when I felt somewhat rejected and didn't really have the close loving family setup that most people enjoy. Not that my family were not loving. We were removed from each other and whilst my parents were the caring kind, they weren't the tactile close knit touchy feely type.

At school there were day boys and boarders.

The day boys attended school during the regular hours 9.00 to 5.30, Monday to Friday and the boarders stayed 24/7 during term time, seven days a week.

No ordinary childhood

For us boarders there were nominated weekends in which we could return to our families and the school would be like a ghost town. Of the c. 500 children some 7 or 8 would remain behind who were unable to go home for whatever reason. These were some of the most difficult for me, and the handful of us who remained at school whilst the other kids would be picked up by their parents, return home and treated for the weekend.

In this small group I found myself feeling somewhat abandoned, isolated and unwanted.

During these times in the evening, I´d sometimes think of the other children in the warmth of their homes, with their families and being treated to even some of the most basic things in life which you cherish. A cake, a cup of tea and sitting in their lounges, with the fire and TV on, all warm, loving, secure and cosy.

Boarding school was cold and austere.

At times like this, I felt very much left behind.

Despite this, boarding school had some plus points. Whilst mine was one of the lower ranking ones in terms of academic performance they were big on discipline, manners and expectations of the kids were higher.

I felt privileged and I do believe that the majority of people who go to boarding school feel likewise.

However, you don't get the support and encouragement of Mum and Dad in your studies, they're not there to ask about what you did or didn't do in class. They're not there to check you are doing your homework or to ask about things you don't understand. And they're not there to support you emotionally.

In my school years I lacked focus, was somewhat of a dreamer and I failed to apply myself which I now regret.

My mind moves quickly, I´m someone full of ideas and I struggle to concentrate on things which do not interest me. In addition to this I´m impatient which means I move fast – often I´ll be reading the next question before having fully answered or written down the answer to the one I should be focused on.

There´s an upside to being quick thinking but there´s also a downside. My exam results were invariably poor. Aged 11, when the time came to move on

No ordinary childhood

from the prep boarding school to the secondary boarding school, I failed the initial upper school entrance exams but thankfully passed my re-takes.

Aged 12, I moved from the preparatory school Bronte House to its big brother upper secondary school Woodhouse Grove.

This was also a Methodist school, which was very strict, disciplined and firm on punctuality.

One of the undoubted positive aspects of my time at boarding school was how it instilled in me a deep appreciation of discipline, respect and punctuality which are characteristics I have been fortunate enough to appreciate and apply as best as I have been able throughout my life.

These are behavioural qualities which I value greatly and are linked to dependability. This boarding school environment had a very positive impact on me and for which I am very grateful.

Woodhouse Grove was set in a beautiful location, in a valley with a river running through it and had an abundance of sporting facilities, which I loved. I participated actively and fully in all the sports; rugby, cricket and athletics, and represented the school sports teams in swimming and tennis.

When I was aged 13, Mum and Dad left Lebanon, a civil war had started taking place and they moved temporarily to Greece.

Which meant that when my brothers and I were on vacation with Mum and Dad in Greece, they took us to see the Greek historical places of interest, including the Parthenon temple on the rock hill of the Acropolis of Athens, Marathon from which the event Marathon originates today and Olympia, birthplace of the Olympics back in 770BC.

Mum and Dad didn't stay in Greece long, perhaps a year.

My father was then posted to Iran. This was another promotion. He managed a joint venture business there, as Managing Director. The business had a manufacturing facility as well as sales and distribution functions.

This business was 50% owned by Goodyear and 50% owned by an Iranian business. Foreign businesses could not fully own businesses in Iran, they had to be joint ventures.

Previously, when Mum and Dad were in Lebanon, it was half Muslim, half

No ordinary childhood

Christian. Iran in contrast was and is very much a deeply Islamic country.

I remember when my brothers and I disembarked from the plane at Tehran airport (the capital of Iran), and when into the arrivals area, passport control and baggage claim, all the signs were written not with conventional letters as we know them but with Islamic script, like a scribble.

The people didn't speak English, why should they? It was quite daunting being in a strange country, in which you don't speak their language, can't read their signs and are not familiar with their culture.

Tehran is a monster of a city, it's huge, around 15 million people today, it's a similar size to London and is surrounded by snow-capped mountains.

Scorching hot in the summer, 37C degrees, it's arid (dry)! And at times blisteringly cold in the winter, -4 to 12C.

I remember when we first arrived there was so much traffic, noise and grit.

At the time a place of extremes, many houses like palaces and in contrast others mud like in their image, lots of them, in places cramped together, there was a lot of poverty.

It has a rich history, and the bazaars (markets, like souks) are like a City within a city, captivating to walk around. Their culture very different to our own. They'd butcher animals in the streets… sheep, goats, cows and in many places there'd be blood on the pavements and a rotten stench.

Sights, smells and sounds all alien to me.

Every day, twice a day you'd hear the "Adhan" (Call to Prayer) wailed out by a Muadhin, a loud song like chanting coming from mosques, being magnified by amplifiers/loudspeakers pushing the call out across the City, eerie yet magnificent.

The mosques are beautiful.

The Islamic culture there was very different to Western Culture, you had to be careful about how you behaved and when you travelled about you felt somewhat vulnerable.

Women had to cover themselves and avoid exposing hair, neck, shoulders, arms or legs, which was prohibited. The Iranian women wore black burqas and headscarves, and similarly all western women covered themselves up, wearing

No ordinary childhood

headscarves, trousers or floor length dresses and skirts.

Being a Muslim country, alcohol was forbidden. The whole environment was somewhat alien, scary and yet very exciting.

At the time when my Dad started working there, the Shah was in power (like a King or President). We're not talking about a democracy here. He ruled Iran with an iron fist, their secret police somewhat legendary, tasked with upholding law. The Iranians had little or no free speech, they had to behave and not do anything to question or compromise the Shah's power.

Iran is not all sand dunes….

If you think Iran is a country made up entirely of arid desert plains, think again. It has plenty of mountains only a few hours from Iran's capital city Tehran with several ski resorts!

Iran was an exciting country to visit, obviously culturally very different to the West. For me the skiing there was great and summers baking hot.

Iranian mountains are higher than those in Europe though not as busy nor so tourist oriented. In the winter holidays, my brothers and I would go skiing 3 times a week.

The skiing in Iran was great, the mountains were high, big and snow conditions invariably good, the slopes were steep and with plenty of off-piste skiing available. My brothers and I were competitive, and so we learned to ski well.

And in the summer, the lifestyle for expats (people living and working abroad) was amazing.

There were British and American communities with which we were involved. Through the British Embassy and with my father working for an American firm we got to meet lots of people. There was an active social scene, get togethers, events and parties at embassy and sports clubs, they even had ice skating. I was able to enjoy all of these activities which was fabulous for me. I loved playing tennis on the clay courts and swimming.

And I remember on several occasions going for picnics in the mountains, and swimming in the near freezing water in the rivers.

Iran was one of my favourite places and at the end of each holiday we had to return to the UK and boarding school.

No ordinary childhood

During term time I was left to my own devices, I wasn't particularly interested in the subjects taught at school and didn't apply myself very well. There was no one to check on me, I didn't focus on my studies and was more interested in sports – rugby, football, cricket and for me, the two in which I excelled, tennis and swimming. So, you won't be surprised by what I say next.

My exam results were not good, and this limited my options going forward, not that I wanted to study intellectually challenging subjects like Applied Maths or Physics.

In Iran, a revolution took place which saw the Shah overthrown. He had been somewhat of a modernist, capitalist, pro-Western and his regime was replaced with a strict Muslim one, which was anti-foreigner. My mother departed Iran immediately when troubles could be foreseen.

My father stayed until it was no longer safe for foreigners to live, work or travel in Iran, he would have been at risk had he stayed. It had become dangerous for foreigners to be out and about, so he grew a beard and moustache, in an attempt to look more like an Iranian and less like a Western foreigner.

He shut down the Goodyear office as far as he could and he even managed to get our dog out of the country, and back to the UK – quite remarkable as Muslims are not keen on dogs.

Amazing guy my Dad, bit like a secret agent or film star.

After a few months back in the UK….

So, where next?

New Zealand. When I was 16 Mum and Dad moved to the other side of the world.

Goodyear had a tyre manufacturing plant there, and Dad was posted there as MD. My brothers and I went out there on two vacations. I remember New Zealand being just like England but prettier and 10-20 years removed, set in a time warp.

However, they only stayed some nine months before returning to England. I was aged 16/17, my brothers 18 and 20 (one about to go to university, one at university). Mum and Dad felt they were too far away from us, at a time when we were all reaching big changes in our lives.

No ordinary childhood

Whilst Mum and Dad were always supportive of us, we were apart more of the time than we were together.

My Mum and Dad are not the type of people to talk about emotions, nor are they the touchy, feely, cuddly sort.

They are from a generation in which many families do not openly express affection nor emotion.

Whilst we were not a close-knit family my mother and father did support us as best as they could even though they were obviously absent through much of our childhood.

When my father told his employer Goodyear that he wanted to come back to the UK or Europe and give up his job in New Zealand, he effectively gave up any chances of further career progression.

He chose to put his family before his career.

Understandably most employers who place people into senior roles, when there is a lot at stake and much cost involved, are looking for those people to prioritise on their work (put the company first).

There's the direct cost and a bigger indirect opportunity cost, the idea being that that person positively impacts the business at a strategic level and with a broad ripple effect. The more senior the role, the greater the ripple.

For a business to deem someone in a senior or specialist role to be successful, they'll typically expect the person to be in the job for a meaningful period of time. They probably expected and hoped my Dad would be in the job for 3-5 years not 9 months.

Most businesses would not want to repeat things which have gone wrong. When Dad gave up this job, he gave up chances of further promotion.

I've subsequently come to realise throughout my recruitment experiences, that there are times in your working life when you can, and times when you cannot make a big change. I'm talking about things such as taking up a new job, assuming a promotion, undertaking a career transition, moving to a new house….

These will typically relate to issues in your home life or in the workplace, notably family issues or personal health, disruptive events affecting your employer or

No ordinary childhood

an economic crisis.

Which means that when timing is right, your interests are likely best served by seizing your chances. Opportunity for positive change is not always available.

From my birth to the age of 17, Mum and Dad moved houses 10 times. I didn't have the settled fixed home family environment that most people have, and my only friends were those I had when I was at school.

The upside of my childhood years were the amazing foreign vacations which I've mentioned, the downside was the separation and isolation. In hindsight I probably craved for love, to be part of a close-knit family and most likely, my Mum and Dad would have wanted that too.

However, the upside of this distanced family set up, were the privileges of boarding school and the travel experiences, which I guess positively shaped me and my aspirations in life.

I remember my final year-end report, written by the headmaster when I had completed my 5th year, aged 16, which read:

"Not a glutton for academic punishment", a sentence which most resonated with me then and to this day.

Unfortunately, I wasn't interested in Latin, Physics, Chemistry, Biology… and therefore lacked concentration, and failed to apply myself. Unless I could see how I would apply such subjects to life or work, I found such subjects theoretical.

I performed poorly at school. Whilst I did well in the easy subjects i.e., Geography, English, Arts etc I struggled with the difficult ones and this was reflected in my exam results.

My father must have been very disappointed. I'm sure he would have felt I had this privileged education, which he had gone out of his way to provide for (whilst his employer company paid for the school fees, it was his success and efforts that enabled this) and that I guess he must have felt I was bone idle.

Had I known then what I know now I would like to think that I would have fully seized the opportunity. That said, different people have different abilities, interests and motivations.

No ordinary childhood

Whilst my peers were developing deeper voices and facial hair, I felt left behind, though it's completely normal for adolescence to begin at any point from the ages of 8 to 14.

Most of my classmates changed at 12 to 14 years of age, but for me, it wasn't happening.

Throughout this period, the other boys shot up in height, broadened out in the shoulders, developed deeper voices and I felt very much second rate.

They got bigger. Initially I was quite tall for my age, I played in strong positions in the rugby team, but as they got taller and I become smaller in comparison to them, I took up the weaker positions in the team and went further down the pack.

Similarly, in the friendship groups.

Would I ever develop from being a boy to being a man? It did worry me…

For me, adolescence didn't happen till I was 16. And in the years leading up to this, I felt inferior. I felt small, boyish in comparison and left behind. This very much knocked my confidence.

Whilst my exam reports were poor, my boarding school education together with my trips to these fascinating places made me think big or to put it another way a dreamer.

I was just a little too young yet to think about career plans. The aspirations which I had, had no substance whatsoever, although in my mind, I thought I'd have an important job or as if by magic I'd set up my own company. I envisaged I would travel the world, would marry one of those beautiful girls you see in the movies, have 2 or 3 children and live in a large house.

I was most interested in sports, particularly tennis and skiing.

In my mid to late teens, we were fortunate to go on skiing holidays every year in France and Italy. Mum, Dad, my two brothers and I enjoyed skiing vacations in Chamonix, Les Arcs, La Plagne and Bormio, these being some of my best memories.

When I was aged 17, Mum and Dad returned to the UK, setting up home in the Midlands. So I left boarding school, spent a couple of terms at the local regular comprehensive state school before going to the local college to study

No ordinary childhood

Business Studies. A year later Mum and Dad moved yet again, he'd been posted to London, which meant I left one college and resumed studies at another.

I guess with all these transitions in my life, I lacked some stability, security and confidence.

Having attended an all-boys boarding school and with my parents abroad, I didn't get exposure to girls at school and had very limited interactions with them in the holidays. Which meant that in my early years, I lacked experience and confidence when it came to talking to girls, and the prospect of chatting them up.

All this upheaval was unsettling, but I found Business Studies interesting.

This was a good time in my life, I enjoyed living at home with my Mum and Dad, my elder brothers were at university and I remember when they came home to stay, we'd go out as a family.

At that time, and in some of the years which followed we'd go to restaurants every once in a while, this was quite a treat. In those days people did not go out as often as they do today, and the world was less sophisticated, at least the cuisine in the UK was. I remember we'd go out and have a starter course of a prawn cocktail salad, well done steak with peas and chips for mains followed by Black Forest gateau.

Your early years shape your personality and my early years most certainly shaped mine.

I was okay talking to girls but in the context of courting them didn't know what to do and found them mysterious.

The first girl I kissed was called Amanda.

She was gorgeous, a tall brunette with long hair, blue eyes and naturally beautiful, and she liked me.

However, I didn't know how to develop a relationship, so it fizzled out really quickly.

At the time, generally, I felt as though my peers, who had been in mixed school environments, had socialised with girls and had had girlfriends/boyfriends for many years. On the other hand I had lived in an isolated environment.

Perhaps I'd developed a stigma about it. In hindsight I should never have

No ordinary childhood

considered them such a mystery.

Even whilst I was at college, I was shy with girls or to put it another way shy when it came to trying to chat them up.

One of the girls that caught my eye was Nina!

Slim, long jet-black hair, tall, long legs, she wore tight black leather jeans or short skirts.

She was a German pop star, who hit fame in 1983 with her hit…

"99 red balloons"

I loved the song and am not sure what captivated me most, the song or her.

The lyrics to this were:

"You and I in a little toy shop

Buy a bag of balloons with the money we've got

Set them free at the break of dawn

'Til one by one, they were gone

Back at base, bugs in the software

Flash the message, "Something's out there!"

Floating in the summer sky

Ninety-nine red balloons go by

Ninety-nine red balloons

Floating in the summer sky

Panic bells, it's red alert!"

And at this time there really was a red alert, a sexually transmitted disease called AIDS was spreading. The world was facing a new and unknown virus, one instilling a fear across society and at the time with high incidences of death.

I guess this instilled in me an additional element of uncertainty about romance.

I was a young man with a broad yet narrow outlook!

My childhood was one with two extremes. It was privileged yet lonely.

With many changes in my life both at school and socially, there were many

No ordinary childhood

situations when I felt like an outsider. I wanted to fit in and in hindsight I guess I was constantly seeking approval.

There's a relationship between the things you find interesting and how well you perform in them. In areas in which you are interested, you become more engaged, you think about them more, your thoughts are positive, and you have a better focus. The opposite also equally applies.

You will generally excel in those areas in which you are interested, as I came to appreciate in my late teens, and you can apply this connection between interest and ability to learn and excel in your career choices.

I found business studies interesting, did quite well in my studies, for the first time in my life I thought of myself as being reasonably bright, capable and having potential.

At this time, I was living with my Mum and Dad, and I was able to talk to my father about my studies. We had some really good conversations, and he was very supportive.

For about three years I lived at home with my Mum & Dad, aged c. 17-20 and these were good years, ones in which my father took an interest in my college work, encouraged me and subsequently helped guide me into my career.

It was good spending time with Mum and Dad, and having been apart for so many years, my only complaint being that my dad repeatedly beat me! Beat me at tennis that is… Dads aren't supposed to do this.

In contrast to my poor school exams my college results were more promising.

I didn't plan on starting off my career in computer sales nor to ultimately become a head-hunter and run my own business.

In my early teens at school, I wanted to be a tennis player!

I wanted to travel the world winning the big tournaments at Wimbledon (London), Roland Garros (Paris) and the US Open at Flushing Meadows (New York).

Like many other people this wasn't my only fantasy, one of my others was to run a hotel in the Swiss Alps, providing ski holidays in the winter and outdoor pursuits in the summer.

Rather than progress into an elite fast track sports academy and on towards

No ordinary childhood

the pro tennis circuit, I went to college and gained a Business Studies diploma.

I had a natural affinity with the whole area of business. There is a relationship between the things that interest you, your focus, levels of attention and ability to apply yourself which translate into effectiveness and success. For me this meant I was doing something worthwhile and on the right path.

I studied Accounts, Tax, Economics, Law, Business Organisation, HR and Sales & Marketing, the latter really sparking my interest.

By this time my expectations were becoming more grounded and at the time of leaving college the economy was in a state of recession. My goal was to pursue a career in business specifically in sales, but good jobs were hard to come by.

So, I'd finished college, passed my exams and was then in job search mode.

The economy was in a state of recession (this was 1983) which meant there were very few choices available to me.

This was to be my first personal experience of what I am referring to in this book as a career impacting event.

Three years earlier the economy had nose-dived, unemployment had risen from 5% to 12%! Can you imagine that? More than 1 in 10 people were unemployed.

At this point in time, there was one of the most famous prime ministers of all time, Margaret Thatcher, the UK's first female prime minister, known as "The Iron Lady".

She was seen as a strong woman, strong leader, a lady with purpose and mission, so much so that the government at the time became known as "The Thatcher Government". Under Thatcher's leadership the government had cut public spending to reduce rampant inflation, they wanted to move the economy from being a manufacturing one to a service based one.

The economy was in a depressed state and at times like this job openings are few and far between, I was not able to pick and choose what kind of job I took up, nor in what kind of company.

My performance in my school exams was well below average but in my college studies I was above average.

To go to university or not to go to university? That was the question that I was faced with.

No ordinary childhood

In those days privileged children, with well-off parents went to university, paid for by their parents. My mother and father had already paid for my two elder brothers to go to university, and whilst my eldest brother had done well my middle brother had struggled. He'd initially chosen the wrong course – for him studying Computer Science seemed like a smart idea which it was, the only problem being that his skills and interests were in other areas, less scientific and less analytical.

He checked out of one subject area and into a new one, he found his groove becoming a teacher and progressing to become a highly regarded headmaster.

Bearing in mind that my school exam results were appalling, I was very concerned that if I went to university, I would be wasting my mother's and father's hard earned money, which was one reason I didn't go.

Perhaps a bad decision not to go to university. With my poor school exam results and modest colleges ones, I was overlooked on the management development programs which were highly sought after by people without degrees.

And when it came to interviewing, I was nervous.

I didn't get one of the sought-after jobs with one of the prestigious blue-chip companies.

My career plans would have to wait.

I needed to work, and to earn, so I took up a seasonal job working in the ski department in Harrods, Knightsbridge whilst keeping my eyes open for the right job vacancy. Working in the ski department at Harrods was a great experience, I got to meet some interesting people working there and I loved skiing, so I had an interest in the skis, the ski equipment and the clothing.

At this point in time, the Irish terrorist group, the IRA was active and had planted bombs in England which had exploded, and more were to follow! High profile targets in London included Harrods.

Towards the end of December 1983, it was Saturday, I remember, I was on the fourth floor. There was a huge boom, with a shock which rocked the building a second or two after. It turned out that the IRA had planted a bomb which had exploded at street level on the side of the building.

It was on my side of the building! I was on the fourth floor, it's a massive

No ordinary childhood

building and for the whole building to shake, meant it was a powerful bomb. I was immediately worried. Will the floor collapse, will it fall through and will I be crushed to death?

We´d been warned that a bomb might go off. Of course, Harrods being famous all over the world, was a flagship target for the IRA.

It was scary. I was worried there might be another bomb or even a sequence of bombs. However, it was a single bomb which exploded, killing 3 police officers and 3 civilians.

We were not allowed to leave the building for safety reasons. If subsequent bombs were to go off, there was a great danger of exploding glass and the injuries which can result from it.

Perhaps an hour later we were let out of the building, sent home early, the team I was in went to the local pub and had a whisky. I worked with good friendly people, the camaraderie of the staff at Harrods was really something, people felt proud to work there, felt as though they were part of a team and with a purpose to provide exemplary customer service.

I think there are times in our lives when we have a lucky escape, I think we all get several chances. For me, I felt like this was one of them.

On the Monday morning, we returned to work for business as usual, but not for the 6 innocent people who lost their lives.

As I said, the economy was on the floor, there was a shortage of jobs.

❈ ❈ ❈

Chapter 2

On the way up…

In the fullness of time I would come to realise that recessions take place about every 10 years. And the implications of these on the availability of jobs are severe.

These are disruptive, career impacting events!

For me, this was the first time I came across circumstances which would affect my job prospects and career options, and of course those of everyone else.

I would come to appreciate that these would come in the form of economic downturns and recessions generally affecting the whole of the economy and that there were three types: severe, shallow and slowdowns.

And that they'd also come in the form of industry specific events such as disruptive changes, and also company, or let's say employer specific events.

The impact of such changes could be positive or negative.

I got my break into professional B2B sales with a US owned computer manufacturer (data comms equipment) working in their UK office based in Slough near London. For me this was the real starting point of my career. Aged 19, I started off at the bottom in a sales admin role, and worked my way upwards.

The computer industry was very much in its infancy at the time and undergoing exponential growth. I was lucky to get into this industry, there was lots happening and tons of opportunity.

I made an early observation of the people around me, whom I'd met at my employer company, and at external training courses and trade shows. They didn't seem to make much of an effort nor apply themselves well. A great many people didn't present themselves, articulate themselves or their ideas very well, let alone being familiar with what they were selling.

Which meant they lacked credibility.

This was the first time I noticed how people fail to make the most of their career opportunity.

On the way up

I was keen to learn, keen to develop strengths and used to take the manuals home to read up on the company's products. I familiarised myself with the products. Too many of my peers were lazy.

I also started reading self–improvement books.

Normally, I'd be the first into the office and last out. And this worked well.

I was like the office junior. I was the youngest, lowest paid… I was the sales admin and the telesales guy.

The others came in late, and many of them didn't do much.

I was the office junior. The other people in the sales team were paid more than me, were given company cars and guess what? I wanted that too.

I was keen, I was happy to cold call and, whilst many of the people I called said NO, the more calls I made the more people said YES.

I was doing better in an inside sales job than my external more senior counterparts. I could see London was a massive patch, completely under exploited, so I asked my boss for a promotion.

"Give me half of London, a field sales job and a company car – and you'll never look back."

My boss had to ask his boss, and I got what I asked for.

I should say the company car was a Renault 4GTL. The GTL bit sounds good doesn't it? Conjures up images of alloy wheels, turbo charged engines and lots of bells and whistles!

No this was a really basic car, small engine, no electric windows… it was like a Citroen 2CV. However a Citroen 2CV has panache… this had, I don't know what it had but I do know we used to laugh about it…

We'd joke with one another, that when we went to visit customers, we'd park around the corner so that our customers didn't see our cars. Our peer group in the competitors drove cars one, two or more levels up.

We were young, we were junior, having a company car, even if it was a Renault 4GTL, was a privilege and it was free.

Sure enough, my move into field sales proved a successful one.

Some 12 months in, I'd been successful in field sales and was one of the top 3

On the way up

sellers. I was talking to one of the other guys and we said we were worthy of better company cars than these. So we visited a BMW showroom and had the people there send our boss a brochure and quotation.

Silly us, in hindsight we should have told our boss first about this rather than them arrive as a surprise… cheeky!

We didn't get BMWs but we got welcome upgrades to Fords.

I've come to observe and appreciate that if you are not progressing you are regressing.

I did well. I advanced my career at this computer manufacturer over three years, from sales admin into telesales, field sales and then team leader. I had found my groove.

I was on a roll, buying my first house at the age of 22, with money in the bank and a fantastic lifestyle. This was the life.

The reality of business is that it changes. Markets evolve, companies innovate and those that don't regress.

Your employment prospects are likely best served by moving with the times.

Whilst these may seem boring points the fact of the matter is, that when you look around you, and you look at people whom you care about and even love – you see that their livelihoods, their happiness and wellbeing are all dependent on work.

And how well they can manage their work opportunity.

You and your work opportunity perhaps.

Your income or that of your loved ones.

Your continuous employment or that of your loved ones.

Your fulfilment and opportunity to realise your potential (and that of your loved ones).

Your happiness and wellbeing (and that of your loves ones). Priceless…

And this went for me too.

By this time the tech company I was working for had reached a plateau and other companies' offerings were getting stronger, were more forward thinking and they were growing more rapidly.

On the way up

I felt as though I had learned what I could learn and that my development had peaked.

I wanted to sell the best, work for the best and to be the best I could be.

I went about looking for a new job and was interviewed by several companies.

If I'm honest not only did I realise that my employer was slow to move with the times but also one of my colleagues had recently left the company to join a highly innovative, high growth organisation.

Whilst I did not have to move jobs, I knew my interests would be better served with a new company, able to present me with new experiences and I guess I was drawn to the excitement of a change.

I did something which I believe has universal merit and which I think is important to most people who are ambitious. I moved jobs when I did not have to.

The best time to look for or be interviewed for a new job is when you don't have to. Because in situations such as this, you will only move if the opportunity is a better one, more progressive and markedly beneficial to you, or your career interests over and above your current one.

Whereas when someone is in between jobs they are more likely to take up a position which is of a like for like nature.

And I joined an ambitious company based in the heart of the City of London with a broader portfolio of offerings, with a growth-oriented culture and belief set based on being the best.

London had a big attraction for me, it was big, buzzing, exciting, mysterious, a global capital, a worldwide centre of commerce, full of glamourous, successful people, I wanted to be part of it, to rub shoulders with them all.

Most of the biggest companies had head offices in London, I'd be in the centre of it, the companies with the biggest spends would be on my doorstep.

This was a fantastic move.

This was to be my time.

The economy was on an upwards trajectory, the market sector I was employed in was in a state of hyper growth and the conditions for my success were all in

On the way up

my favour. This company invested in its people, including me, providing both classroom-based formal structured training and more informal coaching.

As a consequence of working in a high quality, highly motivated team I was able to learn from others. I was working in a company with smarter people who were more pro-active, ambitious and pursued excellence. Simply by being around these people I was able to personally develop.

Whereas my previous employer sold only data comms networking equipment, my new employer sold a much broader range of products, services and solutions: PCs, servers, software applications, consultancy, software development, networking and cabling services.

When I joined they had 55 people and when I left three years later, they had 350.

The company had great leadership, I was surrounded by people who had a real sense of purpose and whom I respected.

This was an amazing chapter for me. The company was doing extremely well, it was in the mid to late 80s, it was the time of the Big Bang (de-regulation of the financial markets) and the markets and broader economy was booming. I sold my out of town starter home and bought a flat twice the price in Fulham, West London.

This was the first time I really felt elated about what I'd started to achieve in life. I'd bought my flat in one of the better parts of Fulham, an upmarket road, I felt like I'd arrived and felt proud and posh.

I decorated it in quite a classical style, giving it an elegant yet warm feeling.

Few people of my age could have afforded this.

In my age group, I would have been in the top 1% of earners.

Over a period of three years I enjoyed a sensational time with this company, attributable to the success I enjoyed and the people with whom I worked, and whom I held in such high regard and with such fondness.

We were I guess what were known as "Yuppies" a fashionable young middle-class person with a well-paid job. Stereotypical 1980s yuppies obsessed with material objects and financial success.

On the way up

Yuppie, short for "young urban professional" or "young upwardly-mobile professional".

These were great times in my life, I was at an age when so many things which I was experiencing in life were a novelty. We'd go out to the fashionable and upmarket bars and clubs in The West End of London, Mayfair and Chelsea.

Some are even famous to this day, all these years later, like "Raffles", a private-members club, in recent years frequented by Prince Harry and friends. For me, still no girlfriend, I was shy but slowly developing an ever increasing self-confidence.

I was socialising with my friends, we were all doing well enough to fully enjoy London life but we spent all the money we had, we'd go out late into the night and the early hours of the morning.

One of the things I always enjoyed was getting a taxi home afterwards.

I've always loved looking at things. I found driving through London at this time of night uplifting.

It felt so special, I felt privileged to be in this magnificent City.

At midnight and in the early hours of the morning, there was no heavy traffic, it was quiet and in my eyes, at its most beautiful.

London, steeped in history, illuminated at night, it had a special feeling.

I would look at the streets lined with elegant terraced houses, many 6 or more storeys high, quaint white stucco-fronted homes.

I loved passing these elegant, historic, expensive places, what would they look like inside? Who could afford these million and multi million pound houses?

They must be aristocrats, landed gentry, Middle Eastern Kings and Queens, ambassadors' residences and homes of the rich and famous.

London has a vibe and magic about it, I was impressed living and working there.

The place was buzzing, I was realising my goals, I was learning a lot, becoming wiser, more sophisticated and I was working in a great environment, which was fun and had a winning formula.

I increased my earnings by upwards of 50%.

On the way up

We were young, doing well, we all had a high opinion of ourselves, we all had big egos. When I look back, whilst we were respectful to other people we were cocky, we felt mighty, I felt mighty and I'd become mightier in the years to come.

When we are young, we can be unintentionally big headed. We were, I was, and it wouldn't be till many years later when having achieved spectacular highs and then my life collapsed around me that I really came to discover humility and to act with it myself.

As well as the company having a positive vibe about it and a culture of success, it had a great social feeling and we'd regularly go out after work either in the City or in the West End.

This was fantastic for me. Having moved around so much in my life, most of the friendships I'd developed were lost so I had very few friends. Whilst working at this company there was a ready-made social scene. I formed lasting friendships with some of these people but most of these were work friends.

I remember one year in the period running up to Christmas feeling very fulfilled with my life. However, returning home at the start of the Christmas break, I realised I had nothing to do over the holiday period, i.e. no social get togethers, no friends to see. Not because I didn't have any friends, I just had too few, and the handful I did have were doing other things. Most were going back to their families.

All good things come to an end.

If you think you can travel through your working life and not be negatively affected by economic downturns, radical market change or company failure you are mistaken.

The tech sector I was working in was dynamic, the market moved fast and three years into joining the company it ran into some cashflow issues, which stemmed its previous cadence, pride and ambition.

It was impacted by two negative events. Firstly it was not collecting its debts very well, customers were taking a long time to pay, and many invoices went unpaid and secondly…

Black Monday!

On the way up

This was another potential career impacting event.

October 19, 1987. The Dow Jones industrial average plunged nearly 23 percent, i.e. there was a stock market collapse amid worries about a slowing global economy and high stock valuations. This became known as Black Monday.

Companies cut spending, my employer's revenues and profits fell.

The company had grown to 350 people. We were all told to go to two different hotels, two different groups of people.

The group in which I was placed numbered some 250 people. We were told that the company had run into some cashflow difficulties, needed to cut costs and that our colleagues, friends in the other hotel, were to be let go.

This was dreadful, not only because you don't want bad things to happen to people but we were a close-knit community. Most of the people they let go were good at their jobs and were people who I, and everyone else respected, valued and cared about.

For me this coincided with a sense that I had become very familiar with what I was doing and selling. I had reached a plateau. If I'm honest I'd probably got a little bit bored.

It was at this time that I first met Caroline. She had long straight dark brown hair, was 5 foot 7 inches tall i.e. an average height for a woman, she was slim, a size 10/12 and looked her best, when she was smiling.

She was the first real girlfriend I had.

Caroline was a vibrant personality, very quick thinking, with a sharp sense of humour and a rich vocabulary.

George, her biological Dad left her and her Mum when she was two years old.

Her father had had several business ventures. One was a car garage and another a hotel in the medieval City of Wells, the smallest city in England which is graced with a magnificent cathedral. His business ventures proved to be failures and he emigrated to Canada.

Leaving Caroline with her Mum.

Some years later Caroline's mother met Ron who was to become her stepfather. I remember Caroline telling me a story… she was in the local town, being taken

On the way up

care of by Ron. He was walking, and she was riding her bicycle. I presume Caroline felt she and her mum made for an acceptable "two's company" scenario and that now with Ron on the scene this was more a case of an unwanted "three's a crowd". Caroline peddled as fast as she could, took flight and managed to lose him.

This happened when Caroline was around eight years old, so you can imagine how worrying this would have been for poor Ron, who in the fullness of time proved to be an exemplary stepfather.

Caroline's mother, being a single mum, had some resentment towards her. I think she felt burdened by having a child. I recall Caroline once saying her mother had repeatedly hit her in the bathroom and pulled her hair out.

Although Caroline's Mum re-married, I think Caroline's childhood lacked proper parental discipline.

In her early teens, her Mum and stepdad lived in Cyprus for several years during which time Caroline had a horse called 'Cherokee'. My understanding is that it was a tranquil, safe horse which she rode slowly. She adored him and when they left Cyprus, she was distraught to leave him behind.

Ron was employed in the military, and was a radio communications engineer, communicating and deciphering Morse code. I suppose you'd call him a wireless radio ham. Based in Cyprus, he later moved to Ascension Islands, to its main island St Helena.

You'd be forgiven for not knowing where St Helena is. It's located in the middle of the Atlantic between Africa and Brazil, one of those places claimed by the British Empire in days gone by, a strategic naval or military posting.

Desolate, in the middle of nowhere, it was on this remote island in 1815 following France's defeat at Waterloo that the deposed French emperor Napoleon Bonaparte was exiled after 10 weeks at sea and who ultimately died six years after arriving on the Island.

He wasn't imprisoned – but he and his entourage were confined to this remotest part of the planet where he lived a life of luxury. I guess the British held him with such great respect that they treated him like a Prince.

If you like walking, bird watching and your own company, it's probably an ideal

On the way up

place to live. Rather than move to this remotest part of the planet where there is little or nothing to do, Caroline chose to stay in the UK, live in the family house and did her own thing! At the time, she was perhaps just 17 or 18.

Living by herself, in a 4 bedroom house in Taunton... I'm not familiar with all the shenanigans but I think she was a wild child at this time, did what she wanted, when she wanted, with whom she wanted and as I understand there were lots of parties.

Not properly disciplined, her mother somewhat resented Caroline in her earlier years. Caroline was a free spirit, stubborn and independent.

When it comes to human behaviour, in many situations in life there's a narrow line between what's acceptable and what's not acceptable. This is an aspect of emotional intelligence, in so far as understanding how others feel and how your actions (or lack of action) affects them.

If you cross the line on certain issues, you may upset someone or fail to show them respect. Frequently we all need to think first about our actions and the implications of them, be considerate and maintain self-control.

There is a grey line between what's acceptable and not acceptable behaviour, and Caroline used to cross it.

Caroline was not averse to upsetting people, she had a sharp tongue.

She loved history, and I have little doubt had she gone to university to study history she'd have breezed her way to a first-class honours.

Fascinated with European royal families, the empires that had ruled over the years and with British aristocracy, Caroline was very patriotic. Proud of being British, proud of being part of our heritage, society, beliefs and of the armed forces.

Her passion was reading books, newspapers and magazines. She had an extremely good memory. She found politics and politicians intriguing, and, like me, she was a capitalist.

Caroline had a first-class command of the English language, powerful vocabulary and articulated herself well. This gave her credibility.

People who pronounce words properly in an eloquent manner and who have a comprehensive vocabulary, are easier to understand and more convincing than

On the way up

those who do not. Caroline read the newspapers, watched the news and current affairs programmes, she knew what was going on.

Both well read and well spoken. This gave Caroline a very credible and convincing personality.

Over the years, I've observed it pays to be good with words.

Interested and interesting. Caroline was interested in others. What she had to say was interesting and this translated into her having a very engaging manner.

Caroline's first job was working in an accounts department in her then home town, Taunton, in the South West of England.

Very provincial, very rural and very remote. In her early 20s she chose to move to London. She took up a job as a recruitment consultant and excelled at it, becoming the top biller in a team of six or seven. Doing very well for herself, albeit with a wildly variable income.

Around the time I met her, she'd only recently bought a flat in Stoke Newington, North East London, which is adjacent to its posh neighbour, Islington.

The flat she bought there in Cedra Court was really nice, built in the early 1960s in the Art Deco style, and in its day highly desirable. Stoke Newington was seen as one of those areas which had potential to be one of those of an "up and coming nature" with scope to develop and for potential for property prices to accelerate.

I remember Stoke Newington and our times there fondly. Caroline had a dog and we'd walk him in the local park.

His name was Sherlock. He was a mongrel, a mixture of an Alsatian and Labrador, dark brown, athletic and strong – he had a handsome manner about him. He was that perfect type of dog, always happy, well behaved, loyal and easy when off the lead. He didn't get into fights with other dogs. If you wanted him to come back to you all you had to do was to click your fingers.

The majority of dogs give unconditional love. Sherlock was no exception.

Sherlock immediately took to me.

Man's best friend.

I guess I walked him and talked to him, and Caroline was slightly indifferent to

On the way up

him, whilst I immediately found Sherlock was a dog I could love.

I think with Sherlock, we could often look at one another and he'd kind of know what I was thinking. For example, if I went into the other room, he knew I was going to feed him, or best of all it was "walkies".

He had good posture, like an Alsatian but more upright, slimmer, his coat was a black and brown one, he had adorable ears, whenever I stroked them they felt like silk.

Well behaved, and easy. Can you believe it? When we walked, he'd ordinarily walk on ahead of us then come back, walk behind us almost in circles, tremendously loyal and always with a wagging tail.

Stoke Newington wasn't the best of areas. In fact it was somewhat run down, poor and had a certain edginess about it, which meant that sometimes if we went to the pub I'd be sure to avoid being loud and coming across as being the kind of posh preppy boy whom perhaps some of the regulars might want to take a punch to.

It was a mixed race community and on many an evening the road would be cordoned off, and the police frequently undertook a drugs raid.

There were several mornings on which, when I got downstairs to my car, it would have had its windows smashed in and the music system stolen.

I didn't like that but I did like the diversity of the area.

The road in which Caroline's flat was located, Cazenove Road, is primarily a Jewish one, in fact a particular 'Hasidic' sect, which was very strict. It had several synagogues located along it.

Whenever we walked the dog along the pavement, the Hasidic Jews would cross over to the other side of the street.

I found them fascinating and have a liking for much of what the Jews represent. They live by age-old traditions.

All religions have some good in them. What I like about religions and religious people is that they tend to have an effect of keeping families close together, close knit and, on a broader basis create communities.

I do believe most religions espouse the virtues of people living in harmony,

On the way up

appreciating one another and the enjoyment of the simple, important things in life rather than materialistic ones.

They were a fascinating community to observe. The Hasidic men are generally bearded, wear long dark frockcoats, large brimmed black hats, sometimes furry hats, and on the sides of their faces they wore long curls of hair platted together, these uncut sidelocks being called "peyots".

The women also dressed conservatively, and most wore wigs, which all seemed exactly the same, black, mid length curling over on the shoulders. Covered up with a scarf, some were like the Amish style you may have observed in documentaries or films.

I think there's a certain charm about most religions and Hasidic Jews come top of the class.

In contrast to peaceful concepts of religion was Creda Court, the particular apartment block in which Caroline had her flat.

It was this block of flats in which the infamous Kray twins had once lived.

Ronald "Ronnie" Kray and Reginald "Reggie" Kray were English criminals, the foremost perpetrators of organised crime in the East End of London during the 1950s and 1960s.

With their gang, known as "The Firm", the Krays were involved in murder, armed robbery, arson, protection rackets and assaults.

The Krays had lived in Cedra Court prior to Caroline's arrival and as she was fascinated with the Krays, this no doubt pleased her very much indeed.

In fact I wonder if the estate agent selling the flat may have told her as much, which would no doubt have elevated her interest.

Stoke Newington is very accessible to the West End and the City of London and was a great base from which to visit the historic sights of London.

Caroline was hard working; she hated the fact that many people sponged from society and despised people who could work, but would not work and who chose to live off benefits.

Her biggest passion was animal welfare. She loved animals and was a champion against cruelty to animals. I believe had she had the opportunity to live her life again, I think she'd have worked for an animal charity.

On the way up

Not long after getting together with Caroline there were some early warning signs of her aggressive nature. I remember my Swedish downstairs neighbour from my flat in Fulham, who had met Caroline and had some nasty interactions with her. She said: "you shouldn't be with that girl, she's trouble." She was right.

I was beginning to see signs of a difficult personality type. After one altercation I said to Caroline: "This isn't working, let's break up." However, a friend of both of ours persuaded me not to.

As I stated earlier, I felt I'd reached a plateau in my career. I wanted to move up the value chain.

I got interviews with top end firms including HP, ICL and Wang. At the time these were the Googles, Amazons and salesforce.coms of the world.

I then made what was to be both a great and bad move. I joined Wang which was on a downward path, but I didn't know it at the time of joining.

This was a time prior to the internet. In today's world with just a few clicks you'd get an accurate and up to date perspective on an employer's financial standing and outlook.

For me it was a bad move. Having previously enjoyed explosive growth, Wang was now imploding. The company withdrew from selling into the UK retail sector and I was re-assigned to a role selling into the manufacturing sector.

The company was on a downward spiral, their solutions were outdated and had not kept up with what the market wanted. Wang was hitting the news for all the wrong reasons. Revenue decline, increasing losses, layoffs…

Inside three months of joining the company I knew I had made a mistake. I should have got out sooner.

If I recall properly, they had 55 salespeople in the UK at the time, and 49 were below target. I was one of the 49 rather than one of the six.

Eight months after joining, my boss quite reasonably said I had to sell more, and very quickly, or he would have to fire me. Of course, I already realised this but I was struggling with the idea of what to do next.

I didn't want to step back to what I had previously been doing. However, what were the choices?

It was now 1988/89, the economy was teetering on the brink of a recession and

On the way up

in a state of low / no growth. There were very few job openings – at times like this, you've got to take what's available.

I moved back to my former employer. This wasn't so much a progressive move, more a practical one. I've been of the belief ever since that going back to a previous employer is generally not a good idea.

My previous employer company had been acquired so I re-joined what was now a larger operation with 2,000 employees rather than 350.

It had a very different culture to when I had worked there previously, when the place and people I worked with, were dynamic and it was exciting.

It was at this time that Caroline and I moved in together.

Snowy by name and snowy by nature.

Caroline had read an article in the newspapers about Siberian Husky dogs and seen photos of them. She wanted one. You know the ones, the sled dogs which are the closest thing to a wolf.

However, we didn't have to go to Siberia to buy one, we bought Snowy from a breeder in Essex. All of the pups in the litter were cute but when Caroline spilled her tea on the floor, Snowy stepped on it, tippy toed off the hot tea in a dancing kind of manner and that was it, this was the pup Caroline wanted. Just eight or nine weeks old, tiny, the size of a small rabbit, he looked like a little cuddly toy white bear with the eyes of a panda toy.

Snowy was a black and white Husky with a blizzard of thick fur. Huskies have striking looks and come in all sorts of varieties, any mix of black, white, copper and red.

A young pup, like a teddy bear, everyone wanted to pick him up and cuddle him.

It was also at this time that we moved from London to a house in Leeds, in the north of the country.

My middle brother was living there. He was married with two young daughters, and my elderly grandmother lived there too, but we knew no one else in Leeds.

Now living with Caroline, I saw a lot more of both her positive and negative traits.

On the way up

Caroline was very good company and also challenging. She had a nasty side to her, she was somewhat of a Jekyll and Hyde personality type.

My life with Caroline was always interesting, doing much of the stuff couples do, and her personality was such that there was never a dull moment. There were occasional arguments, some of which gave rise to concern one of which sticks in my memory. I remember early one evening Caroline coming at me with a kitchen knife. I was on the middle floor of the house we were living in and couldn't get out.

I didn't really know what to do. I'm not sure trying to tackle someone who has a kitchen knife in their hands, who is temporarily out of their mind, is a good idea. Even if you are stronger than them, the odds are against you and an altercation is going to result in a bad outcome, the question simply being who gets hurt and how bad.

What do you do in a situation like this? And who do you speak to?

I hadn't connected with my brother that well. I didn't really know who to turn to for help, who to talk this situation over with, nor where to go.

I couldn't really tell my brother. "Oh by the way, can you help me. My wife is trying to stab me with a nine-inch kitchen knife?" And I didn't want him to know my problems.

I was stuck on the middle floor. To get out of the house, I'd need to get past this temporarily mad woman with a knife.

This was such a serious incident that I called the police! They arrived, somewhat calmed the moment, asked if there was anyone I could go and stay with... And so, I ended up staying at a hotel that night.

The following morning, in the cold light of day I put it down to a one-off incident. Or was it that? I wonder if in hindsight, the prospect of splitting up was so daunting, we were living away from friends and family, and there were complications like financial ones, and our dogs.

I returned hoping it would never be repeated.

She continued to lose her mind, she had no self-control button.

In most relationships someone has the upper hand. And in our relationship Caroline had the upper hand.

On the way up

I'd been to boarding school, I was used to being told what to do and in hindsight I was weak at standing up for myself, something that wasn't to change until my 40s.

Often in relationships there comes a crunch point, when an argument or point is to be won.

Someone's going to win and the other gives in!

I think this then sets a precedent, and unfortunately for many people, in most relationships someone has the upper hand, man or woman. The ideal of course being a relationship on an even basis.

Life isn't ideal, there are lots of relationships in which one party, either the man or woman is abusive, nasty, controlling, violent or manipulative.

At work I had a very good couple of years, selling larger more complex networking projects and managed services, including winning several multi-million-pound deals.

I exceeded my goals but I felt I was treading a familiar path.

The reasons I had previously left my employer were attributable to issues which for me were largely the same when I went back! Whilst the company was bigger and in some ways more sophisticated, I felt I'd reached a peak before and I was doing very much the same job I'd been doing for several years.

For me at that time, my primary motivation was to grow and maximise my earnings. My employer, in contrast, wanted to control earnings, especially commission.

I was 26 and when I looked around me, I could see that my peers were more mature, more credible and more streetwise than me. I wasn't going to be in contention for promotion and the earnings were somewhat restricted at the company, which was run by an accountant who didn't like paying big commissions.

Your motivations and interests change over time, influenced by experiences, opportunity and priorities, much of which is determined by the age we're at. Implications such as being young and ambitious, having children or as you get older nearing retirement.

We were young, what was referred to at the time as being Dinkies… dual

On the way up

income no kids. I got married to Caroline at a young age, 26, just a year or two after meeting her.

Caroline was a self-employed recruitment consultant. At the time she was quite a high earner, big spender and fundamentally bankrupt. She'd bought a couple of flats before meeting me, then the housing market fell apart. Interest rates rocketed upwards, at one point reaching 15%, the monthly repayments people were making soared, people sold their flats and houses. Desperate to sell, people dropped their prices and repossessions took place.

House prices had crashed, the borrowings which Caroline had on her flats were greater than the value of her flats, she had negative equity and owed money to the banks.

I was better placed, I'd put more of my own money into my property, I'd got a modest equity in my West End flat and was regularly earning well.

However, I wanted something bigger, and more out of my work life than my employment was giving me.

At the end of the year, I got my commissions and bonuses which were to give me an opportunity!

People's goals change over time.

I wanted something new and challenging.

Some career decisions will be low risk but for me the next one was to be a very high risk move.

I made the decision to set up in business with Caroline in recruitment, and resigned from my relatively stable job leaving behind the security of my regular reasonably predictable assured income.

There's a similarity here, between my change from employment to being self-employed and a career change.

Would it work, would I like it, would I earn, would it give me the income I required and dreamed of?

The risks were high, would the change be worth it?

Some business ventures or career changes are more likely to meet with success than others.

On the way up

Success is more assured if there is evidence that a new direction will work, whether this is freelance or setting up a business on another pathway. And conversely, if something is fundamentally new it will be alien to you, is therefore unproven, and presents a higher risk.

Caroline was already in recruitment and I was already familiar with selling and tech sector knowledge.

And so we set up our recruitment business in 1990. Initially called Northern Recruitment, reflecting the fact that we were based in the North of England and recruiting into positions based there.

Do or die.

This presented a very big risk.

We only had enough money to get by for three months but sales cycles at that time were short. So long as we rapidly picked up vacancies, moved the interview processes along and chased for prompt payment, we could expect to be able to survive.

Up till this time, I had had the benefit of having a company car, but when I resigned and gave up my job, I gave up my company car. Rather than spend money buying a car, we chose to wait and walk.

We had to make this work.

When I started in recruitment I took up what is an occupation which is high in intensity and pressure. From this point on, I was subject to an unpredictable income, which would bring with it stress and anxiety.

Very soon after setting up in business we decided to return to the South of England, to Windsor near London, and of course the name Northern Recruitment was no longer appropriate and so…

Arena Search & Selection was born. We were embarking on what was to be an exciting journey.

And so began what was to prove the most successful chapter of my professional working life.

To start off with sales cycles were short. I got lucky, leveraging my people network to pick up a vacancy, secured my first deal inside seven days and was

On the way up

paid the fee inside 40 days, i.e. under two months.

Fast forward to the present day and in the areas in which I specialise in headhunting, the cycle from taking an instruction (vacancy) through to completion is much more sophisticated, prolonged and getting paid is more like four to six months from start to finish.

In the early days, recruitment was dynamic, exciting, fast paced, rewarding, and I got a thrill out of it.

If a company wanted to make a hire of a specialist nature, using a recruitment firm was in the majority of situations the best if not only realistic approach for the employer.

Working with recruitment companies gave employers immediate access to a candidate pool, in our case a very specialist one, initially recruiting IT sales managers and execs.

At this time, which was pre-internet, recruitment companies with a candidate database and a people network had a winning set of cards.

It's obvious isn't it? The best people get the best jobs.

The recruitment model we applied to start off with was simplistic and one which is often referred to as file search.

It was an agency-based model, sourcing candidates from file/on-record and through advertising.

We would present our most relevant, strongest and best candidates to the best clients, to the exclusion of the weak ones.

The weak ones fell into three categories:

Firstly, those who didn't present themselves well ordinarily characterised by poorly written and styled CVs. This type had a complacent approach to preparing for interview and their personal presentation was poor.

Secondly, those who had hopped from one job to another and had failed to perform well in their jobs.

Thirdly, older people, employers wanted to hire young or middle aged people not older ones, the only exception being when they were hiring into the more senior positions.

On the way up

Survival of the fittest, the dynamics of the employment market is such that, it's kind to some and cruel to others…

Here's an analogy for you…

You're familiar with reality TV shows? The ones where people are dropped off on a desert island or parachuted into the jungle, they're called things like "Castaway".

Team-based contests, competing for a challenge and starting with a selection process.

Where two captains are appointed, and they pick people for their teams one at a time, one captain chooses and then the other, then back and so forth.

The first ones picked feel proud, elated and smile, the last ones feel like also rans, somewhat rejected and downbeat.

There's a kind of human nature which takes place in selection.

People pick the strongest specimens. The biggest, strongest, prettiest, quickest, sharpest, most confident, most forceful and most articulate. They choose the most impressive over the smaller, least attractive, quieter and timid ones.

When it comes to hiring, decisions are largely made on the basis of first and early impressions, a bit like dating.

I noticed this early on in my recruitment experiences.

Decisions are made largely on the basis of how well people present themselves (CV, image, conduct and manner) as they are on a deeper analysis of competence.

What is surprising is how easy it is for people to get it right, and how easy it is for them to be complacent and get it wrong.

People in job search mode attending interviews underestimate the importance of how they present themselves, how they conduct themselves at interview and generally undersell themselves.

It can make or break people, and it can be very costly.

I noticed that at all levels people failed to properly showcase their credentials, 20% would showcase themselves well, 40% presented themselves in a very mediocre way and 40% did such a bad job, they compromised themselves, their future potential and in some cases their family welfare.

On the way up

We set up in business in 1990, during an economic slowdown.

Not only was this tough for us but at times like this the majority of companies are letting people go rather than taking people on. So, for us, being in recruitment picking up vacancies required a lot of hard work, a lot of cold calling and a lot of rejection.

Moreover, it was tough for those people looking for work.

It's at times like this that many people's lives fall apart.

This was another period in my life when there were career impacting events. For me, I was okay, I just had to work hard and do so under pressure. However, I observed a lot of hardship.

There were very few jobs available, and there were more candidates than vacancies.

Even good people were losing their jobs.

And finding a new one was challenging, difficult and costly.

Imagine being out of work for three, six or nine months.

How would you cope? Do you have the money in the bank to cover your costs for the next three, six or nine months?

Imagine running out of money.

Could you borrow money? I observed people getting into serious debt.

What if this happened to you? Or what if it happened to your husband, wife, father, mother, brother, sister, son or daughter?

What I noticed about people who were unemployed at this time, was that missing out on a summer holiday wasn't an issue.

What was really punishing were things which were acutely embarrassing or brutal…

I remember interviewing one candidate, who didn't want to tell their partner they were unemployed and who had been getting up, as if to go to work for several weeks, putting on their suit, picking up their briefcase and getting in their car to go to work.

Spending the working day in their car, driving around and at the end of the day no doubt returning home, having pretended to be at work and remaining

On the way up

employed. On more than one occasion people told me they had to take their kids out of private school and put them into the state comprehensive schooling system. They were so embarrassed about this, breaking such news to their wife or husband, to their children and to their social circles/peer groups.

Unfortunately the reality is that some people who are out of work have weak credentials, which means that their chances of getting back into a commensurate role with a commensurate salary are minimal. I saw a lot of people take up jobs which didn't meet their expectations and in some extreme cases, people were in for a fall! One guy I knew went from having a prestigious high paid six figure salary software sales job driving around in his Mercedes car to driving a van for a living.

No longer young, he was into his late 40s, early 50s.

His track record had become weak, he had become tired, he looked out of shape and was out of date.

No return into high paid software sales for him. However, after around 12 months of driving a van up and down the country, he took up a job selling kitchens and tripled his earnings.

Whilst it didn't have the same status as software sales, he was able to feel like he was in a winning groove once again.

Losing your job is crushing mentally and financially, and the implications can extend to your family, and loved ones…

I spoke with people whose marriages fell apart.

The jobs market at this time was very depressed, I frequently came across guys who had lost their jobs, struggled to get back into work, their lack of income compromised their lifestyle, and they suffered a loss of self-esteem and self-confidence.

Failing to secure a new job meant that wives lost respect for their husbands. If I recall correctly I observed two people whose marriages fell apart as a consequence.

I appreciate I'm talking more about men at work than women, that's because back then the world was less inclusive of women. Today it's much more of an even playing field.

On the way up

Being sacked, made redundant and being unemployed can carry a stigma. And at times like this the consequences can be brutal.

People don't know where to turn to for career advice, or at least back then they didn't.

Which meant often I'd find people looking to me for advice ordinarily in respect of their CV, their interview technique and also on occasion a more complex issue, their choice of career pathways.

I had the benefit of observing people on both the candidate side and employer side.

Not only did I start to gain considerable insight as to the qualities employers like and dislike in candidates, but I also started to develop an interest in career coaching which I have since become passionate about.

At this time, in my early years in recruitment, many of my observations were superficial ones. However in the fullness of time my experiences would mean that I'd not only develop deep, specialist knowledge but also a sixth sense, something you can't learn at college, you only gain with broad in-depth experience.

If you meet as many people as I have done, you come to realise that some people attending interview are a NO the moment they step foot in the door.

Most people present themselves in a mediocre way at interview.

Which would at minimum compromise how employers felt about them and in a worst-case scenario could mean they'd be disqualified completely.

When it came to giving advice, Caroline was more pragmatic than me. She'd be polite, concise and avoided giving her time away for free.

On more than one occasion she would tell someone: "You're going to have to shave off your beard and moustache."

I remember Caroline saying this to several people and most took extreme offence at her recommendation. However, the fact of the matter was that at that point in time for the kind of roles we were recruiting into, hiring managers were negatively disposed to people wearing beards and moustaches. They had a perception that people who wore beards were misfits and not as sharp.

The decision makers in the hiring seat wanted to hire people who were

On the way up

clean cut. The definition of clean cut is that someone would present themselves with short-combed hair, clean shaven face, well dressed, clean breath and a non-smoker. A similar concept applies with ladies, a neat, tidy appearance.

Fast forward to the present day, there's a fashion for men having beards and moustaches in professional and managerial roles. I guess they're copying role models who are self-made billionaire types, actors, footballers or singers/pop stars. However I'm not seeing many of the executive business leaders wearing them.

How people present themselves isn't so much about what they think, it's what others think which really makes the difference.

No one wants to be told their children are ugly.

In recruitment, when you give feedback, it's highly personal. People love it when they're complimented, but when its negative feedback of a critical nature they tend not to want to hear it, not to want to accept it and to take offence at it.

People are easily insulted. However, the fact of the matter is that when employers are interviewing people a great deal of weight is placed on how well someone comes across. Most people are mediocre but think they are impressive, being blind to their shortcomings. And there's always an abundance of job seekers who are the weaker specimens of society.

However they're all God's creatures.

By this time, I'd met a variety of people.

Some candidates really impressed me in the first 15 minutes and there was also a contrasting group, best described as quieter types who failed to impress me to start off with but came good over time. Initially unimpressive, what they had to say was smart, the questions they asked were poignant, they kept gaining ground, and the longer I spoke with them the more impressed I was.

Rarely are the best-looking people the most intelligent.

I was meeting people who were slick, well presented types and, make no bones about it, these people excel at interview and in life. However, what I was beginning to appreciate is that I don't believe there's such a thing as a bad candidate.

Just some people who are better suited to certain jobs than others.

On the way up

The point I am making is that if you want to do well in your professional life, you should never underestimate the importance of having a commanding physical presence, which means presenting yourself well and having strong communication skills.

In my position as a headhunter I'm getting feedback on candidates all the time, when you get feedback, it can be good or bad.

When an employer gives negative feedback it can be bitchy, brutal and interviewers' comments may be lacking in context. Interviewers make mistakes too.

We all have our strengths and shortcomings, there's good in every one of us.

Being unkind and superior is unwarranted, and in recruitment and interviewing there is an absolute need to exercise respect to everyone. Until such time that people (including you) recognise this, you are only half human.

Communicating good news is easy, communicating bad news can be mentally draining. You've got to be sympathetic and diplomatic, and you need to make a judgement call about whether you communicate the real feedback or not.

If the feedback is about something a candidate cannot change and will hurt their feelings especially if they are unemployed, what good will it do? You've got to think about the implications of what you say.

Sometimes people lie, both employer and candidate side. More often it's that they are telling white lies or withholding the truth, sometimes buying time. Employers and candidates often have other options!

There is the need to be patient, diplomatic and keep your head.

It's not often that employers or candidates will thank you for your time or effort, and more often than not they will have little idea how much time you have invested in them. And each time there's a re-arrangement or a change of plan, it costs time, which is money.

What tends to be worst, is that when a candidate messes around at interview, or fails to take up a job or is a bad hire, it reflects on you.

You can cover as much ground as possible with other good works or replacement candidates but recruitment is unpredictable, people are unpredictable and every year I tend to lose a client because of a candidate's behaviour or action.

On the way up

Recruitment is a mentally demanding job, you can do as much as you like to try to be perfect but there are so many variables.

Living and working with Caroline had its plus and minus points. And in doing so, commenced a roller coaster of a ride, with many highs and lows in our income, with massive peaks and troughs.

Even though I was working with Caroline the reality of being self-employed and the isolation of just being the two of us slowly came to dawn on me.

There's a difference between thinking about how something will be and living it.

The novelty and excitement to start off with of working from home, of not having to commute and of being entrepreneurial was accompanied by loneliness, and absence of the social interaction and support that you benefit from in a workplace, and from working for a company.

Sometimes I would miss the substance and depth of support I'd previously had behind me at a company.

However we did well, we quickly prospered from having enough money to pay the basic bills to having a surplus.

And this surplus became ever increasingly significant.

For most of the years in which I worked in recruitment with Caroline it was very lucrative, so much so that the immediate years which were to follow gave us an affluent lifestyle, and the opportunity to pay down or pay off mortgages as we moved up the property ladder.

However, it wasn't all roses!

Soon after we had moved to Windsor Caroline read an article in a magazine about caged, factory farming of animals which greatly upset her. She proceeded to have a temper tantrum and got aggressive with me in front of a couple of our friends.

Why she chose to target her abuse at me I do not know, she'd done this before, and it became a repeated theme.

Many years later, one of the friends who witnessed this was to say, "I don't know how you put up with her for so long".

On the way up

Caroline was happy to humiliate people in front of others. At times she was one of the most difficult personalities, but 90% of the time she was very much the best of company, vibrant, engaging and with somewhat of a magnetic personality, she was interesting and interested.

What I wanted most in life was to love, and to be loved. And whilst work was going well, our relationship left a lot to be desired.

Caroline was a highly intelligent woman with a personality disorder.

Rarely would a week go by without there being an incident, sometimes directed at me, sometimes directed at other people, often strangers.

I remember a couple of incidents around this time. We had been food shopping in the town centre and were carrying numerous bags. I was probably carrying three or four, one or two in each hand and had just started walking home.

I can't remember why she decided to kick off. She went into a rant in public, shouting and being abusive at me, and then decided to drop the shopping. I laugh at the thought now. Much of the shopping fell out of the bags and onto the street, and there were some loose oranges making their own way down the street. She'd stormed off, and there I was rounding up the oranges.

She was happy to humiliate me and her abusive manner wasn't something she just inflicted on me!

Another event, quite typical of Caroline, was her getting into an argument with the barber (hairdresser) who was next door but one to us, his shop had a small back yard. He would often take his dog to work and the dog would be put in his yard.

Caroline took it upon herself to give the barber a ton of abuse, stating that his yard wasn't big enough for the dog and it was cruel. This was not only ridiculous but also rich, because we had three large dogs ourselves and we only had a small back garden.

She was a complex character. Her love for history meant she was an avid reader, with a particular interest in royalty, and this translated into an interest in visiting royal palaces and country houses.

So we would go on regular trips to visit country houses, one of our favourites being Hampton Court Palace, built in 1515 adjacent to the River Thames.

On the way up

It was built for Cardinal Thomas Wolsey, a favourite of King Henry VIII.

Caroline was able to tell me all the history behind these people and places.

Divorced, beheaded, died, divorced, beheaded, survived.

Why women are captivated by morbid stories such as those about serial killers I do not know. However, Caroline had such a fascination and she was particularly intrigued by Henry VIII.

Caroline loved reading books about Henry VIII, and I loved hearing Caroline tell me the stories (the histories) about him.

She'd tell me how Henry had been initially handsome and how as he progressively became older he subsequently became a horrible man.

She explained how he came to the throne when he was 17, tall, handsome and athletic. Yet when he died aged 55, he was obese. Initially charming, latterly, a tyrant.

Not only did Caroline read about Henry VIII but also his six wives and their spectacular stories, and their fate…

Divorced, beheaded, died, divorced, beheaded, survived.

People are amazing, Henry VIII was amazing. He supposedly composed the classic song 'Greensleeves', play it on YouTube if you're not familiar with it, you'll recognise the tune.

Caroline was able to tell me intriguing real life stories.

Such as how Henry VIII's son Edward VI died aged 15 of tuberculosis, and was succeeded by Queen Mary. Known as 'Bloody Mary' she had 300 protestant men, women and children burnt to death.

Following Mary's death Elizabeth succeeded to the throne.

A redhead, she was extremely white-faced and a dedicated follower of fashion. Elizabeth I, one of the most iconic figures in history, is sometimes called the Virgin Queen and saw herself wedded to her country. It was under her reign that the England defeated the Spanish Armada.

One of the wonderful things about Caroline was that she'd regularly be organising things to do socially with others and the two of us, day trips or weekends away most often related to historical events or country houses/

On the way up

palaces. You'll have heard of the expression, "do you live to work or work to live?"

I'm one of those people who is a workaholic.

And on the work front, one of the things I loved was words, expressions and making content engaging for the right reasons. I was constantly thinking up smart ideas and putting some of them to good use, creating compelling ads resulting in a strong response and in us developing a powerful brand.

If you want to be good at recruitment or as a head-hunter, you need to be able to present your clients' interests well. You need to be able to showcase the employer and their job openings.

This is something I love about my job; I love doing a really good job for my clients, which means finding them the best people and doing so promptly.

To take our ads to the next level, I engaged the assistance of a professional copywriter and designer.

I'm one of those clients who has their own ideas. I'm not without talent. Most of the straplines, most of the power messaging and most of the design concepts were ones I conceived. I needed someone to add final touches with copywriting, grammar and visuals.

We were beginning to work on more senior vacancies, with more demanding and more prestigious clients.

I don't think its unique to me. As humans I think we strive to be the best we can possibly be. For me, this is an underlying motivation, I want to be at the top of my game. I always want to be improving.

Real headhunting is based on the ethos that the best people are employed. The school of thought is that it is the weaker people whom companies sack or make redundant. There is much truth in this but that is not to say this applies to everyone.

Headhunting differs from other forms of recruitment in so far as it tends to be focused on the more senior hiring requirements. Ordinarily head-hunters are paid a proportion of the fees up front, then completion fee/s and will be working on a vacancy on an exclusive basis.

Headhunting… the term conjures up images of someone being identified, tracked down,

On the way up

pursued and manipulated, it's actually a compliment to be headhunted.

It's a tag line which sounds brutal, many headhunters and headhunting firms prefer to be called executive search firms and executive search consultants.

The term 'headhunted' applies only to someone who has been specifically identified for a position, approached for that role then hired into the company, unlike an active job seeker applying to a company or being introduced via a staffing firm aka recruitment agency.

Headhunting is challenging and highly rewarding, you're looking to identify people with specific qualities, to engage with them in a confidential dialogue and to simultaneously develop their interest in something whilst also checking them out and measuring them up. Once you have engaged into a dialogue with them and meeting with them, you need to establish if they really have the qualities, credentials and motivations required.

Frequently it's all got to be expedited with a lot of secrecy both employer side and candidate side, sometimes employers do not want the outside market to know that they are looking to make a key appointment, more often they don't want their existing staff to know they are hiring and in particular, if they want to replace someone, which is known as a cloak and dagger scenario.

It can be exciting, sometimes it's like being on a secret mission!

My first real headhunting experience was with an artificial intelligence company. I'm talking about AI a quarter of a century before Alexa entered your life.

This company wanted to hire some very special people into sales and pre-sales/technical sales roles. The MD did not think the kind of people he wanted would be openly available and accessible on the jobs market, nor through advertising. He wanted a headhunting based approach.

I'd met good leaders before but none with the polish and executive presence this man had.

This MD made a lasting impact on me.

If you are ambitious you need to understand that in the sweepstakes of life, you should never underestimate the importance of having a commanding physical presence.

The greater the level of seniority you operate at, or aspire to operate at, the

On the way up

more sophisticated you need to look. A CEO does not wear a $300 suit, he or she is likely to wear a $1,000 plus suit.

Good posture, clean cut, expensive clothes and shoes.

And in the world we live in today, in which in some industries dress codes are less formal, a similar principle applies.

This MD communicated well and had intellectual firepower. Intelligent, he had a way with words, an eloquent manner, a powerful vocabulary and articulated himself with a clarity you'd associate with a TV broadcast news reader.

This guy had real leadership quality. Beyond looking the part, he was inspirational.

He outlined his employer's line of business, explained in simple terms the value they brought to their clients, how they applied AI (back then very much in its infancy) to drive meaningful business outcomes and benefits. He told me why the role would appeal to someone who was heads down and happy or faced with many choices.

He was clear about what qualities he wanted in candidates, why this was important, and made me feel as though what I was doing was important, made me feel empowered and gave me conviction about the merits of the opportunity.

This was a game-changing experience for me.

I leveraged my people network, filled the roles with exceptional hires, got three big fees and, more importantly, beyond money, I'd completed my first headhunting assignment and delivered it well.

By this time, I'd been in recruitment for perhaps three or four years and had been in the job long enough to appreciate some of the harsh realities of it.

Whilst I'd only recently completed the retained headhunting job with the AI vendor, it was then back to business as usual, working with clients on a success-only fee basis.

For a recruiter/headhunter there are advantages and disadvantages to retained and success-only recruitment models. At its best recruitment is an exhilarating job and financially lucrative.

At its worst, being in recruitment is like being on an emotional rollercoaster of highs and lows, and not being able to get off.

On the way up

Being in recruitment means undertaking a job with little or no certainty. It's got many moving parts. One minute you can be on Cloud Nine and the next you can feel like life is crashing down around you.

At this time I was around 30 years old, and most of our friends were of a similar age. For me this was a really exciting era, with so much in life to look forward to.

Like most other people of this age, you're not really affected by poor health or crisis. Caroline and I lived with constant pressure, recruitment is full of highs and lows.

Around this time, we'd got this Irish chap living in London a job offer which he had accepted with a prestigious, high growth company. This was a good move for the candidate, it could be expected to positively move his career forward.

He was smart, well presented and had that Irish charm.

He'd resigned from his current job and was working his four weeks' notice. The week before he was due to start, he called to let us know he wouldn't be joining as he had won the Irish lottery and decided to pack up work, return home to the Emerald Isle and buy a farm.

The invoice to be raised for his introductory fee was no more.

Here's the thing, imagine how I felt and I'm not alone. This applies to other people as well.

Imagine you've got a deal. It's a lot of money. Perhaps 10-20k or more, after tax that's 5-10k or more. I'd need one deal minimum to cover my costs, housing etc. However, if you get two or more deals you've hit the jackpot.

At times like this, you think you've got a deal. I would think I had a deal.

Imagine that being taken away from you. It's always a kick in the teeth when a deal falls through.

It's a bit like someone has agreed to pay you 20k or whatever, and then takes it away, changing their minds.

If I were you reading this I would think that this is simply part of the job. However if you were to sit in my shoes and feel the pain, you'd appreciate the low points of doing the job can be subject to spectacular pressure and anxiety, if you don't bill, you don't earn.

On the way up

And of course, I'd not only feel like I'd taken a kicking, but I'd also have to call the client and give them the bad news.

Employers don't like this, it's inconvenient and impacts on their success, and in cases like this, the employer will somewhat view it as being me who has failed them.

Recruitment is a gamble. Working in recruitment is like a lottery and the expression "the harder you work the luckier you get" applies.

There are times when you can suffer one setback after another for reasons beyond your control.

Around the same time, having worked hard on a vacancy with a business intelligence software company over a period of some three weeks, I'd found them a superstar, progressed the person through the interview cycle, the person had started, I'd sent the invoice and we'd been paid the fee.

I had a call from the company to let me know that the candidate had subsequently resigned four weeks into the job. He'd been offered several hundred thousand pounds for a story, which he sold to a TV Channel and so was giving up work.

Which meant I had to pay them back the fee.

I appreciate these two stories may seem somewhat far-fetched but that's the truth. Whilst these are extreme examples, recruitment is a job full of many moving parts and those parts are people, whose lives are unpredictable.

At this point in time I'd only undertaken one recruitment campaign for which I had been paid up front. Everything else and for many years to come would be success only recruitment.

No hire, no fee.

And there's a lot which can go wrong.

Guess what? Most of what can go wrong is client side, or candidate side – not the recruiter, headhunter trying to make the right matches happen for the right reasons.

But can you imagine this? Can you imagine working hard for your employer company for a month, being committed to them, going out of your way to do not just an average job but a great one, and being paid on the last day of the month?

On the way up

And then two weeks later they ask for their money back. And you pay your salary back to your employer?

That's the reality, the job of recruitment is subject to many twists and turns.

It's an emotional rollercoaster, full of extreme highs and extreme lows.

One of the more common lows is when a company decides not to go ahead with a hiring requirement, and this is quite commonplace especially when the economy is on the floor. And this was happening a lot to us at this time. The economy was in a poor state.

Often, we would be working for weeks on a vacancy, and it would go on hold.

In retained search, we and others would be less exposed to things going wrong or being cancelled but the retainer part of a recruitment fee doesn't cover all of the cost of the time involved.

The job of being a recruiter and headhunter requires resilience, determination and constant high work rate. It's a tough job, there's a lot to endure.

I have often thought, "why am I doing this?"

Why am I doing things for other people who are giving me little or nothing in return?

In recruitment you often feel you are doing other people a favour, investing time in them.

Identifying, tracking down and engaging with people with very specific profiles and skill sets is time consuming. Invariably you'll be giving a client your best people "AAA quality candidates" and often offering candidates the best openings in the industry.

There's not a lot of gratitude in return!

At best clients and candidates come back with demands. They're often unrealistic, unresponsive and unreliable. In recruitment you need the patience of a saint.

Whilst I seek to apply excellence, often the people I am trying to help only respond when they want to, which can be challenging – imagine going on a date, giving your date a compliment and them being unresponsive.

That's what people do, both client and candidate side.

On the way up

Delays are deadly, resulting in employers or candidates going cold on one another and then afterwards we've got to pick up the pieces.

Imagine going on a date and not hearing back from the person for a few days… "I'll think about it."

This kills people's interests and egos, and we've got to bring it back to life.

Looking inwards with respect to how I feel about it, the moment someone is unresponsive to me, it compromises my own belief in them and investing my time in them.

Do you give someone the benefit of the doubt when often 9 times out of 10 they may be trying to mislead you. Understand this can happen both client and candidate side, do you call them out? What are the implications of the various options available to you, including doing nothing?

The feelings I'm talking about aren't unique to me.

I'm sure you'll experience awkward people issues yourself both in your life at home and work. However, I do believe they are magnified in recruiting and headhunting.

When dealing with hiring both managers and candidates, as a recruiter/headhunter there's the need to apply a lot of emotional intelligence.

This is something which has become an area of interest for me over the last 10 years.

Here's the technical description of it… Emotional intelligence: "The ability to understand and control one's own emotions, together with the ability to manage relationships through the recognition and understanding of other people's emotions."

Emotional intelligence accounts for 58% of performance in all jobs.

It's shaped by five dimensions:

Self-awareness. The ability to understand your emotions as well as recognise their impact on relationships and performance. This relates to accurate self-assessment and self-confidence.

Self-management. Controlling your emotions and using your awareness of them to stay flexible and act positively. A critical aspect in business is the

On the way up

ability to keep any disruptive emotions under control in changing situations and overcoming difficulties. This relates to transparency (trustworthiness), adaptability, achievement orientation, initiative and optimism.

Social awareness. Your ability to identify emotions in other people and to understand their perspective and take an interest in their concerns. This relates to empathy, organisational awareness and service orientation.

Social skills/relationship management. Your ability to use your awareness of your own emotions together with your understanding of the emotions of others to manage interactions successfully. A critical aspect in business is the ability to take charge and inspire others while sending out clear, convincing and well-tuned messages. This relates to inspirational leadership, influence, developing others, change catalyst, conflict management, building bonds, teamwork and collaboration.

Motivation. The final personal skills aspect of emotional intelligence is motivation. This refers to your inner drive to achieve and improve, and your preferences, it involves our reason for doing.

Here's the non-technical description of emotional intelligence:

What your mother called charm and your father called common sense.

One of the challenges in recruitment is giving people bad news.

I've come across all sorts of feedback. There's an expression, no-one wants to be told their children are ugly, it's personal, it's hurtful…

In recruitment, when you give feedback to a candidate it's invariably personal.

No room for Humpty Dumpty here.

That's what one of our friends said when we recounted this story.

One of the candidates Caroline submitted to DELL attended an interview with them. The interview was on the second floor, the candidate was big, really overweight and the interviewer at DELL took the stairs as she always did.

By the time the candidate had reached the second floor he was completely out of breath and the interviewer was understandably concerned for his health, so much so that she wondered if the candidate would have a heart attack, and if they did hire him what risk would be involved, if any?

On the way up

Whilst DELL did not go ahead with the candidate for reasons other than his weight, it may well have been a contributing factor.

There are no perfect people.

Do you give the real feedback? Do you tell a candidate that they have been rejected because they had halitosis (bad breath). It happened with one of my employer clients and candidates. One of my clients rejected someone because they had bad breath, I did explain to the client I'd met the candidate and they didn't have bad breath then but he still said thanks but no thanks.

The saying "You only get one chance to make a first impression" has much truth. However, often someone can start off poorly and become impressive with the passage of time.

Back to my point, when dealing with candidates… Do you tell someone what's on your mind?

Call me a prude.

I think you're showcasing the wrong features.

I remember on one occasion interviewing a marketing lady. She wore a tight-fitting white blouse which was too small, which meant it was being pushed out by and emphasising her chest.

Men in an interviewing seat would think such an image clumsy and compromising at best. Women in a hiring seat would think what a 'xxxx'.

If she went out on interview, wearing this kind of top would reduce her likelihood of being successful, she'd be qualified out on the basis of lacking a professional and credible image.

Whilst this may just seem like one thing, often several perhaps seemingly minor issues collectively become enlarged into a 'no thanks'.

Sitting in my shoes, I often have to tell people things they do not want to hear, may not respond well to being told and which, from my perspective, can be awkward.

The reality is that when interviewing for jobs at senior levels in professional non-creative environments, a conservative or neutral image is best, so I discussed the matter with Caroline first. She agreed, best to tell her to wear

On the way up

a larger shirt and not one in which her buttons were being pushed out by her breasts.

At the more senior levels, the strongest candidates are those who are high in both IQ and EQ (emotional intelligence).

And in my capacity as a headhunter I'm required to assess people.

Ordinarily I'll get into a dialogue with a candidate and quite early on I'll need to talk about the position I'm recruiting into and the employer company.

Whilst I'm doing this and afterwards I've got to make a decision. I have one of four choices:

Firstly to submit to the client with a recommendation. Second is to submit and be neutral. Third is to submit and be negative. And there is the fourth choice, which is when I will simply say to a candidate that there is a gap between both sides and there's no match but let's stay in touch.

Often the reason I'd reject or do not recommend people, is if they are poorly qualified for the role or weak in comparison to others. The critical areas of strength I look for include…

Relevant experience including their track record (scope and scale), having an ongoing curiosity, motivation, growth potential, emotional intelligence, interpersonal skills, values, intelligence, wisdom and education.

The reality is that often I'd conclude that someone lacked the gravitas or impact which was required in most of the jobs I was recruiting into or the… specific skills, experience or track record to give confidence they'd be able to do the job with motivation being essential for any match.

But you can't tell someone they're a Dumbo, you've got to be diplomatic.

Most people who are high in EQ will be self-aware and therefore present themselves well. However, when someone doesn't have the gravitas, executive presence or interpersonal communication skills they probably will struggle with relationships and impact.

I was increasingly coming to understand what separates out the best from the rest at the most senior levels (my own learning) and one of the most important areas is that of critical decision making, and the execution which must follow.

In another life I could have been a counsellor!

On the way up

As a recruiter/headhunter you've got to ask questions and be a good listener. If you were to sit in my shoes, you'd be surprised as to how few people ask anything about me. The best candidates tend to have good people skills and tend to not only tune into the company I've approached them about but also make a point of establishing a connection or rapport with me.

Many of the people who I interviewed, I concluded to be very average, attributable to the fact they made little or no impact.

You can't field someone who will compromise your reputation as a professional recruiter or headhunter.

I frequently have to think long and hard about how I reject someone. You've got to work out what you're going to say and, if it is appropriate, to share the real feedback, which may be constructive or in some way damaging.

Invariably I think about what are the implications of the feedback I give, what I choose to say or not to say. Will it damage the candidate's confidence? Is it constructive? Will the candidate benefit from the feedback? Will the candidate embrace it or fight back?

Telling people they've been rejected is at best an art and at worst an emotional drain on me or anyone who is communicating the bad news.

I tend not to delay, get it over and done with, move on. Do so with diplomacy, respect, and finish on some sort of positive note.

In my earlier years many of my observations were of a superficial nature, in the fullness of time I would gain deeper experience at the most senior levels.

I was increasingly meeting with a variety of leaders and managers. This enabled me to compare different people's strengths and weaknesses, and to reflect on what impressed me and concerned me about them.

One of the qualities which sets apart great leaders and managers from the rest, is their ability to successfully hire the best and brightest talents.

Whilst a desperate candidate will take any job, someone who is employed, of a high quality and sought after, will be selective and needs to be sold to.

If you want to hire a "Triple AAA" quality candidate, then the hiring manager needs to be able to properly position the opportunity to the candidate.

I was beginning to develop the experience and skills to be able to assess

On the way up

leadership qualities. One of the key qualities a leader needs to possess is the ability to hire good people, and to hire the best, you need to come across as someone A players want to work for.

A five-star manager has a magnetic effect on landing the best and brightest talents.

One of the managers I met was great at this. When I first met her, she was a first line manager and in time she would go all the way to the top. She had natural leadership qualities: she had a strategy and vision, she made you feel valued and that what you were doing was important

She was great at positioning the opportunity and objective, along the lines of: "This is what we are going to make happen, this is why it is important, and this is how we will make it succeed."

The clarity with which she spoke was truly impressive not just in her first-class command of the English language, the crispness and eloquence with which she articulated her words, but also the content. Easy to understand, precise and powerful.

Too many people think leadership is all about inspiring people - wrong! That's just one part.

It's about strategy and vision, clarity of purpose, inspiring others and driving execution.

She exemplified these qualities.

Her personal presentation was immaculate. Sharp, well-cut expensive suits, neutral in colour typically navy or black, minimal mix of colour. Neat, tidy hair, good posture, clear desk, firm handshake, a clear smile and positive greeting: she exuded professionalism.

I knew she was destined for the "C" suite, the ultimate level of seniority.

Leaders invariably have a calming manner about them. I remember her once saying, what people need to understand is that when faced with critical problems there is always a way through.

One of the fabulous things about being in recruitment is observing what makes people special.

At this time, we were living in Windsor. A great place in which to live, a fabulous

On the way up

town to walk around, graced with the River Thames and Windsor Castle.

This was a largely enjoyable chapter of my life.

We'd already got two dogs, an Alsatian cross Labrador "Sherlock" and a Husky "Snowy". Caroline wanted another Husky and so we got "Timber". Huskies are mischievous dogs, not very good off the lead, they don't come back and too frequently get into fights with other dogs.

Timber was to become the love of Caroline's life.

Both Snowy and Timber has the classic Husky coats, grey and white. Huskies are also born with other types of coats mainly all white, or predominantly black, or with brown rather than grey/black patches.

They had brown eyes, although some huskies have grey eyes and some have one grey, and one brown!

I think they look more friendly with brown eyes… by the way, when they go to sleep their noses dry up, and that's so that they don't get frozen noses if they were out in freezing weather or snows.

We got Timber when he was just six months old. Unusually for a Husky we were able to let him off the lead and most of the time he'd come back. He'd been trained by a breeder to come back although he couldn't be relied upon to do so.

At six months he had that baby dog manner and look about him, not quite an adult, a little smaller than a fully-grown dog.

He was black and white, slim in comparison to Snowy – Timber was very athletic.

You know when you sometimes look at people and they aren't good looking but have an amazing appeal about them, Timber had this, a certain X factor. There was a kind of beauty in his slightly gawky look. And he was an alpha male dog, hugely confident.

Timber was a real head turner from when he was six months and in the many years which followed.

People would stop us in the street and ask to say hello to him.

Timber and Caroline were very much a double act. Always together. They

On the way up

adored one another. Timber would always be at Caroline's side, he'd sleep on the floor on her side of the bed, sit beside her when she was sitting on the settee or at her desk.

Caroline liked taking Timber everywhere including to the shops.

He was such a striking, good-looking dog that more often than not we'd get away with taking him into the shops. I'm not talking about food shops but clothes shops, even department stores.

Yep we had three seats in the aircraft: two for us, and one for Timber.

One year we took him on a weekend away to one of the Channel Islands and, strange as it may seem, in the tiny aircraft which had 9 seats, people were allowed to take dogs.

We were beginning to lead an extravagant lifestyle.

I always found walking a great way to relax. Whenever I walked by myself it gave me thinking time, particularly at this time and in the years to come. Exercising releases endorphins which help make you feel good and walking gave me the time to chill and think about how I could make my work better and come up with creative ideas.

Every day we'd walk in and around Windsor. There was a lot of fun in our lives, we had a large sports car and we'd pack the three dogs in the back. It wasn't ideal, but it worked. Just.

For us life was very much dominated by work, dog walking, going to the pub and socialising.

In our late 20s, early 30s we were drinking too much, Caroline more so than me. It's not unusual for people to drink too much at this time in their lives but I do believe there's a mistaken belief somewhat associated with the middle class – that they don't get drunk.

There's something of a perception that it's the working class who get drunk, not the educated white-collar ones who wouldn't be seen drunk in public. WRONG.

They drink and get drunk mainly behind closed doors.

There's a grey line between what is acceptable and unacceptable behaviour. Caroline used to cross it every week, with me and other people. At times she'd

On the way up

lack self-awareness and self-control.

An abusive personality type, she would regularly lose her temper and attack me, kick me, punch me and try to pull my hair out. How do you handle a woman who is physically abusive?

I was on the receiving end for some 13 years of her physical aggression and mental abuse. When I reflect back on it, I wonder "Why did I put up with it for so long?"

What I should have done in hindsight was to say to Caroline that her behaviour was unacceptable and that we should take some time out, spend two weeks apart and during that time she could reflect on the relationship and her behaviour.

And then when I returned if she was abusive once again, I should have explained I'd take another break until such time that she changed her behaviour or we'd have to go our separate ways.

Or simply to have left, which seemed daunting to say the least.

I stayed.

Work was full on, quite pressurised and stressful. Work hard, play hard.

It wasn't so much that we were going to clubs and staying out into the early hours of the morning. We'd work flat out in the day. Recruitment requires a relentless work ethic, it's demanding, you take a lot of rejection and the people you deal with are often rude.

Often, you'll work hard on a vacancy, invest a lot of time in it, on behalf of the employer company, the hiring manager and or candidates, only to find the people involved do not have the courtesy to answer, return calls or get back to you.

This happens more often with lower and mid-level roles, and with lower and mid-level individuals than it does with senior ones. In the years which would follow this would ultimately become less of an issue to me as I came to recruit into more leadership and senior roles.

But back then, this happened quite frequently because at the time we were recruiting into a lot of specialist mid-level roles and the economy was in a depressed state which translated into a lot of job openings being placed on hold or cancelled.

On the way up

Most of the work we were doing was of a success-only nature, no hire no fee.

At the time recruitment cycles were quite short, and the amount of work required manageable, which meant that the money we were earning handsomely compensated for the stress of the job and the failure of people both client and candidate side to be responsive, express manners and gratitude.

When people are rude, unresponsive, unreliable or disrespectful, such behaviour is mentally punishing to accept. We all crave for respect.

I think it's human nature that people wish to be kind and generous to others, giving makes us feel good about ourselves.

For anyone in a recruitment or headhunting seat, the ongoing emotional battering is an endurance to bear.

Can you imagine working for free and people being rude and unreliable? HR professionals are frequently nasty, vindictive to and talk down to external recruiters and head-hunters.

Recruitment consultants are subject to a lot of bullying.

Sometimes this can be simply people being patronising or having a superior attitude, in a kind of master/slave relationship.

Often it is peoples behaviour which is lacking in respect both employer and candidate side, people tell a lot of white lies to recruitment consultants, often people are not transparent and a white lie is a lie.

And at times, an employer client or candidate may go quiet on you, there's a term for this, "being ghosted".

The more senior the level of the position, the less likely it is that the employer client will ghost you but candidate side that's not always the case.

Regardless, I do believe that "Manners maketh man or woman" without which you will never be the best version of yourself.

The recruitment profession is one which is subject to taking big gambles on an ongoing basis with a heavy dose of uncertainty, headache and stress.

In any occupation, there are the people who pursue excellence and those who are cowboys. This includes doctors and lawyers. I think in each and every type of job….

On the way up

We have the opportunity to be as professional as we choose to be!

The amount of rejection you have to take in my job and that of everyone else like me, is extraordinary. However I've always managed to keep my head up, put on a brave face, avoid looking or sounding down when given news I didn't want to hear and bite my lip when people were rude.

Recruitment is extremely unpredictable, requires a relentless work rate and comes with a lot of pressure.

I take pride in what I do, and endeavour to apply excellence at all times.

Undertaken properly, recruitment and headhunting can transform the success of businesses, the teams within them and change lives for good.

We'd drink in the evenings after work. Just one glass of wine turns into just one more, two into three and perhaps a whole bottle each or more.

Heavy drinking has mental and physical consequences. Not so much a pick me up, alcohol is often referred to as being a depressant.

Unfortunately, Caroline didn't know when to stop. When she drank too much, she'd become somewhat rude, aggressive and sometimes semi-comatose.

She'd often get into that swaying state, you know what I mean, when you see someone who has obviously had too much to drink and they either can't stand up properly or walk in a straight line.

Caroline could be quite stubborn. If someone said something or did something which she didn't like she'd speak up. And if someone's response was anything other than consolatory, her response would be to insult the person and/or to become aggressive.

She was a difficult person to live and work with.

Her personality was a like a time bomb.

You wondered when it would go off.

Caroline would get upset, annoyed or easily fall out with all sorts of people: neighbours, waiters or waitresses, shop assistants, parking attendants. The list goes on, which was a great shame because her positive qualities were equally extreme.

She was a complex character.

On the way up

Financially we were doing very well indeed. We paid off the mortgage on the first house we'd bought in Windsor inside three years, and then repeated this on the next bigger, more expensive property.

I'm going to try to make you laugh or smile with this little anecdote.

Our second house in Windsor was a 3 storey town house, we were going up in the world, our previous one was a two storey one.

Nick our next door neighbour was a good fun guy, his house had exactly the same layout as ours, it was like being in our own house.

He'd got divorced a few months after we had moved in and so he had parties every so often.

One night, he had a big party, a late one, loud music, lots of booze.

Caroline and I both got drunk, and I can't remember the end of the evening. However, the following morning there was a knock at the bedroom door.

As I woke up, lifted my head up and turned around, looking over Caroline who was lying next to me, I could see Nick at the door… "Good morning, would you like a cup of tea?".

We'd got so drunk, that when Caroline and I went to bed, we must have thought we were in our house, but we were in Nick's and we'd slept in his bed thinking it was our own.

We were working flat out and up till this time had never taken a holiday. There were only two of us at the time, and we didn't want to be unavailable to our clients nor for them to realise it was just the two of us.

Whilst we were doing well, our income was however like being on a roller coaster ride, exciting and scary. We went from experiencing accelerated high fee income to equally low points, sometimes with slow recovery. Our income was continually subject to peaks and troughs.

During the first four years of being self-employed and running our business we didn't take a holiday. We didn't work on weekends and public holidays, we were very much heads down, focused on making a success of the opportunity available to us and intent on avoiding failure.

As we began to feel increasingly more secure and financially well placed, we

On the way up

started to take holidays, to start with over Christmas and New Year so as to avoid taking time off.

Our first holiday was to Barbados. On the way out, I remember buying a Brietling watch at the airport, it wasn't a planned purchase.... we were doing so well, we were beginning to experience having spending power.

Amazing, fantastic place, great weather, I loved Barbados. On the west coast there are the best hotels and beaches for swimming in the sea. On the east coast the seas are rough, dangerous to swim in and there are few hotels. The east coast has been described as being like Scotland. Atlantic facing, it's lush with greenery, windy and with stunning hilly landscapes.

Caroline loved history, which meant Barbados was an ideal vacation for her. It has a rich legacy and stories emerging from the slave trade and sugar plantations which were fascinating places to visit, read about and travel back in your mind as to what it would have been like.

In years gone by it would have been an amazing existence for the British and awful one for the slaves.

Our second extravagant holiday was to Antigua. The departure flight was delayed and so to pass the time I bought a What Car magazine. Land Rover had just released a new Range Rover model... of course we had three large dogs and a sports car... and money in the bank.

Back then there wasn't as much money around as there is today. I called the local dealer and asked about pricing and availability, what specs did they have available? I'm back from holiday in a week's time, bring one round, and if I like it, I'll buy one. And sure enough when I got back they brought one round and I bought my first Range Rover outright, no loan.

Whilst this all sounds like an ideal lifestyle, Caroline's behaviour compromised it.

In Antigua the British Navy were in town, and on New Year's Eve they were partying at the restaurant we were at. Caroline got drunk (as usual) and come midnight she was dancing with an 'officer and a gentleman' not with me.

We'd been joined by an American couple and so I was sitting down with them looking on, feeling somewhat embarrassed and belittled.

On the way up

Confused thoughts were going through my head.

"She's drunk as usual, am I upset or am I not?

"I like her as a business partner and her company but this is not the relationship I wanted in life, and I'm worth more than this.

"Should I go and get her, tell her to stop dancing with the officer? It would cause a scene, upset people, what use would it serve? There was no point."

In common with most of the evenings when we went to a party, she'd got into a semi-comatose state and I carried her home.

Why did I put up with it for so long?

I think the life we were living had become spectacular, exciting and extravagant, and that this compensated somewhat for her destructive side.

Our lifestyle and being able to pay off the mortgage was funded in part by not having to pay tax till some 12 months after receiving our fee payments from our clients. This, combined with our increasingly high earnings, enabled us to make capital repayments against our mortgage while some of the money should have been put away for tax liabilities.

If you're not familiar with this, this means that if you are self-employed or have your own business, your tax liabilities and payments are subject to a delay which means you are often sitting on cash in the bank which in the fullness of time you'll need to pay in tax.

Whilst we were spending large, we were financially pushing things to the limit, so we were constantly living with a tax liability, for which we continued to need to earn BIG in order to be able to make the payments when they became due.

There were times when I thought I should split with Caroline, but this seemed impossible, firstly because of these tax liabilities which had to be met (and which we always paid). Secondly, there's a kind of security in a marriage, in a marital home and of course Caroline and I were not just linked in marriage but also in our work. And thirdly, our dogs, which I loved.

I felt somewhat trapped.

Our earliest years were before email.

Quite unimaginable today, we used to fax or post CVs to clients.

On the way up

From 1991 to about 2000 we were making very good money. We'd be sending cheques to the mortgage lender every three months, often monthly, for £5k to £10k, as capital repayments to pay down the mortgage.

We were increasingly getting good ad response, from good candidates, and becoming a well-regarded firm.

I constantly sought to get ahead, I wanted to be the best… I'm sure we were one of the first companies to scan CVs using OCR and certainly one of the first to use email. I always sought to present a great image. For example, we were one of the first companies of our type to have music on hold on our switchboard.

This was before LinkedIn.

At that time, any recruitment firm with a good candidate database was in a strong position. By this time our advertising was becoming increasingly recognised and when we met prospective clients, they would say they had seen our adverts and liked our style.

We were building our brand. "Arena Search & Selection" was becoming a recognised name in the marketplace, one associated with excellence and as the 'go to' company.

"Countdown to a new career"

This was the first of many headlines which would set us apart from the rest of the crowd. The line "Countdown to a new career" was accompanied by a powerful, fiery image of the space shuttle, dramatic and eye catching, intended to stand out from the crowd.

"Your new job starts in California"

That was one of our many attention-grabbing headlines.

This meant that new hires would start in their new jobs by attending training courses in San Francisco.

"Going for gold"

We used this at the time of the Olympics. We used this attention getter together with an athlete carrying the Olympic flag, with the inference: there were great jobs, great achievements to be had and people's aspirations would be better realised working with us.

On the way up

Our adverts were head and shoulders above the rest and our brand was well recognised and associated with excellence.

In fact we even used the strapline "Head and shoulders above the rest" to describe what we were looking for, for one of our clients, and we used a giraffe image to get the message across… typically we were always looking for the best candidates.

Competitors started to copy our style, so I came up with an idea to further distance us from the rest of the pack.

Recruitment companies were largely advertising the same kind of jobs, so what could we do to make job seekers more likely to read and respond to our ads?

I came up with a slogan, concept and content:

"The first value-added recruitment company".

I came up with the concept of giving people tips in the advert to make them more engaging: "how to write a better CV, how to ace the interview, how to negotiate a salary increase". We'd put these tips on the left hand side of the advert and the jobs on the right hand side.

From the early years when we set up in business and on an ongoing basis our success was not without challenges. There were lows, real lows.

We spent large, made substantial capital repayments off the mortgage, becoming mortgage free on our first and then second more expensive house in Windsor.

However, we would face astronomical tax bills for which all too often we had failed to set aside an adequate amount of money. At these times the pressure was massive.

By which I mean that we had to win deals and get paid the resultant fees. otherwise we would run out of money.

Up till this point I was normally working 8.00 till 8.00 and doing some work at the weekends, and perhaps we'd take 5-10 working days off a year.

Whilst our income was unpredictable and subject to spikes, generally it was increasing each year. However, on a daily and weekly basis we could be up one minute and down the next, by perhaps as much as 10-50k.

On the way up

It was exciting, and high pressure.

When we weren't working, we'd be going out, seeing friends, going to the pub and on dog walks, and because Caroline loved history we'd regularly go on trips to visit country houses, palaces and places of historic interest.

I loved this too.

One of the clients for whom I was recruiting and with whom I got on well kindly gave me a lead:

"Robert, you should get in touch with this chap at IBM, he's recruiting, his name is Tim…"

When I called the IBM switchboard I wondered if they would put me through. Often companies screen callers. However, sure enough they put me through, I was a little nervous, this could be the start of something big or alternatively people can be dismissive, rude even sometimes.

And he answered the phone. A make or break call!

This was exciting, at the time IBM was the most prestigious tech vendor on the planet.

He answered the phone and, after a short call, I'd picked up his vacancies and suddenly I'd opened the door into the #1 vendor in the business.

Back then there were fewer women in the workplace and especially in the tech sector.

This chap Tim wanted to recruit several salespeople into IBM to sell software. He wanted candidates who were of a high quality and with very specific skills by which I mean familiarity with product types and market sectors.

We had many software salespeople, it just so happened that the best three we had were all girls. And he hired them.

Each of them was bright, ambitious and very good looking.

This made me smile for more than one reason.

When Tim hired these girls and they walked around the office, apparently they were referred to as Tim and his hareem.

Obviously it was a complimentary thing for people to say but I'm not sure people would make this sort of comment today.

On the way up

These ladies not only proved successful hires but one of them went on to become a member of IBM's senior EMEA leadership team, another proceeded to become one of the industry's top 1% of performers and the third did well at IBM for several years. I lost track of her.

Long before the days of LinkedIn.

So the hiring of these 3 AAA quality candidates was the starting point of our relationship with IBM.

❋ ❋ ❋

Chapter 3
Hitting the big time

Around this time, we'd been living in Windsor for some six years. However, with three dogs and more money, we wanted a house with a large garden. The houses in Windsor had small to regular sized gardens and we found what we wanted 10 minutes' drive away between Windsor and Ascot.

Looks can be deceptive.

When Caroline showed me the estate agent's picture of the house, I didn't want to see the place. It didn't look good from the outside, in fact it looked really quite dull from the front. What prompted us to view the property was its enormous garden.

Just two steps in from the entrance, I was standing in this amazing hall.

You could fit a house in the hall itself. It had a grand fireplace, a sweeping staircase spanning two sides of the hall and a balcony on the third side. The hall was upwards of 30 feet in height. At the top was a magnificent domed ceiling and a cupola with several glass windows letting an abundance of light into this grand hallway.

I knew instantly that we both wanted to buy the place.

The house had an extremely large garden, which many years earlier had been landscaped. It was like a small park and ideal for our three large dogs.

It was the wing of a former mansion house, and whilst it had just three bedrooms, the room sizes were huge, and the garden extended to approaching three acres.

So we bought the place.

However, the décor, kitchen and bathrooms were all dated. We went about refurbishing the place and, given that we were making a lot of money, we were able to be extravagant in our tastes. We started to furnish this historic Regency property, which had large, elegant rooms with roots going back to the 17th Century, in a classical style with antique furniture and paintings.

We were on a high but were soon brought back down to the ground with a

Hitting the big time

hard landing. The accountant we'd worked with for several years had died. He was a sole practitioner, which caused a six-month problem. He had been in possession of our previous annual accounts and his work in progress was an asset of his estate! This meant that until such time that his will and affairs were sorted out, our accounts remained under lock and key at his office.

So when his estate was eventually settled half a year later, we were able to pick up our accounts and we appointed a new accountant.

When he first came to the offices in our house, his behaviour was chauvinistic, which upset both Caroline and me. He picked up some paperwork which was no longer needed, crunched it up and chucked it on the floor of the room – in our house! How rude. Caroline quite rightly thought, you male chauvinist pig!.

There was no place for his behaviour and Caroline understandably took great offence, on the basis that she was tremendously successful, hard-working and very smart.

He subsequently incorrectly calculated our tax liability.

He'd under-estimated our tax by some £30k. This was partly due to nuances in the tax system, its various complexities, multiple types of tax, payment dates etc, but also a failure on his part to put tax liabilities in writing.

When we first instructed him we had been very specific. Our number one requirement was that we needed very clear notifications as to our tax liabilities, amounts to be paid and dates these needed to be paid. However, he had omitted a large tax payment.

I was annoyed by this. Had we been properly advised we would have spent less money. I found his failure incompetent, I explained to him that this was a big mistake on his part and terminated him as our accountant.

This was a tremendous setback. A £30k tax underassessment means you've got to earn £60k to recover…

I do think small businesses are dealt a harsh set of cards by banks.

For my business, I've typically always had quite a lot of money in the bank, tens of thousands of pounds purely to cover tax liabilities and then money to cover bills. Up till this point I'd quite regularly had £20-50k in the bank (in the future considerably more!). Nonetheless, when you go to the bank asking

Hitting the big time

for a business overdraft you feel as though you're going cap in hand, asking to borrow £30k when they can see you've regularly held this and more with them, and you can show a forward projection.

They give you a stern look, a bit like going in front of the headmaster at school when you've done something wrong. Today a business overdraft of that amount is simply a few clicks away.

Back-to-basics then. And whilst my shortfall was not insurmountable, I had to get a temporary overdraft to pay the tax, and banks don't like this. Banks want to lend for investment and to fund cashflow. They don't want to provide overdrafts for people who have incorrectly assessed their tax liability and overspent.

Having explained the situation to the bank, they granted us an overdraft and recommended a very good firm of accountants which I use to this day.

Two weeks after I terminated our work with the accountant who had incorrectly advised us, the taxman came knocking at our door.

We'd had just one previous tax inspection some three years earlier, and I don't see it as a coincidence that the tax inspector's visit came so soon after we terminated the work with the previous accountant. I don't think he liked me pointing out his errors, and reckon he suggested to the taxman to check us out purely out of spite.

Whilst a tax inspection is a distraction and time consuming, we were squeaky clean, nothing irregular, nothing found, nothing going on which was wrong.

But that doesn't mean to say you don't worry. The tax inspection didn't particularly worry me but our shortfall of £30k did, which at the time took the wind out of our sails.

With no guaranteed income, you're always wondering where the next deal will come from. When will it be, how much will it be, when will it get paid and is it a good deal?

A good deal is one where everyone wins… where the employer is hiring someone into an opening where the odds of them sticking, staying and being successful are very much in their favour.

For someone taking up a new job there is a similar logic. Can they do the job,

Hitting the big time

will they be successful, and will they be happy?

And for us, all the above plus us getting paid. Anything else is a compromise.

There are many risks involved. And for us, importantly, sustaining an income was a constant worry.

Can I/we make it happen? What if we don't get the deal?

The uncertainty and the pressure do make you anxious.

At this point in time, it wasn't the end of the world, whilst a major set-back equating to two to three months' billings. Deal cycles back then were much shorter than they are now... deals took weeks to months. Today they're normally months to quarters!

On a positive note, at work Caroline and I elevated one another.

Hard work never hurt anyone, and the more you apply yourself, the luckier you get. We righted our little ship.

Caroline and I made a pretty good team. By this time, we'd been together for about eight years, living and working together 24/7. Whilst my parents no doubt loved me, and went to great efforts for me, I was never with them for a substantial period. For better or for worse, Caroline was like the family I never had.

"I want people with intellectual firepower".

That's what one of the hiring managers at IBM said to me.

IBM's expectations when it came to be hiring were high. I'd got lucky with the three fantastic sales hires. I happened to have access to these three A player types and whom I'd cherry picked from our database (the best of the best).

To deliver well to IBM we'd have to raise our game! We'd need more of these "best of the best" types.

To me IBM represented a once in a lifetime opportunity.

What appealed to me was the opportunity to work with the worldwide number #1 tech vendor.

I've interviewed thousands of people and, for the majority, work is something bigger than just the money, and most people believe that if you do the right thing, money will follow.

Hitting the big time

And I'm no exception.

What appealed to me most was the challenge and the prestige associated with finding the best people, which I knew would be a big ask with such a client.

I was already making big money and could do so without IBM. However, I was cognizant that being such a big company, with so many potential hires to be made, that this would represent my biggest billing opportunity.

Over a period of three years IBM quickly became our biggest account.

I didn't expect to bill a million pounds into IBM.

And I didn't realise what an education IBM would give me, nor did I realise how difficult it would be either.

Not only was I drawn to this big, most prestigious and powerful company in the world, but I knew others would be too.

Working for such a renowned, truly globally recognised prestigious blue-chip company like IBM, is something to which most people aspire to. In fact, let me use the words dream of.

And for mums and dads, girlfriends and boyfriends, partners and grandparents, when someone you love or care about goes to work at such a company, it's something people are tremendously proud of.

It's like joining an elite country club: "You're not coming in if you don't meet our high standards."

Only the best get in. The brightest brains, those with the best degrees from the best colleges and the people with the best credentials. In many cases these are people with privileged backgrounds, characterised by those who have had the benefit of a good education and family background, are most likely to be well presented, well spoken, using correct grammar, well mannered, confident, well read and worldly; in a nutshell "credible". At an advantage.

In contrast, a significant proportion of people who may have had a poor education and less privileged upbringing are likely to be at a disadvantage, being less well presented, less eloquent, having a less proficient command of the English language (good grammar, broad vocabulary), being less confident, less well informed and less able to impress. At a disadvantage.

It's possible to address gaps such as these, but without strong personal qualities,

Hitting the big time

a lot of these people just won't get into the club.

Some of these attributes are coachable. And this has become an area of interest for me, and in the fullness of time became an area in which I'd develop expertise.

IBM recruited from me what they called experienced hires (i.e., not graduates, not people embarking on their career journey).

They were people who had very specific knowledge/skills, strong track records of accomplishment, the best of the best, usually the top 10%.

I changed people's lives.

Many of these hires progressed through multiple promotions and multiple levels of seniority. Several became senior execs managing hundreds or thousands of people.

Others were able to take their careers in new directions, into new occupational types and/or business units, fulfilling career aspirations and dreams, taking pathways they would not have been able to go down elsewhere.

For all the hires IBM acted as a catalyst and a platform on which to develop themselves, realise their full potential and become the best they could be.

Just because IBM was a big name this didn't mean recruiting for them was easy.

In fact, to the contrary, their expectations were sky high. However, they were paying the same or less money than people were already being paid!

Here's how I made it happen:

Firstly, through file search and advertising. I selected the best people who were already on file, on our radar and from powerful, well thought out advertising.

Secondly, I networked, using various intelligence gathering techniques to identity people.

IBM wanted to hire people who were AAA quality types, high achievers, with high potential and, importantly, with experience in market areas/product areas which IBM either wanted to move into or wanted to expand further into. These included business intelligence & data warehousing, supercomputing, hosting, ITO, BPO and ecommerce.

They wanted to hire people with experience in new, emerging areas and guess

Hitting the big time

what...? These people were in short supply, hard to find and hard to move.

My approach was to firstly identify the hunting ground, from what industry types/niches and specific companies might the best person for the job be employed within?

This meant determining a clarity about the sector, and competitive landscape. For IBM, this often meant several niche sectors rather than just one. One of my first vacancies with IBM was in their speech recognition business, and as time went on several were in business process outsourcing.

Having determined the immediate market type and direct competitors, I'd then look to broaden out the hunting ground by identifying adjacent market niches and the companies within them.

Once I'd identified which companies were operating in the sectors IBM wanted to hire from, I'd then identify the people working at those companies in the relevant job types I was recruiting into and then approach them.

This wasn't easy, this was before LinkedIn. It meant I had to do a lot of networking and much creative work!

You might think calling people is easy. However, whilst sometimes I might have someone's mobile number, this was not often the case, which meant often I'd have to try get them by dialling through the switchboard.

I'd have to be clever to get past the gatekeepers.

And people don't often pick up on the first call anyway...

I was calling people to whom I hadn't spoken before, persuading people who were employed, often heads down and happy, and not actively looking to move jobs. I had to grab their attention, uncover their motivations and interests, and talk about the merits of the opportunity. Whilst simultaneously sounding them out and trying to work out how good or average they were!

One of the merits for me in working with IBM was refining my approach and fine tuning my skills. Applying a headhunting approach, I came to see things in different ways, a more consultative one, more considered and with a pin-point kind of accuracy.

In addition to identifying people working in like-for-like positions, in like-for-like types of industries/tech sectors, I leveraged my people network for broader

Hitting the big time

based searches and to stretch out the net.

Who knows what, and who knows whom?

A major obstacle was that invariably people would offer up someone who was actively looking for a new job, who were unemployed, had been let go or who were under performers. This is a common issue which headhunters like me face...

Recommend a failure? No thanks.

Which meant I had to be pushy and firm to get people to open up with the names of strong, relevant people who might not be actively looking and who may not even want to be called.

Of the 97 people I recruited into IBM, one in two were people previously unknown to me, who weren't on our database nor people who had responded to adverts.

I was persuading people who were heads down and happy and well regarded in their employment to move jobs.

Whilst I appreciated that different people had different motivations, my experience with IBM, for whom half of the people I recruited were ones whom I had headhunted, ingrained in me the critical importance of tuning into what different people wanted.

I developed my own catchphrase for this...

A benefit is only a benefit if it is relevant to someone.

And I learned how to best uncover what people's motivations are and how to use this to my advantage.

Persuading someone to give up their existing job isn't something you can do overnight and is something you should only do if you genuinely believe there's merit in the person making the move.

It's a gradual process, where you need to build a prospective hire's interest and confidence in an opportunity.

As a headhunter you can encourage both the hiring manager and candidate but both sides really need to build on this as the hiring experience progresses through interview stages, and the calls, and follow-up in between them.

Hitting the big time

Generally, a momentum needs to be maintained without which interest levels will tail off on one or both sides. It's imperative to keep both sides warm.

In my capacity as a headhunter, I looked to ensure this was maintained… conversely if one side really isn't interested, and it's not going to happen, you need to highlight the gap, and most likely stop the process.

Most of the time the follow-up required is more considerable than you'd imagine.

You cannot be overly forceful, that is counterproductive.

Often headhunting someone out of an existing job requires both a push and a pull factor.

This means there is something missing or which someone is unhappy about in their current employment (push factor).

And there is something meaningful to be gained in the new opportunity (pull factor).

It's not always the case that a new opportunity will give enough of a carrot to someone who is head down and happy, performing well, well integrated in their existing job and well regarded, in order to give up what they've already got.

The third catalyst for my success was hard work, long hours and packing a lot into those hours.

Someone once said to me:

"You work 6 times harder than everyone else."

IBM tended to pay the market rate and the people whom I was after were highly sought after, in demand and high earners.

Often these people would be generously paid, which meant they may have to either move for a like-for-like salary or perhaps take a modest salary cut!

No-one is going to put their hands up and say "YES, I'll take a salary cut."

I knew IBM could offer more than just money. Which meant I would look to tune into the right people for the right reasons and to re-frame their thinking.

I identified two angles on which I could establish a strategic and superior positioning for IBM.

Before I explain these, I should say that in a recruitment or headhunting

Hitting the big time

situation, you have got to tune into people's motivations.

This is because a benefit is only a benefit if it is relevant to someone, so you could offer up to someone what you may think is a plus point but others may think it's a negative. For example, with IBM this would often be "IBM's the biggest company", which meant this appealed to some but others didn't like the idea of working for a big company!

If you want to be a good recruiter or headhunter, you need to be honest with yourself and with others and recognise when there is a match, and when there is not.

My approach was to… ask people what their priorities were, what their goals were, and how they wished to develop their career.

My first angle was around personal & career development and leadership.

If they were career minded and wanted to develop themselves as much as they could do, to be the best version of themselves, then this could be a good sign.

People would talk about how they wanted to grow their careers, build new skills and, in some cases, they liked the idea of brand IBM.

I would aim to get them to elaborate further about their aspirations and then position IBM as being able to meet these: "and, by the way, the salary may not be quite as good. However, you can expect to enjoy accelerated career growth, personal development, bonus payments and progression through pay grades."

My second angle was in respect of the power of IBM to be able to perform better over a longer period of time… many of IBM's competitors would be successful for a few years but fail to innovate on an ongoing basis.

IBM continually evolved. Working for IBM you could join in one business unit and move into another, even if you stayed in one business unit. IBM is great at bringing new products to market.

People could enjoy more sustained success with IBM.

I did a lot of work for IBM, my biggest client: 97 hires over three years, that's £1m+ in fee values, in today's money perhaps the equivalent of £3m!

Beyond the money, I feel so proud to have worked with IBM which, for me, is the prime example of what a company can be at its best.

Hitting the big time

IBM has respect for people. Quality first – that was their motto in recruitment. Apple's still in catch-up mode; IBM's the only tech company to have continually re-invented itself over so many decades.

IBM was our flagship account. However, we were rocking and enjoying runaway success with other big-name vendors including but not limited to HP, Oracle, Sun Microsystems…

If you stand still you actually regress…

I was continually looking for improvement. If we were not the first with a website, we were one of the first, and we invested in a good database, good software and network.

In life there's always someone bigger and better than you, and who knows more than you.

My confidence was about to take a knock.

Something happened which was to influence my approach very heavily.

Lotus, one of the IBM divisions, had got in touch. They wanted to hire people but at the time there was a shortage of the kind of people they wanted. I had presented some good people, but Lotus were dragging their feet.

If they did not act swiftly, other companies would offer my candidates jobs, IBM Lotus would lose them, and I would lose prospective deals. It was possible for me to place these candidates into other IBM divisions or other clients of ours.

I explained this to Stephen, the IBM Lotus HR manager, but what I thought was a realistic point to make was misinterpreted. They asked me to come into their offices, the whole thing backfired on me, and the HR manager proceeded to give me a dressing down.

His interpretation of my comment was that I was trying to pressurise them, and he deemed my approach unprofessional.

He had taken offence at my position and proceeded to make the inference that they were recruiting professionals but that my manner was unprofessional.

He implied that they were expert at interpreting hiring requirements and assessing talent but that I was not. In hindsight, in reality to an extent he was

Hitting the big time

right; I was expert at attracting the right people but had gaps when it came to assessing them.

I knew things which he did not! And he knew things which I did not.

I take a lot of pride in what I do, and I felt very humiliated. However, I bit my lip, reflected on what he was saying and apologised if I had acted in haste.

In recruitment there is the need to keep everyone on side, client and candidate, even when you think you are right, or know you are right, you need to be cautious.

Eating humble pie had a payback.

The following afternoon I received three successive calls from him, each one offering one of my candidates a job: three offers, three acceptances.

By the way, that really was a one off, to have 3 successive calls offering people a job. For the type and context of recruitment which I do this really is very unusual.

Obviously, I was delighted about the prospect of the resulting fees, but I did think perhaps his patronising behaviour towards me had been unnecessary.

Importantly it did serve to supercharge my sense of purpose and my determination to be the best.

I didn't want to be second best to anyone.

There's always someone bigger than you and better than you, and when it came to interviewing, Stephen knew things which I didn't.

You would not have expected it, but I developed a good relationship with him; in the fullness of time he became a mentor to me and friend of mine.

His input shaped the basis on which I have refined parts of my approach to interviewing, appraising and benchmarking people.

In the years which followed, I undertook work with him as a client and had the privilege of having him work for me, when undertaking some large scale and senior level recruitment search campaigns.

I adopted two of his principles and use them to this day among my arsenal of interviewing techniques. The first is the importance of taking and maintaining control of the interview, and the second being around how to best explore

Hitting the big time

candidate suitability, including structuring questioning in a logical sequence: past, present and future.

In the fullness of time I would come to interview lots of people with him. In addition to his pragmatic approach to interviewing, I've observed that he has a certain sixth sense. Headhunters and people who are truly expert at recruiting, which Stephen certainly was, are able to see things which others do not notice. This does not come from a textbook alone; it comes after many years of experience.

And that was an attribute I was beginning to develop myself, and in years to come people would say similar things about me.

As I said before, I wanted to be in the "best of the best" category.

To be the best I could be I needed to become more sophisticated in my approach and smarter.

Neither Caroline nor I had a background in one of the large professional search firms, we were unaware of the best practice they applied and how they applied it. We'd have to work out it for ourselves how these elite headhunting firms operated, and determine how we could elevate our modus operandi to their kind of level.

I did some research trying to discover what their methodology was, what techniques did they use which we were unaware of, and what their secrets were. Eventually I found what I was looking for. It was a book, an expert guide, available only in the USA. if I recall I paid £100 for the shipping fee alone. In today's money perhaps £300-500.

This was before the existence of a plethora of info on Google, and the arrival of Amazon and Kindle.

It was worth every penny.

I read it and was able to apply the best practices outlined to me and our evolving team.

Not only had I developed my approach to recruitment but similarly Caroline's had become much more sophisticated. She read and watched the news and she had an amazing memory. Politics has much alignment with history and Caroline developed and maintained a good knowledge of the goings-on in

Hitting the big time

politics and government, which she leveraged to her advantage in recruiting into roles which had a government focus.

The government was outsourcing a lot of IT and business processes and this resulted in her recruiting business unit directors/GMs, sales directors, bid managers and heads of innovation.

Some of the people we recruited architected, won and delivered contracts in the tens of millions of pounds, hundreds of millions of pounds and a handful even £ billion plus.

Her approach to people was very different to mine, being extremely personal, high on personality and low on detail, whereas mine was more pragmatic.

We were proud, we'd taken risks and worked hard. Whilst what I am about to say may seem big headed, such was our success that we were above our peer group in terms of financial career success and status.

Whilst we were earning big money it didn't come easily, it required a lot of hard work. You can't manufacture people, and for specialist roles it takes a lot of time and effort to find them. And there were continual surprises, pressures and lots of emotional ups and downs.

By this time we really were living the dream.

Living in this grand house was the happiest time of my life with Caroline.

As I said, Caroline loved history and country houses. Having visited so many in recent years, each time this would inspire Caroline (and me) to restore our house to glory, copying the themes we'd seen in these houses.

She had good taste; this was primarily her passion, mine to a lesser extent.

We replaced and restored sash windows which had become rotten or previously removed.

We populated the house with antiques and fine art, having magnificent bespoke high-end curtains made and fitted complete with pelmets (a stylish classic encasement which hides away any unwanted fixtures) and tie-backs. There was an endless list of more subtle finishing touches like fitting crystal door handles.

I loved it. It made me feel aristocratic, like the lord of the manor. We had spending power and could afford what to most would have seemed extravagant.

Hitting the big time

When I reflect back on those times, there was an aspect of arrogance about us. It wasn't deliberate, though some people probably thought of us as Lord and Lady Muck.

The garden had been landscaped dozens of years before. It was so large, mowing the lawn on a ride-on lawn mower normally took two to three hours. It was almost like a small park and featured a pond for which I bought Caroline the smallest of rowing boats.

And every morning and every lunchtime Caroline would walk her favourite dog, Timber, round the garden, normally a 15-minute walk. This was her time and normally she'd come in with a smile on her face.

With spending power came confidence.

We were getting kicks out of having money. It wasn't a matter of pushing it down other people throats, more a case of self-satisfaction.

Concorde used to fly over our house every day from London, usually to New York, transporting global execs and rock stars. It also flew people to Barbados in under four hours.

As I said, Caroline was very resourceful and got the travel tour operator on the phone. They'd put together packages, flights and hotels. She negotiated the price down by perhaps 10%.

And so we flew to Barbados and back on Concorde; we felt on top of the world.

On entering the aircraft, I was struck by how small the cabin was and how beautifully finished.

British Airways navy coloured leather seats, two on each side of the aisle. It wasn't big inside, Concorde had a long thin body.

We sat down in our seats; it was so exciting.

"Would you like Champagne?" No ordinary Champagne on Concorde: Louis Rodriger, one of the exclusive top end brands, perfectly chilled.

Once in the air, I thought I'd take a photo. I felt somewhat self-conscious about doing so, although no sooner had I stood up and taken photos, then everyone else followed.

Hitting the big time

Our flight took off from London Heathrow Airport after we'd had a champagne breakfast in the Concorde lounge, and we were having a late lunch by the Caribbean sea just a few hours later.

This was our second time to Barbados. This time round we were richer and able to afford to go to some of the better restaurants which had begun to appear. At the time they were in their infancy but are now quite renowned, like The Cliff, which is in an amazing setting, its torchlit terraces set above a floodlit cove, simply majestic, and the Lone Star, which at the time had a wow factor, it was very contemporary.

Before the return journey, I remember having our photo taken at the airport on the tarmac adjacent to the runway, with Concorde in the background which we were about to board.

I tried to put my arm around Caroline for the photo, but she refused, being in a mood for some silly meaningless reason. She was difficult, as I have repeatedly said. Such a shame.

On the return journey I remember looking out of the window and being able to observe and consciously pay attention to the curvature of the earth. Concorde flew higher than other jets, and I remember as I looked one way and then the other, I could observe the differences in daylight, daytime and night-time in different time zones.

You'd have thought a holiday such as this could not be beaten!

A lot happened in the period 1998 to 2001.

'You do not have to say anything, but it may harm your defence if you do not mention when questioned something which you later may rely on in court. Anything you do say may be given in evidence'.

We'd originally bought what was the left-hand side of the mansion, which had a small number of massive rooms including three bedrooms. Then the middle part of the house became available, it was similar in size but had three floors and many more rooms, including eight bedrooms. We bought it.

So we now had a house with 11 bedrooms.

This was obviously a major expense. Extremely run down, we went about having it renovated; a huge project, back then an investment upwards of £200K

Hitting the big time

and in today's money perhaps double or more. We had the roof and much of the fabric of the building rebuilt.

The house's origins went back to the 1800s and was grade two listed. This meant it was subject to various historic building preservation orders, and planning consent was required for anything other than minor repairs.

There were limitations as to what you could and couldn't do. Whilst we were doing a lot, we were not doing anything which shouldn't be done. However, someone must have tipped off the local authority and planning department. The collective size of the works meant planning approval was deemed to be required and without this we couldn't continue. Furthermore… they cautioned us!

'You do not have to say anything, but it may harm your defence if you do not mention when questioned something which you later may rely on in court. Anything you do say may be given in evidence'.

Both Caroline and I were quite offended by this. We were extremely hard working, paid huge amounts of tax and had invested big money in renovating this property, with works carried out sympathetic to its era.

Caroline, being Caroline, lost her temper with the people from the planning department and, when they were leaving the property, she proceeded to slam the door of their car shut, trapping one of the ladies' legs between the door and the car body.

Whilst this didn't cut any skin or break any bones no doubt it caused some pain and bruising.

This was typical behaviour for Caroline and completely unreasonable. Whilst these people were doing things we did not like, they were simply doing their job.

Any margin of flexibility was now gone out of the window.

The project had to be put on ice, we had to pay some damages to the builders in lieu of loss of work and for proper planning consent to be written up and approved.

This caused a six-month delay.

This was a large project; once resumed and completed, with the left wing and

Hitting the big time

central parts of the house now reunited, we ended up with a massive house, complete with 11 bedrooms.

Soon after we'd recommenced the building work, there was another incident.

"Mr Tearle, can I have a word?"

I was in the bank; I'd been going there regularly on Fridays for perhaps over 12-18 months, every Friday with the exception of the six-month delay, and each week I'd normally take out £2k to £10k in cash.

It had come to the bank's attention that I was taking out large amounts of cash. "May I have a word? Perhaps we can talk in the room here".

It turned out he wanted to understand what the cash was being used for. Was it perhaps being used for something illegal or untoward? I explained it was being used to pay the various builders, tradesman, craftsman and for materials, which he was happy with.

Our offices had been in the original part of the house, but we now had large offices and interviewing rooms in the newer middle section, and this coincided nicely with us expanding the business, and growing it to a peak of seven strong.

When I look back at this time, the amount of work I was doing was tremendous but because most of it was so positive and so exciting, my energy levels and drive must have seen me firing on all cylinders.

I would start work every day at 8.00. I'd be at my desk at 8.00 and I'd be on it at 8.00 not making a coffee, not reading an industry magazine, but working.

We didn't take much time off. In the early years of the business we didn't take holidays and when we became established, we still worked relentlessly.

At this time, we'd take just five to ten days off a year. Caroline worked 9-5, five days a week – she took care of most of the domestic stuff, I worked considerably longer and took care of all of the business affairs.

I was working flat out as well as managing all the goings on associated with the house refurbishment, development, admin and expansion of the business. I'd work on admin tasks and accounts at the weekend.

I raised and chased every invoice, I paid every supplier, I raised the employment contracts, I paid the employees, I produced and submitted the accounts, I wrote the adverts and I constructed the platform on which our business operated.

Hitting the big time

I bought the desks, the chairs, the filing cabinets, interview room furniture and moved them all around.

I fixed up the computer networks and telephony.

Back then, connecting the computers together and into the broader internet wasn't so much the drag and drop, menu kind of set-up you have today. It was all more hard-wired, coded. I smile as I look back at it. I made it work, I'm an ideas person, talker, enthusiast not a tech wizard.

As I said, there was a lot going on, hiring people, training people, coaching and managing them.

I felt responsible for their success or failure. When you run a business, the buck stops with you.

And this was a big worry. When people are doing well you don't get concerned, but when they are failing, struggling and not applying themselves well, and when you have questions over their ability, you worry about them.

Is it possible to turn them round if you confront them and tell them they're not doing what they're supposed to be doing well enough? Will you demoralise them? Will you have to carry them, support them, is it worth it? And if you have to sack them, wow! You'd feel really bad.

As the business got bigger, I worried a bit more about managing cashflow. As a small business owner, I always paid my bills by return but our client companies would take 60, 90 days to pay and in some cases longer.

Occasionally, I'd worry, will I run out of money?

This was a great experience - employing and managing the team, hiring people using my own money and investing my own money. When it comes to hiring, exposing yourself to a prospective loss is very different to hiring people if you work for a company, and are spending a company's money.

And if things go wrong, you've only got yourself to blame.

I found I'd be thinking about how to get the best out of these people and when they were not doing the right things or struggling, I'd be worrying about them.

And there's a balance to be achieved between motivating and encouraging with positive comments and being clear about criticising shortcomings. How do

Hitting the big time

you say something without upsetting someone, how to say what you mean and mean what you say? You need to be clear when managing people.

Being the boss of the business felt like I was the Daddy of the team. The buck stopped with me.

When you run your own business, no-one will be as motivated as you are.

By this time, I'd undertaken a lot of work for IBM and developed some good relationships across the business including HR and Recruitment.

I was invited into a supplier meeting with IBM, multiple suppliers had been invited. IBM wanted to move into eBusiness, hosting and eCommerce.

At the end of the meeting: "Thank you for coming in today, would Robert Tearle please stay behind…"

IBM wanted to run a large Sunday Times advert. A massive £50k full colour ad. They wanted me to exclusively manage, screen and shortlist the ad response.

IBM wanted the marketplace to see the company as being less stuffy and more contemporary, and with this in mind, the ad design by IBM's advertising agency reflected this initiative.

The ad featured an image of 5 teenage-looking young adults jumping into a lake, it was really refreshing and very much of a stand out nature.

At the time this was the greatest accolade that a recruitment firm such as ours could dream of.

It was a successful campaign, resulting in four hires (sales and consulting) which met both IBM's and our expectations. The ad was not just about attracting candidates, it also had a broader objective of promoting the IBM brand and, importantly, IBM as an employer of choice.

If you want to be successful in recruitment it requires a non-stop relentless work rate. It has a constant set of pressures; people are unpredictable and emotional. Recruitment is a job with lots of moving parts which create difficulties and anxieties.

And walking the dogs was my way of relaxing and recalibrating; it was my favourite time of the day.

It gave me thinking time.

Hitting the big time

I adored our dogs. Every morning and evening I'd pack the dogs into the Range Rover and off we'd go to a park. They'd be in the back, all excited, and I'd talk to them. And most days, whilst driving along, one would often push its head around the headrest, and place its long nose and head on my shoulders.

And often I'd feel the wet end of their nose on my face.

This was my time of day, I loved being with them, me and my three dogs, our little pack.

I remember one day there were two giant poodles in the distance, making their way over to us. Giant poodles are not small dogs, they are very big, athletic and strong. They were running flat out directly towards us.

Timber had wandered off and was perhaps 100 yards away and I had got Snowy on an extension flexi lead. Sherlock was close by me. Snowy was an escape artist. If he was let off the lead he wouldn't come back, so he was always on the lead when we were walking.

These two giant poodles, the same size as my dogs, perhaps a little bigger even, came bounding into us and started trying to attack Snowy. It's difficult to break up a dog fight at any time, especially when you have a dog lead in one hand, and two other dogs to split up.

In the distance, Timber had seen this happening and came full speed to the rescue.

He came bounding over and saw them off.

And so the trouble then dissipated.

It's interesting how dogs have a pack-like behaviour and attitude, our little pack, our little family.

Most of the time I'd walk the dogs by myself. It gave me my own bit of time, my own peace and quiet and time away from Caroline. However, on occasion she'd also come dog walking, but when she did sparks would often fly.

One of the places where we walked the dogs was on the land within the racing circuit at Ascot racecourse. The track is huge and at the time contained a golf course which was quite easy to walk around. However, Caroline would insist on walking over fairways and putting greens; she lacked consideration and respect

Hitting the big time

for others. The golfers would complain and shout at us to get the dogs off the course. Caroline would invariably become abusive towards them. I remember on more than one occasion one of the golfers saying: "you should control your wife" – well Caroline wasn't someone you could control.

All too often her difficult personality compromised what should have been many relaxing, enjoyable times.

Whenever I bought Caroline presents, she would invariably be unhappy with them and take them back, she could be a very difficult person to please.

With our spending power came confidence.

We were getting kicks out of having money and I'm pleased to say it wasn't a matter of pushing it down other people throats. More of self-satisfaction.

Our income enabled our excess!

As I said before, Caroline was fascinated by Henry VIII and his six wives: Catherine of Aragon, Anne Boleyn, Jane Seymour, Anne of Cleves, Catherine Howard and Catherine Parr.

Her interest prompted her to read numerous books written about them and for us to visit some of the places where Henry VIII and his wives had lived, including the Palace of Westminster, Hampton Court, the Tower of London, Windsor Castle, Hatfield House, Leeds Castle and, Caroline's favourite, Hever Castle.

One year, in the days preceding Caroline's birthday, this fascination prompted me to buy a set of 7 porcelain figurines of Henry VIII and his six wives – they were exquisite and came with a price tag to match, £900 back then – double it in today's money.

When I came to give her these on her birthday, I was excited. Surely, she's going to love them and will be delighted and appreciative of the thought I'd put into them. Bought with love, fondness and consideration.

"No, I don't like them, I don't want those."

I had to take them back, which I always found embarrassing. By this time, having become familiar with Caroline's behaviour, I'd checked with the retailer before buying them that I could take them back, and so I did.

Okay, so what do you want Caroline? "I want jewellery".

Hitting the big time

We'd been to Asprey before. Located in Mayfair, London's most exclusive retail area, it is a chic showroom for fine jewellery.

Asprey has had a royal warrant since 1781 and is one of the stores the Queen shops at.

The items which they have for sale are magnificent, including the finest pieces of jewellery, one of which was a pink tourmaline diamond necklace costing £17,000.

I paid for it with my black Amex card.

What next?

A love affair with horses and polo.

My morning routine was always the same. I'd get up early, shower and then walk the dogs. This was always my time, an escape and often my favourite time of the day.

I found the exercise made me ready and energized for the day, had a calming effect on me and that whilst walking I had many of my best and most creative ideas.

Not only did I walk the dogs every morning but also at the end of every day, which gave me a break from Caroline, especially when her temper was at its worst, and when I was at my unhappiest in my relationship with her.

After dog walking, my morning routine included taking a juice and newspaper up to Caroline and waking her up; she always got up later than me.

By the way, if I haven't already said so, Caroline didn't drive. Peculiar as it may seem.

One morning, having woken Caroline up, she immediately asked me to go and get her a copy of Horse and Hound magazine. She wanted to buy a horse.

We pretty much had most things in life.

Several hours later, having looked through the horses for sale section, she'd found one she liked. "I like the look of this one" she said. It was one of the most handsome and perhaps most expensive horses available for sale. "Let's go see him." A truly magnificent horse, Mitch, a dark bay gelding, about nine

Hitting the big time

years old, over 17 hands tall, we're talking a big horse, a magnificent one. We'll buy him.

If you're not familiar with horses, dark bay is characterized by a brown body colour with a black mane, tail, ear edges, and lower legs. Seventeen hands tall. Mitch was a stunning horse, powerful and a real head-turner.

This was not the right way to buy a horse. Caroline hadn't ridden for over a quarter of a century! If you buy a horse, it needs to be the right horse for you, the right type, right temperament, for the horse to be matched with the rider and with a suitable level of power for the rider. You don't want to be over-horsed.

99% of people who buy a horse ride it first before buying one. You really need to ride one to know if it's for you.

She wanted him, she hadn't ridden him, we bought him.

Realising this would probably be a passing fad for Caroline, an interest which would come and go, I thought I had better learn to ride. And I wanted to move the horse to a new stable with better and bigger fields for him to roam around in.

I found a wonderful new facility. Having viewed it and thought it over, I called the manager, Steve, told him I wanted to go ahead and for him to move Mitch to his set up. "Steve, I need to pay you. Where and when can I meet you to pay you the deposit and advance payments?"

"Meet me at the Royal County of Berkshire Polo Club (the Berkshire)." Where's that? It turned out the place was literally within a half of a mile from my house.

I'd had very little exposure to polo before. I'd watched Pretty Woman in my younger years, read about it in glossy in-flight magazines, and the previous year I'd been to a high-profile game.

This was an event at the UK's most prestigious polo club, the Cartier International at the Guards Polo Club, in Windsor Great Park. The place oozed sophistication, numerous rich and famous people graced this, the highest profile match of the year, and the winners were presented with the trophy by the Queen.

Society's most elite.

Hitting the big time

The ladies epitomised the word glamorous, dressed in designer outfits, accessorised with matching coloured metallic clutch bags, diamonds, and largely heavily made-up. Invariably posing, cutting elegant figures, showing off their toned legs, and some leaving little to the imagination. The men looked rich, successful and powerful.

So, I went to meet Steve at the Berkshire polo club. Wow!

The place is a world class polo club located near Windsor, Berkshire, a magnificent set up, set in a 230-acre estate and one mile from Ascot racecourse. Vast, comprising six polo fields and home to some of the most coveted high goal trophies in polo.

To start with I found the polo scene very unfamiliar and quite daunting. The whole world of horses was very alien to me, and I knew next to nothing about polo. The club struck me as being elite and as far as I was concerned, I was rubbing shoulders with the rich and the famous.

Polo is like football on horses, but a horse can run at speeds of up to 65 km/h. A polo field is equivalent to the size of five official football pitches and a polo ball can travel as fast as 160 km/h.

As soon as I stepped foot on the grounds of the club, I instantly knew polo was for me.

When I started going to the "Berkshire" polo club, I was impressed by the sports cars, lots of 4x4s, and there was an exclusive feeling about the place, complemented by a chilled kind of vibe.

In fact, occasionally you'd see someone fly to the club in their helicopter.

Sometimes you see what you want to see and what you see is shaped by your perceptions. At first I was slightly intimidated, and I was taken aback by how upmarket the whole set-up and scene was.

Everyone and everything had an air of exclusivity about it, and both the women and men were glamorous.

Polo gear! There's a defining set of clothing and accessories…

I remember being struck by how dazzling people looked the first time I properly took notice of what polo players were wearing.

A tall handsome Canadian man and stunning American/Italian blonde rode

Hitting the big time

by me on their ponies, wearing polo helmets, boots, colourful team shirts and bright white jeans.

White jeans and polo shirts. Most team shirts are in colours other than white, so the contrast between white jeans and coloured T-shirts creates a very marked style. Together with an accompaniment of accessories such as gloves and protective knee pads, this all forms the basis of the official polo gear.

It was not long before I met a couple who lived in London's West End. They were both investment bankers, they looked every inch the power couple.

The horses at the club were like athletes, muscular and impressively fitted out with saddles, saddle pads, reins, protective bandages etc.

And so, my love affair with the game began.

The most complex of sports, the basics being:

Polo involves two teams of four players. A full-size field is 300 yards long and 160 yards wide. There are tall goalposts at each end of the field and the object of the game is to score the most goals. Polo teams change sides after each goal to compensate for field and wind conditions.

A polo game has periods of play, known as chukkas (also chukkers or chuckers). Depending on the level of the game, four, five or six chukkas. Each chukka is seven and a half minutes long. Between chukkas, and sometimes during them, the players often switch to fresh ponies.

In the lower levels of the game, players may have as few as two ponies, alternating between them. Even at the lowest level a player will ideally play on three or more ponies in a game. The demands on the horse are high. And at the very top end of the game it would be quite usual for a player to play on eight or more horses.

It's a game with rules, penalties, interruptions and intervals; from start to finish most games last 60 minutes, and at a higher level 90.

To say that riding is difficult is an understatement. Simply hitting the ball whilst sitting on a horse is challenging, and playing the game even more complex.

Prior to sitting on a polo pony, I had only two riding lessons. I couldn't ride, let alone hit a ball whilst riding. We've all got to start somewhere, and I was going to make this work.

Hitting the big time

Welcome to the most difficult game in the world. Riding a horse is really one of the most difficult things to learn to do well. And OMG, the rules applying to the game of polo are extraordinarily complex.

When I started riding I'd be thinking, will today be the day when I fall off? How bad will it be…?

There's walking, trotting, cantering and galloping. The faster you ride, the more dangerous it feels.

I'd be thinking, will I fall off, get trampled on, break my nose, collar, shoulder, arm, leg or perhaps two or more?

Once I became more familiar with the place and its people, I came to understand that people were interested in polo and the polo scene for different reasons. Some simply liked the glamour, most liked the sport and the ego which goes with it, some the sport and the glamour — and of course there's the occasional contingent of single girls hanging around trying to bag a rich prince.

One of the best things about polo is that it's an inclusive sport, men and women play side by side.

And not all people in the polo community are rich. However, they all have one core common interest — an absolute passion for all things polo.

I have always played sports and have good eye/ball co-ordination, I played tennis in the school team and was both a reasonable rugby and cricket player.

However, to hit the ball on a horse, you need to be able to control the horse well and maintain good balance — as you and the horse move, change direction, accelerate, slow and stop… reach down and across, get bumped around in ride-offs — all at speed.

Fast, furious and featuring an incredible partnership of human and horse.

And with others in close proximity to you.

It's a dangerous sport. Expect to get hit by the hard, synthetic ball or other people's polo mallets, to take knocks with other players and horses. It didn't take long to find out that when you fall it hurts. It can happy really quickly, there's this thump on the ground, you having fallen to the ground from the height of a horse.

If you're travelling at speed, you fall at speed.

Hitting the big time

Technically you're supposed to roll to break the impact of the fall but that's easier said than done.

What I found was that whenever I fell, I was taken by surprise, it all happened very suddenly and normally my fall would be broken with me rolling somewhat.

Often one part of you will hit the ground first and, depending on your fall and how you fall, may mean you either get off lightly or perhaps break something.

My falls have all so far been minimal ones. As soon as I hit the ground I've felt a thud, and my immediate thought is am I OK? I haven't blacked out, but this is quite common.

Often there's an immediate feeling of being hurt but it's often 2 days afterwards, when the bruising comes through, that you feel at your worst.

Sadly, there are occasional fatalities on the polo field and these can be of professional players as well as amateur ones.

This is of course extremely rare. More likely that if you have a bad fall and are severely injured, you may get airlifted to hospital by an air ambulance if one is available. Indeed, this tends to happen several times a year.

If you take a high level view of the game it's extremely dangerous!

Ironically, in the first year of taking up the most expensive game you can imagine, I was at my wealthiest, my earnings at a high point.

Learning to ride takes time, it's not something you'll learn properly in a week. If you're unfamiliar with riding, it may look easy and effortless. On the contrary, it's one of the most difficult activities you could do in your life and far more exhausting than you'd ever imagine.

In my early years of playing, there were many occasions on which I was frightened about the speed of the horses and being able to stop them.

I felt the faster I travelled, the greater the danger I would be in, and that I'd lose control. How would I be able to hit the ball or ride the opponent off without losing my balance and falling off? Or what if someone bumped into me and I fell off?

And at the time I was regularly worried about whether I would be able to stop the horse. This isn't much of a worry at a walk, nor a trot, nor in a canter, but at full gallop I was scared, often intimidated.

Hitting the big time

You know when you see someone bumping around on a horse, perhaps in a movie, that was me to start with.

I had lots of lessons and in many of them I found the prospect of riding the horse scary. In some of these lessons I'd be tasked with riding quickly alongside a wooden wall, then stopping on a sixpence and instantly having to turn completely around, perhaps a bit like rodeo cowboys. I found this frightening. What scared me most now was falling into the wooden boards.

However, I wanted to play polo and knew this was part of the journey.

I came to appreciate that riding horses is for me the most wonderful thing in the world, and anyone who has spent a considerable amount of time riding will no doubt share my passion.

There is a certain beauty, smoothness, a kind of ballet when you ride, that's assuming you ride well or reasonably well. It requires a continual focus, absorbs my mind, and when I ride, I try to be at one with the horse.

To flow with the horse, give it gentle, considered commands; riding well really is a challenge.

The big thing in riding is balance. And in my early riding years, achieving this and doing it most, not some of the time, wasn't easy. As I progressed, I'd try to ride with good balance all the time, not most of it.

When playing in a game in my early polo years, perhaps my first two, my mind was often consumed with a fear of falling off.

My fear was offset by a determination to be able to ride well, play the game well. which I came to appreciate were skills which take a long time to develop.

It takes years to become truly proficient. To start off with, I felt that getting on the horse was intimidating and scary. However, as I became more competent my fear turned into excitement.

I bought my first horse, second horse, third horse and fourth. I was now playing the Game of Kings.

However, after getting involved with polo my earnings dropped somewhat. Ridiculously expensive, but I was smitten. Polo is addictive.

It's often said polo is like a drug habit and once hooked, it's like handing over your bank account details, passwords, pin numbers, with an open remit to debit

Hitting the big time

your account at any time, for things you both expect and don't expect.

Polo has speed, it's exhilarating, tremendously complex and challenging. A dangerous sport; when you ride and play, there's a certain edge.

There's an ever-present exposure to falling off the horse, bumping into other players or horses, being hit by the ball or someone else's mallet.

In my early years of playing polo I felt a constant state of anticipation, nervousness and motivation to play well. I still feel this to this day.

Prior to a game I'm all excited. How well can I play? How well will I play? Who are the competitors, how strong are they, who are their strong and weak players? Do they have any aggressive players whom I need to be aware of?

What's going to happen? I had a nervous set of anticipations with two extremes, firstly what I want to happen… I want to play like a professional, I want to excel and be the most valued player, or secondly, I might suffer a serious injury.

I'd envisage myself playing well, to be the best player on the best horses… in reality when you first start playing you're the worst on the field. Then my mind would wander towards the negative…

Will I fall off? What if I get trampled on or trapped by a horse weighing upwards of 1,000 pounds, 450kg, that's more than 10 times the weight of a human? And if I got trampled on, how bad would my injuries be? Might I break an arm or leg, or shoulder, or what if I suffer internal injuries?

What if a ball hits me on my elbow or in the face? Or if I get struck by someone else's stick? Will I get hit in the teeth by the ball and have my teeth knocked out?

These things happen in polo! One of the girls I know who plays polo had her new set of teeth knocked out just two weeks after having them fitted.

Next to ice hockey, polo is the fastest game in the world. You've got to be quick thinking, to keep up with what's going on and to anticipate what will happen next. And the rules of the game are complex. The game is so dynamic, everything happens in the blink of an eye. You've got to be constantly focused, engaged and switched on.

The invention of the game is dated variously from the 6th century BC to the 1st century AD! Its exact origins are unknown, although China, India, Iran, Mongolia and Pakistan all claim to be the birthplace of polo.

Hitting the big time

Whilst the roots of polo are from the Middle East and Asia, today the game is dominated on the other side of the world by Argentina.

I came to appreciate that one of the main reasons for this is that in Argentina there's an abundance of land and horses. The Argentine cowboys, referred to as gauchos, use horses to herd cattle and they can be credited with some of the breeding, horsemanship and management skills in keeping horses at their best, by schooling and training them. Many polo professionals have their roots in the pampas, the farmlands of Argentina.

It is the Argentine elite who have dominated the top end of the game. The high goal players usually come from polo dynasties where their families have large estancias (cattle ranches), they're large land owners, have huge farms in Argentina and breeding programmes geared up to produce exceptional polo ponies.

These professionals travel the world playing polo. Paid to play by billionaires in the USA, UK, Spain, Dubai, France, Switzerland and, more recently, China.

In the UK, there's a large contingent of Argentine professional polo players and grooms. Many come over purely for the summer polo season, some leaving broken hearts and more behind when they return.

I find the Argentine a fascinating type of person, and few of them speak English. Those that do often do so in a broken kind of manner. That said, I don't speak Spanish particularly well either.

The Argentine population has much of its origins from people who emigrated from Spain and Italy in search of a better life. Largely dark haired and olive skinned, they're well mannered, have a certain charm and an alluring accent.

Those with Latin European roots are often quite beautiful or handsome. Sexy and sensual, many of the girls have alluring sultry looks and likewise the guys look hot.

There are also those with more indigenous roots, with a sort of nomadic, Latin American-Indian look about them.

Almost two extremes. Those into fashion, glamorous and looking good. And a more earthy farmer type, a kind of Inca.

Hitting the big time

About this time, Caroline and I took our first trip to Argentina, about a 17-hour flight. We travelled up front with Aerolineas Argentinas – the Argentine airline – our holiday began when we stepped on the plane – largely Argentine travellers, and the crew spoke little or no English.

I remember the first time I went to Buenos Aires, Argentina's capital.

Magnificent, a huge city, three million people in the centre and a further nine in the greater BA conurbation. In the heart of the capital high rise buildings and flats dominate.

In central BA they have the widest avenues in the world – 7 lanes across in each direction. An eclectic mix of European cultures: Spanish, Italian, French and English styles.

We were there in their summer. It was baking hot, 29 degrees and humid. I always find the extreme heat and dryness of a big cosmopolitan city give it a certain feeling. Argentina is the source of tango, which has its roots in the docks of Buenos Aires…

It's a distinctive dance with a similarly accompanying type of music, really quite enchanting. I came to learn that it began in the working class port neighbourhoods of Buenos Aires.

Apparently, prostitutes used tango to seduce sailors, coercing them into parting with their hard-earned money. The sailors no doubt were intent on returning to their families with their small fortunes, but no doubt a great many were tempted into spending money with the oldest profession in the world.

There's little doubt that tango is the sexiest of dances.

I was captivated by the beauty of Buenos Aires, and in parts contrasting decay. It's rich in style; in the 1920s and 1930s there was a population explosion and economic boom, the city expanded quickly.

BA, as Buenos Aires is known, is a vast capital city, in the centre of which there's an abundance of truly elegant town houses and apartment blocks, European in their styling, representing the best of Parisian, Italian and Spanish themes.

Back then Argentina was so rich it was lending money to France.

I find there's a certain allure and sense of intrigue when I'm abroad. Especially

Hitting the big time

when people don't speak your language – and few people in Argentina speak English.

I suppose it's logical that Chinese is the most commonly spoken language in the world. However, you may not know that Spanish is actually the second most commonly spoken language, and it's Spanish which is spoken in Argentina.

English comes a close third!

So we'd arrived in Argentina… they don't speak English here!

This kind of makes it all feel daunting, special, mysterious…

However, I'd been listening to language audios and had just enough Spanish to get by. Our trip was partly arranged by a couple who had organised much of my polo in the UK. He's Argentinian, she's English.

After spending a night in BA, we flew to Mar Del Plata on the coast; this is a BIG city.

And we stayed in the Costa Gallana, a five-star hotel, in the penthouse suite on the top floor. At the time everything cost approx. one fifth of what things cost here.

I didn't know what exactly to expect but Argentina made an impression on me; I immediately loved the place.

We were there over New Year, and on New Year's Eve our hosts took us to a fabulous restaurant. It was a great evening up until a few minutes before midnight. Caroline got drunk, semi-comatose, and it was time to get back to the hotel.

She couldn't really walk properly, and of course not only did I find this extremely embarrassing, but sadly it also spoilt the evening for our hosts and me.

There followed the difficulty of trying to help her walk out, whilst trying not to make a scene, and then trying to get a taxi to the hotel. Of course, at midnight on New Year's Eve we couldn't easily get a taxi.

After walking, well of sorts, I was having to support Caroline's drunken state for approaching an hour before we were able to get a taxi back.

Hitting the big time

However, this really was disappointing and I felt we'd let our hosts down. And this compromised and ruined my New Year – yet another one.

This was my first trip to Argentina and on four of the days I played polo beside the sea. I was playing some medium goal polo there. Whilst out of my depth, this was a treasured experience playing at such a level, and in the baking heat.

At this level the game moves so fast, you struggle to be in the right place. There I was, a minus one handicap player (which means someone with quite limited ability) on a field full of four and five goalers (these being very competent, mid to high end professionals).

These players spoke little or no English, making it somewhat daunting but an experience not to be missed.

A polo game typically lasts for an hour to an hour and a half. Whilst it comprises four to six chukkas, lasting seven and a half minutes, the reality is that horses are changed at the end of each chukka and the game is subject to fouls, penalties and other stoppages.

The two games I played there were both five chukka games, in the baking heat of the Argentine summer and at a pace beyond my capability. I was exhausted after the second chukka – but I made it through to the end.

In each of these games I probably hit the ball just three or four times. This is quite usual when you are starting off in polo, but I like to be in the action, I like to make an impact. But that would have to wait.

These players were better than me. Better riders than me, better able to control their horses than me, better able to read the play than me, better able to hit the ball than me and better able to ride off than me.

I wanted to play like a God, not a numpty.

Still early days for me in my polo career!

My first trip to Argentina was certainly not to be my last.

❊ ❊ ❊

Chapter 4

The turning point

In hindsight I guess we'd reached our peak probably sometime in or after 2001.

Around this time Caroline and I took a holiday in the Bahamas, a better holiday by far than when we went to Barbados.

We flew to Nassau. If it sounds familiar it's the place that you'd associate with the Bond films Thunderball and Casino Royale.

And we stayed at the Ocean Club hotel, Nassau's smartest beach retreat which a year later would be viewed by audiences worldwide in Casino Royale…

When our taxi arrived outside the Ocean Club and began pulling in, I was struck by the manicured landscaped gardens, and we pulled up near its magnificent, pillared entrance, with large marble steps leading up towards reception.

It was impressive, we knew we were somewhere special and walked from the hot air outside into the air-conditioned reception, immediately struck by the calm, sophisticated and upmarket beauty of the place.

We turned and smiled at one another, feeling relaxed and pleased with our choice.

In Casino Royale Daniel Craig plays Bond, who arrives in the Bahamas in a waterplane, drives in his Ford to the Ocean Club, smashing into a car on his arrival in its in-and-out driveway.

He then plays a poker game in the library, located just off the lobby, and wins an Aston Martin DB5 at the gambling table.

After the game, in one of the Ocean Club's sea-view villas,, he seduces Dimitrio's girlfriend Solange with champagne and Beluga caviar.

The company who owns the hotel group refer to them as being "The one and only Ocean Club".

It certainly lives up to their claims; the most exclusive hotel on the island, it has a glamourous retro feel to it.

Ocean Club Bahamas is of an elegant colonial style, painted white, just

The turning point

two storeys tall, it's an exclusive elite retreat with just 105 rooms spread out over expansive 35-acre gardens. The hotel features mahogany furnishings, hardwood floors and colourful tropical flourishes. All of the rooms have louvered doors opening onto private terraces or balconies with direct ocean views.

A polar opposite of the nearby Atlantis with 3,805 rooms, the Ocean Club even has French-inspired layered terraced gardens.

In the evening it's super chic, with an elite set of people showing off their expensive clothes, drinking dry martinis, with jazz music playing in the background in the colonial-style main house.

We felt quite at home, Caroline dressed quite well in her outfits bought from Harvey Nichols, Harrods and boutiques, with her Chanel handbags and Cartier watches; she had 5 or 6 such watches by this time.

My style is quite understated. I'm a blazer, crisp pressed white shirt and smart jeans kind of guy. We fitted in well and would start each evening with a glass of champagne in the main reception before going out to dinner.

Our favourite restaurant was the Greycliff, an historic, colonial mansion set in lush tropical gardens. It even has its own cigar manufacturing facility; if I recall the original cigar roller (person who makes the cigars) formerly worked for Fidel Castro in Cuba.

I had a few meals rounded off with a cigar, I probably looked slightly stupid, I personally think cigar smoking is better suited to older people… anyway we enjoyed all luxuries.

We were living the high life. Privileged to be in such an exclusive and wonderful environment. The sort of place you associate with the rich and famous.

On the subject of which… guess who was sat next to us one evening at an Italian restaurant, Café Matisse in Nassau? Piers Brosnan with his second wife… he starred in the Bond Films: Goldeneye, Tomorrow Never Dies, The World is Not Enough and Die Another Day.

Caroline loved outings and she found out about a trip to Harbour Island, a two plus hour ferry trip. Harbour Island is one of the outlying Islands near Nassau

The turning point

and this was a recommended trip.

I wasn't enamoured with the thought of two plus hours on a boat trip there, and again on the way back. However, invariably doing something was always better than simply staying at the hotel or going to the nearest town.

As we approached Harbour Island… "Wow!"

Probably the prettiest place I have ever seen in my entire life.

As this small island came into view, I was viewing it across crystal blue waters.

I could see Dunmore Town, the main and only town in Harbour Island.

It had New England type houses, in pastel colours, set among trees and bushes with a pier, and at the time I couldn't see a car in sight.

I have an excitable personality; it takes a lot for me to become relaxed and as soon as I saw this place, I felt chilled.

The island itself has roots going back to the 1500s when the Spanish came to the Bahamas, captured locals as slaves and shipped them off to work in South America. This sleepy town was apparently known in the 1800s for shipbuilding, sugar refinement and making rum during the prohibition.

We were there before it became famous and before the celebs moved in.

We hired a golf buggy – few cars here, that's the mode of transport. Off we ventured to the other side of the island, perhaps 10 minutes if you're in a rush and 10 minutes if you're not in a rush. This is the kind of place where time stands still.

I felt hugely privileged to be here. What a special place, and when we got to the beach on the other side of the island we were looking at pink sands – there cannot be a prettier place on the planet.

This was heaven. The tranquil beach with only a small number of people dotted around, crystal waters, beautiful temperature. It was such a glorious setting we decided to stay the night and delay our return, and so we stayed in a hotel.

Unfortunately, whilst I felt I was in the most idyllic place on planet earth, I'd been worn down by Caroline's behaviour over the years and had come to despise her somewhat.

This was the best holiday I had with Caroline.

The turning point

We loved it so much that we returned some 7 months later. However, on this second trip, instead of taking the boat to Harbour Island, we flew to the adjacent island, Eleuthera, in a private plane and stayed at the famous Pink Sands Hotel. For me, Harbour Island is as a beautiful place as I have ever seen in my life.

However, my best holiday ever was yet to come!

It wasn't long after our return from Nassau that we made the decision to put Sherlock, our oldest dog, down out of kindness. Once lively, athletic and happy, he was now arthritic, struggling to stand up and looking sorry for himself. He'd been ill and now 16 years of age, he was suffering and in pain and the vet said the fairest thing to do was to put him to sleep.

I had him put to sleep in my arms. The vet came to our house and I sat on the floor, cuddling and holding Sherlock, kissing him on his head, talking to him, telling him he would be going to a better place, doggie heaven, and crying my eyes out.

This was my dog, I was his.

I was his best mate for 10 years, that's 3,650 days of two dog walks a day, that's 7,000 dog walks… 7,000 of the best times in my life.

Sherlock was an Alsatian cross labrador, and he absolutely loved me.

Caroline loved the youngest husky, Timber, liked the older husky Snowy. However, to Sherlock I was his and if I did have a favourite, it was probably him. Caroline, on the other hand, was very indifferent about Sherlock. I simply loved all three.

Sherlock's death was devastating. Everything was on a downward spiral.

We'd benefited from what was known as the "Dot Com Bubble", the tech sector had boomed and now it was about to crash; this was back in 2001/2002.

For many tech sector employees and associated unemployed it was a colossal career impacting event.

And it was disastrous for anyone like us working in the recruitment business focused on serving the tech sector.

The late 90s saw high growth driven by the internet and networking, and Y2K.

The turning point

As organisations approached year 2000, they were concerned their computers and apps would stop working because the software hadn't been designed to accommodate the number 2 at the beginning of the date. It could handle 1995, 1996, 1997, 1998, 1999 but what would happen in year 2000?

Companies were worried their computers would fail and with it their businesses.

This was a major motivating factor prompting companies to implement new improved systems, the latest tech and applications.

There was an explosion in spending in all things software, computing and networking.

This fuelled hiring demand, we benefited from a market wanting what we had… they wanted to hire "A player" people and we were able to find them for them.

Tech stocks surged, they were over-valued and multiplied in value five times between 1995 and 2000.

A massive high and then a massive crash.

What had been a hyper growth market sector was now on the floor; companies in the sector once strong were now weak; revenues were plummeting for vendors across the sector, tech vendors were laying people off.

What was a boom market was now bust.

This was our market, and our livelihood was attached to it.

Just a year earlier the sector had been rocking, tech firms dominated Superbowl advertising (the most watched event on the planet), 17 tech firms showcased their brands on prime-time TV.

Following the bust 3.

The market had imploded.

Then on September 11th, 2001 came the attack on the Twin Towers in New York. Obviously the 9/11 tragedy was such a sad loss for those who died and their loved ones. On a broader basis it served to add to an already rocked economy, including seeing flights around the world go into a lockdown…

One by one our big clients stopped recruiting: HP, Oracle, Sun Microsystems…

Our revenues halved and we had invested significantly in pursuing an

The turning point

expansion agenda; our previous conservative costs were low, now they were high.

We'd been spending big, both at work and at home.

This was probably my first severe crisis in life. And it wasn't to be just a case of a one-off incident, it was to prove to be the first of a series of catastrophes which were about to happen to me.

The collapse of the tech sector and hiring within it also coincided with several sea changes in respect of how employers sourced candidates, happening simultaneously!

Three significant game-changing shifts impacted recruitment simultaneously.

Firstly, companies were now able to advertise their positions on their own websites.

Secondly, they adopted self-sourcing in-house recruiting models.

Thirdly LinkedIn opened up their access to talent.

As the market slowed… With few vacancies both Caroline and I were able to achieve only modest success because we were well connected. However, the people working for us were struggling.

They were earning low commission or none and living off basic salary only. For Caroline and me the cost of employing them was only just covered by their modest billings, and at worst they were costing us money.

This was a very worrying time. I would go to bed at night thinking about how to best help them. And I'd question myself. Were these jobs in their best interests?

I remember one of the people working for me, who was cold calling. Our approach was always courteous, respectful and our team were well trained, and with good knowledge of the industry.

He had been cold calling for weeks, we'd all been doing a lot of this and we were not getting very far.

One of the people he cold called worked for a company called Compuware and told him to XXXX off. He was sitting beside me; I could hear some of what had been said and now I could see he was crying.

Recruitment is a tough job. However, I am delighted to say he went on to

The turning point

achieve great things. I constantly worried about the team. This was tough, was it worth it? And bearing in mind how difficult it was, would these people working for me leave to pursue other occupations once the economy had picked up?

These people were mainly in the formative years of their careers and I did wonder if they would actually be happier doing a different kind of job.

People in employer companies are often rude to recruiters, they can be patronising, make derisory comments or simply fail to respond to follow-up calls, cancel interviews and be generally unresponsive, ungrateful and unreliable.

Much of the time that a recruitment consultant invests in employer clients and candidates is undertaken for free.

Can you imagine how you would feel working for FREE?

Especially when people are rude, and in a job type which is unpredictable, often commission only or low base high commission.

The recruitment industry is working to an old model, largely unsustainable…

You need to be pretty resilient to stay in it, lots of people work in recruitment for 1, 2 or 3 years and jump out.

For Caroline and me, we'd done well in the good times but it wouldn't always be like that!

And back to the person who was working for me, who cried…

I'd like to think we supported him and the others well, we gave them breathing room, by which I mean plenty of time in which to produce billings.

We trained and supported them well, and we paid above market base salaries. However, in the here and now, most of them were not billing, and they were costing us money, which also led me to think how long can we go on like this?

And I'd worry would I have to let them go?

If I did let them go, would they be able to find a new decent job?

In fact, in the years to come I'm proud to say that some of the people I trained in their first jobs proceeded to work for IBM, Oracle, Workday, and some of the top end boutique search firms.

On a personal basis, I was thinking if we cannot get our billings back on a high, we won't be able to sustain our lifestyle.

The turning point

I started to wonder, had we reached a peak?

The turning point.

My career was a runaway success, but my life was a failure.

There's an expression:

"You can always earn more money, but you can never buy your life back."

Within a 10-year period Caroline and I had gone from having assets of £12K to being a multi-millionaire couple.

Over a period of some four years leading up to 2001 a lot was happening on both domestic and work fronts.

However, this also came with pressure.

At the time we had grown to become a seven strong team with recruitment consultants, researchers (research is the head-hunting term for generating candidates) and administrators.

When you are a child, you look up to your parents.

I'll use the word father figure meaning there's someone above you, guiding you, directing you, supporting you.

When you go to school and subsequently on to university, a similar scenario exists… teachers, lecturers above you, directing you. Again, I'll use the word father figure. When you go into the workplace, a similar scenario, your boss, your manager above you, directing you. Again, I'll use the word father figure.

When you set up and run your own business or are self-employed there's no longer any father figure.

The buck stops with you.

I felt as though I was everyone's father, I'm responsible for keeping it all together, so the one to look towards for support.

You're all by yourself.

And as the business expanded and we employed a small team I was the father figure, the Daddy. And with this came responsibility.

Caroline looked after the house, I looked after the business issues and whilst I'd always seek her approval on spending, I was the one carrying the can; the buck stopped with me.

The turning point

We had a high-profile brand. Many people viewed us as being the most pre-eminent headhunting recruitment firm in our niche; if we weren't #1, we were without doubt right at the top of our game.

The brand "Arena Search & Selection" was well recognised and regarded.

Life was good. We owned an 11-bedroom house complete with park-like gardens and by this time we had paid off the mortgage, i.e. no borrowings.

I had a string of polo ponies and we holidayed in the best hotels in Argentina, Barbados, St Lucia, Antigua, Mauritius and the Bahamas, travelling by Club Class and even Concorde.

Most of the time we enjoyed exceptional spending power… we had the interior of the house repeatedly re-designed, spent tens of thousands of pounds on curtains, tens of thousands of pounds on Persian carpets, a quarter of a million on antiques and fine art, with several paintings costing £10-20k each, and Caroline had a row of Chanel handbags.

We'd go to Harvey Nichols and Sloane Avenue, and then lunch at what was in earlier years Lady Diana's favourite restaurant, "San Lorenzo" in Beauchamp Place.

San Lorenzo was my favourite place to go. At the time one of those places where you feel like you've arrived.

With a discreet sophistication, rich and famous clientele, it comprises a sprawl of sunlit, conservatory-style rooms on different levels, done out in alfresco style with vaulted skylights, canvas umbrellas, pot plants and cheeky modern prints.

Italian food is my favourite. People go there for the best plates of zucchini al pesto, spaghetti with lobster, grilled tuna with cannellini beans or saltimbocca alla romana served by staff from the old school of Italian hospitality.

I felt proud of what I'd achieved in life, and the lifestyle was amazing. However…

As I said… You can always earn more money, but you can never buy your life back.

I'd got it all, or so I thought, but I wasn't happy. From the outside you'd think I'd got it all.

Why wasn't I happy?

The turning point

Primarily because I was unhappy in my relationship with Caroline.

Behind the scenes life was far from ideal. You don't know what goes on behind closed doors.

You may think you know someone well and on the surface people may come across as being happy. However, with most of the people you think you are familiar with, and may even think you know well, there's a good chance you don't know what's really going on in their home lives. And this will also apply to people around you: your colleagues, friends and family.

In my relationship with Caroline, I was always going to be vulnerable to being controlled as a consequence of my childhood background at boarding school, where I was told what to do, and I had to do it.

Caroline had a strong personality, was quick thinking and had the upper hand with me.

Pretty much from the outset, she had the better of me but over time her behaviour towards me deteriorated. She became increasingly manipulative and controlling.

You don't know what goes on behind closed doors!

Often, you'll hear people say that he or she is a really nice person, and they think they know that person well.

However, this is very rarely the case.

Most of the interactions you have with people, even some close family and friends, are ones of an arms-length nature. You may be in someone's company or be speaking to them on the phone perhaps 10% of the time, but what about the other 90% of the time?

And in my relationship with Caroline, whilst people could see that she was a difficult character they would not have appreciated how severe an issue it was.

Initially infrequent and quite low levels of aggression morphed into something more troublesome: 15 years of physical and verbal abuse. Physical violence and emotional abuse, regularly and repeatedly.

I felt a great shame that I had been beaten down and in hindsight I realised that I somewhat allowed myself to be beaten down and, looking back on it all, I guess perhaps some people could see it too.

The turning point

Caroline was not a very balanced personality.

She had a Jekyll and Hyde type character; there were two sides to her.

Often when she got angry, she was in such a state that she would be frothing at the mouth.

She had a temper I have not seen in anyone else. She would get so angry. She was quite happy to humiliate people, and the biggest victim was me.

More recently I've read that about two in five victims of domestic abuse are men.

Do you know that?

As a decent man you cannot hit a woman, which means you can't fight back. You can try to restrain the person, but you'll still get hit, kicked, your hair pulled, spat at and bitten.

I was ashamed and felt I could not talk to anyone about it.

The biggest problem was the booze.

In hindsight, the reality was that Caroline had an alcohol abuse problem. She would be in a drunken state five or six nights a week.

Frequently she would turn the music on really loud; I'm talking about the sort of volume which is so great you cannot think.

Numbed by alcohol, she'd get into the sort of state where everything she said was repetitive and then subsequently she'd fall asleep at the kitchen table, with her forehead and nose pressed against it.

I'd go to bed early. Often simply just to get away from her and or the noise.

She'd then come to bed in a drunken state and would become verbally and physically aggressive, hitting me, trying to pull my hair out and occasionally biting me. Initially I'd go and sleep in another bedroom, but this didn't always work; often she'd follow me in and continue in her aggression.

When this happened, and her behaviour became increasingly abusive, it prompted me to go and sleep in one of the bathrooms or shall I say attempt to sleep in it.

The bathrooms were the only rooms in the house with a lock.

My mind would be racing round with confused thoughts. Uppermost on my

The turning point

mind was the thought that she'd slowly been killing the love I had for her, which was making me despise her.

I'd lay awake many a night in the bathroom, quite cold, thinking about our relationship, and I'd wonder how I could get her to drink less or how could I escape from her?

My thoughts about her drinking less were overshadowed by feeling sorry for myself, feeling like a victim and wondering how I could get out of this relationship, tied in by our business, our dogs and our lifestyle.

Nonetheless I still had concern for her wellbeing.

Whilst we would go to glamorous balls and parties, she would invariably get very drunk, often becoming semi-comatose and unable to walk without assistance.

Obviously not a good thing for her or the people she was with, and for me it was extremely embarrassing.

By this time I despised her and had reached a point where I no longer wanted to go out.

On countless occasions I would try to talk to her about the problem, but her response was to get angry.

It was on one night, which should have been one of the best of the year for us, when she got very drunk that I came to the conclusion that enough was enough. I was worth more than this. I was not going to tolerate this any more.

Why did I not decide this earlier? I felt stuck. Why did I feel stuck?

We had our dogs which we adored, and whilst I no longer wanted to be with Caroline, I had some concerns for her and how she'd cope.

And there was a practical lock in: the continual need to make money to recover ground, i.e. continually paying down the mortgage and doing so with a proportion of money which should have been set aside for tax.

We were continually chasing our tails. Whilst the majority of the time we had large sums of money in the bank, these were often insufficient to cover our pending tax liabilities.

In hindsight we should have spent less and saved more.

Our income was continually unpredictable. Which meant that the constant

The turning point

pressure of having to earn, combined with Caroline's aggressive behaviour, made me feel very anxious.

Our relationship was dominated by making money and spending it.

We were getting our kicks out of spending large which compensated for some of the shortcomings in our relationship.

Eventually it got too much, and I wanted more out of life.

For several years we'd been supporters of the Born Free Foundation. The charity's focus is on 'Keeping wildlife in the wild' rather than being caged in zoos, chained or featured in nightclubs.

Caroline was fanatical about the charity; she'd seen the film Born Free in her childhood and was hooked on the cause.

She'd spend many an evening watching the Born Free film and then fall asleep in the lounge.

We were making regular and substantial donations to the charity; I'm talking thousands and tens of thousands of pounds.

If you're reading this and are opposed to people making donations to animal charities, which many people are, I can understand. Many prefer to give to human charities. Cruelty to animals and the abuse they suffer is a result of human choice, inflicted by humans, and both Caroline and I found this disturbing.

And our choices were primarily to give to animal charities.

Not only is animal cruelty wrong and it should therefore be condemned, but there is substantial research that shows people who abuse and are cruel to animals and fail to respect them, have been proven to go on to abuse or be cruel to humans.

Caroline's fondness for animals was admirable.

Prior to meeting Caroline, I wasn't really aware of intensive animal farming, the poor and cramped conditions in which they are kept, nor the factory type breeding and mass production environment in which they are abused.

I hadn't thought much about the cruelty of animals being kept in a zoo, keeping lions in pens the size of a tennis court and whales confined to something akin

The turning point

to the size of a swimming pool. Of course, I buy into the merit of animal conservation of endangered species… however some things are cruel and as a society we are all too often ignorant and turn a blind eye to animal abuse.

Caroline enlightened me and her passion became one which I shared. Ever since meeting her I have always gone out of my way to buy free range meat and eggs.

I don't feel proud of eating meat; in fact, the saying that "we are a nation of animal lovers" is ridiculous when you consider the conditions in which they are bred, kept and how we then eat them!

One of the biggest crimes of the 20th and 21st centuries has been intensive animal farming; if you can afford it, please buy free range. As we move forward new alternatives will emerge, and I believe we will in time as a society become less cruel.

The other charity which Caroline was fond of is the Brooke Hospital for Animals.

Eight million horses, donkeys and mules died in World War I.

Today 100 million such animals are working in punishing environments supporting the incomes of 600 million people, i.e. the owners of the animals derive their income from the work of those animals.

These animals are largely the descendants of those which were left behind in the war; those and subsequent generations have suffered from the heat and from poor conditions and heavy workloads.

The Brooke Hospital for Animals cares for horses, donkeys and mules across the Middle East, Asia and parts of South America, attempting to make their lives better and more bearable.

On more than one occasion Caroline stopped eating meat. If I recall correctly, twice for periods upwards of a year. I hold vegetarians in very high regard.

Being vegetarian is limiting for someone who's been a meat eater. I remember once going to a pub restaurant and Caroline asked for "egg and chips" and the waitress said in a snotty manner: "Oh, no we couldn't possibly do that" to which Caroline replied: "Well I'll have the ham, egg and chips listed here, without the ham".

The turning point

She was quick thinking, which was one of the many things I loved about her.

Anyway, back to the Born Free Foundation.

They were running charity fundraising campaigns, evenings and dinners.

And they set up events at amazing venues. They'd pull in celeb support and sell tickets for a substantial price. And wrap the evening up with a fund-raising raffle.

We'd gone to a few of these events, and here's what happened on one such occasion...

The event was at the Natural History Museum in the evening. It was a black-tie event and we'd gone there in a limousine with a couple of friends.

The set-up was spectacular and we saw several famous faces. We had dinner and drinks, and at the end was the raffle. The animal for which the Born Free Foundation is best known is the lion and they were raffling off a cuddly lion soft toy, it was big, two metres tall.

Of course, Caroline wanted it. No matter what, I was going to make sure she got it, and my final bid of nearly £1,000 secured it, for the £100 cuddly lion.

As usual Caroline had had too much to drink... so at the end of the evening I went outside to check that our limo was ready and waiting, so that I could escort her, in her drunken state, back to the car.

When I came back in, I was disappointed to see, but not entirely surprised that Caroline had been sick on the lion, its colour augmented by Cabernet Sauvignon. I had to support semi-comatose Caroline from the room on one arm, with the lion on the other.

When I got outside I helped Caroline into the car and placed the lion in the boot.

As I turned around, I saw a very famous female celeb getting into her limo. She wasn't drunk, she was renowned for her good looks and I thought there's a lady every man would aspire to be with. There was this seemingly perfect girl.

I'm not a bad looking guy...

And who was I with? An abusive, difficult woman with a serious drinking problem who had refused to do anything about it. She was difficult all the time

The turning point

and at the big, exciting events in my life, such as this, she was an embarrassment.

I'm not saying I'm a perfect guy nor the best-looking guy around. However, when it comes to how people conduct themselves, both in public and behind closed doors, it went through my mind in this moment that I deserved more than this, I was worth more than this kind of behaviour, enough was enough.

This was the defining moment.

I was not going to tolerate this any more, not ever again and this relationship was over.

In February 2003 I told Caroline I wanted to split up.

There was no hurry to split up, given our lives were so intertwined, with us living and working together. And taking into consideration her aggressive personality I wondered if I could get out of the relationship without her becoming even more of a nightmare.

I wondered would it be possible to split up on an amicable basis.

My heart said YES, and my head said NO, she could be really nasty.

How would we do it and what would happen to both of us afterwards?

Whilst by this time I had come to despise her, I did worry about her.

Someone once said to me, "There's not a bad bone in your body".

I did worry about her; how would she cope?

How could we split up, how would we split up, what about our house, the business, the people working for us, our beloved dogs and our customers, what would the mechanics of a split be?

All quite overwhelming thoughts.

I explained very clearly to Caroline that I wanted out of the relationship. I told her how I was unhappy, how I felt abused and unloved. How could someone treat someone they loved as she treated me?

When I looked at her, I would often think I was looking at my abuser.

I wanted to finish. I told her I wanted to terminate the relationship and I told her very clearly. She said could we give it another chance? And I said there was no point. However, when she said, "can't we leave it a little longer?" I thought why not let this sink in.

The turning point

I told her we do not have to split up immediately, but this relationship is over. However, there's a lot to be sorted out and we can take our time about it.

I thought that once I had told her it would be easier and maybe she'd be co-operative.

I'd told her clearly that I wanted out which felt both somewhat of a relief to have let her know how I felt, but also created a pressure. I hoped then that carrying it through might be emotionally and practically less difficult to make happen. I simply needed to tell her again in the days or weeks to come, and escalate the break-up from an announcement to action.

She could come to accept it and perhaps we could split up on an amicable basis.

That said, she was volatile and troublesome, so any split would be difficult, not only in the domestic side of our life but also on a business basis. We ran our business together, this was complicated, and furthermore, all of this followed on from the dot com bubble.

I had it all, but my marriage was an unhappy one and financially everything was now beginning to crash down around me. The last year had been challenging.

The worst chapter of my entire life was now about to unfold.

Caroline collapsed in the hall.

A complete surprise, no warning.

Unknown to me Caroline had been bleeding heavily in the last 24 hours and her blood loss was so significant that she collapsed.

I was unaware that this had been preceded by her spotting (vaginal bleeding outside of normal periods) over the previous few months. She had been to our local doctor and I presume she had hoped the bleeding would go away and had chosen to overlook it.

Caroline had avoided having smear tests over the years. She had been embarrassed about having them and so had avoided them. She felt her private parts were private and a smear test an intrusion.

Following Caroline's collapse, we went straight to the doctor, who said that if we had private healthcare cover, which we did, he could refer her to a consultant immediately, and so Caroline was admitted to hospital.

The turning point

Caroline stayed in the hospital overnight and I returned home. Up till this point, in our 13 years together I think we had spent just one night apart.

We had worked together as well as lived together for the absolute majority of that time.

The following morning Caroline was put under anaesthetic and examined.

The consultant explained they had found a small lump; it might be cancerous, and he had removed it. He was more worried about liver damage as a result of excessive drinking than he was about the lump.

Caroline asked: "What if it's cancer, what are my chances of survival?" He said upwards of 90% and that there shouldn't be anything to worry about.

Various thoughts were going through my mind, it was such a shock it felt like slow motion. My primary thought was, "oh my God, poor Caroline."

It felt like a potential death sentence had been placed on her.

It's difficult to explain how I had such contradictory feelings. On the one hand Caroline was the person whom I cared about more than anyone else in my life and on the other hand she'd abused me for so long I wanted out of the relationship, and had been wanting out of it for quite a long time.

"I hope she gets through it. I can't leave her now, when will I be able to get out of this relationship?"

Whilst I no longer wanted to live my life with Caroline, she was the one person I cared for most about in the world, we had done so much together.

I admired so much about Caroline; she was interesting, upbeat and could often be the life and soul of a party.

History, politics and current affairs, including gossip, were some of her hot topics.

Not someone who's like an entertainer holding court, but in a group of three to six she could be funny, quick witted and her extreme view prompted many a vibrant conversation or constructive argument.

Many of her convictions were good ones, in particular those against the abuse of animals. A lot of people are too weak or shy to argue a point.

She was one of life's high achievers.

The turning point

It was 2003. Caroline had got cancer.

The consultant referred us to a specialist in Harley Street, London, who examined Caroline and told us that her cervix was in a concerning state and that he thought she had a small tumour, and she'd need to have scans.

Ever since I first met Caroline, I knew from things she had said that she had always been worried about getting cancer. And now her biggest worry was becoming a reality.

Caroline asked him for his opinion. What did he think, what were her chances of recovery? He said perhaps 80%.

I recall her immediate thoughts were: "Am I going to die and will my hair fallout?"

Can you imagine how you would feel if you were her? Perhaps you know of someone or are someone who has faced or is facing something similar?

I was concerned for her, I loved her though I loathed her behaviour. You would not wish this on anybody, it is so unfair.

During the treatment, it brought us closer together.

When they diagnosed cancer, Caroline asked me to stay with her until she had got through the treatment successfully. What was I supposed to say?

Of course, I wanted to be there for her, to support her.

I felt I had no choice other than to promise her I would, and I also promised myself I would leave when she got through it.

There was not a single day during her treatment that I didn't want to support her and there were several times when she thanked me for staying with her.

To start off with I think we felt the chances were on our side, but we also realised the chances of it being terminal were significant.

I remember night after night she would be lying in my arms crying and scared of dying. And me too, I was scared of her dying. I felt so sad that she had got cancer, I felt so sorry for her, I was so worried for her.

I still loved her; I just didn't want to live my life with her.

And so, we took trips to Harley Street clinics and those in its adjacent areas for consultations, MRI scans (magnetic scans) and CT scans.

136

The turning point

The machines, in which the patient lies down and whose whole body is immersed, are really quite claustrophobic and extremely noisy. Caroline found these absolutely terrifying. Each time she had the scans taken she would be petrified and literally shaking.

I would be in the room with her, holding her hand as best I could. The consultants/operators gave me a heavy green protective coat to wear and headset to protect me from the noise.

Caroline must have been so scared; I could see the fear in the expression on her face.

In addition to MRI scans, she had CT scans (specialist X-ray type scans).

Different doctors, different consultants, different hospitals, different surgeries and different clinics. The treatment process really seemed very disjointed, very clinical and pushed from one person to the next.

Back to the consultant in Harley Street.

He said Caroline had a tumour, confirming our fears, which was the size of a large strawberry. I think this is a de-facto approach used by consultants to talk to patients... peanuts, grapes, strawberries, apples, grapefruits.

This felt like a confirmation of a death sentence.

At that time, he said the best treatment would be surgery to remove her cervix and womb, that this would be major surgery and she'd be unable to move around for some three to six months, largely confined to bed or a chair.

Once again Caroline asked him his opinion. What did he think, what were her chances of recovery? His response was that from what he was then able to see, perhaps 70%.

And so, the next step was that we went to one of the private London hospitals which was hotel-like in its quality. Here Caroline was to have a hysterectomy, that was the course of treatment that the consultant had proposed, to surgically remove Caroline's uterus and in doing so cut out the cancer, cut it out, remove the problem.

This had been discussed previously; what would follow would be 3 or more months convalescing, not being able to move much and being largely confined to a chair... I envisaged her being like a patient, in the comfort of our home,

The turning point

I could envisage her sitting in the lounge looking on to our park-like gardens, recovering from what would have been a major operation.

Like a patient in a movie, who's had a serious car crash, being cut up on an operating table, stitched back together and hoping to pull through.

Even if the operation was a technical success, which you'd expect it to be, she would then be faced with the issue of whether it had got rid of the cancer or had it spread further, would it still be there?

It all felt very terrifying, both in the here and the now, and for the outlook in the weeks and months to come.

So we checked in to the hospital where Caroline was to have her hysterectomy, and she put on her blue and white patient's gown, the consultant re-examined Caroline and once again looked at her scans.

He then said that instead of going ahead with the operation, it would be better to have a combination of radiotherapy and chemotherapy. He explained the cancer was sitting on the edge of her uterus and therefore may already have spread or might spread during the course of surgery.

Not only did this come as a shock, but it seemed like a change of plan which suggested her prognosis was even worse than we'd been led to believe.

Why were they changing the treatment, had something fundamentally changed?

I'm not an oncologist (a doctor who treats cancer) but why had he had her admitted to hospital.

Why had they bothered to let her get dressed for treatment, only to say I've changed my mind, we're going to take a different approach.

Had he not previously checked the scans, had he left this to the last minute?

I'm not complaining, it was surprising and strange.

A few minutes later it so happened that when I was in the lift, going to get Caroline a drink, the consultant was also in the lift and I asked him, what were her chances of survival?

He said less than 60%... I was distraught and at a loss for words.

It's 17 years since this happened and as I am typing this I am crying.

At this point in time, Caroline said she no longer wanted to know of any other

The turning point

negative changes to her likely survival. She wanted to cling on to a 60% hope that her treatment would be successful rather than subsequently become aware if it were to be even worse.

Whilst we had private medical cover, some of the treatment and consulting was provided by the NHS, a kind of partnership.

We were referred to another consultant, at another hospital, an NHS hospital. Apparently recent research pointed towards the combination of radiotherapy and chemotherapy having stronger, more positive outcomes. This was the treatment now being recommended.

Caroline had stepped out of the room... and I took the opportunity to ask the consultant what the prognosis now looked like.

He said 50/50!

I'd been seriously worried for some time and now the odds were worse than playing Russian roulette; it was a toss of the coin whether she would live or die.

The severity of it all had previously sunk in, but this felt like it was going from bad to worse to fatal.

What followed were regular trips to the hospital for radio therapy. If I recall this was daily or several times a week. Half hour visits. The treatment itself less than a minute. They drew markings on her body and then lined up the lasers and pressed go, it was all very quick.

And for chemotherapy, if I recall properly, it was once a week, and the treatment took several hours. They'd connect a drip into Caroline's bloodstream and pump the chemotherapy through.

This was not like in the movies, it was a living hell.

I cared for and loved Caroline more than anyone else in the world.

Having come to despise Caroline prior to her getting cancer, my feelings were now caring ones.

She had been the most important person to me, in my entire life. I felt worried sick for her and felt sorry for myself.

During the course of Caroline's treatment, on the work front the market had

The turning point

slowed. Caroline was no longer working full time, just when she felt up to it, which became increasingly infrequent, spending most of her time in bed.

In the early days of her treatment, she was working perhaps two or three hours a day. Towards the end of it, just up to 30 minutes a day or not at all.

When people have radiotherapy and chemotherapy, they lose their appetite, and this happened to Caroline.

She had been losing weight, and losing her strength, losing a lot of it.

I continued to work throughout, excepting when I took Caroline for treatment. We had our office in our house, it was huge, and our main office was around 40 x 25 feet.

It now felt very empty, just me and one other.

This was the time following the dot com burst and 9/11, the tech sector had crashed, hiring was minimal and most of the people who had been working for us couldn't see any short-term rewards. Their prospects were better in other lines of business and they had chosen to leave us and get out of recruitment.

The private sector as a whole had stopped spending on significant new projects, but the government was still spending, the public sector spend was healthy.

Most of Caroline's work was aligned to public sector spend, her tech clients were almost exclusively focused on selling into the government, which meant I covered her clients, did her work, not necessarily at the expense of my own clients who had cut back hiring to zero or absolute minimum at best.

Saying goodbye to IBM.

IBM, our flagship client, had been putting out vacancies to us but they would then be placed on hold, i.e. cancelled. We were putting a considerable amount of time into these vacancies for which fees didn't materialise.

Much as we would have loved to retain IBM as a client, it wasn't sustainable, we couldn't afford to do so financially or emotionally.

It wasn't worth it; we couldn't justify it and by this time the business was in a state of decline. Our fee income was cut in half, Caroline was no longer working, we were down to me and Caroline's executive assistant. I had to prioritise my time.

The turning point

IBM decided to outsource their recruitment and headhunting, which meant we would have to work through their new managed service provider, who told us we either needed to work with them as a limited company or not at all.

At the time, our trading entity was me; I was a sole trader/proprietor who employed people.

With all our other demands we didn't want to set up a limited company at that time.

In hindsight this was probably a mistake. At the time we didn't want to be pushed around, told what to do etc.

There were other things to worry about. We didn't really have the time; we were going to the hospital for treatment daily and the work we were doing with IBM was simply not coming to anything.

We could no longer afford to work for free.

We didn't really have much choice other than to say "No". Sadly, it was goodbye IBM.

Several years later, I changed the status of the business to that of a limited company: "Arena Search & Selection Limited".

At some point during the course of her treatment, beyond the half-way stage and approaching the end, Caroline had a further scan to check if the treatment was working, and indeed the scan showed the tumour to be shrinking.

This was of course a promising sign. In an ideal world we'd have hoped the entire tumour would have been eliminated, but we knew if it had been shrunk, the likelihood was that it would be possible for it to continue to be destroyed.

However, it wasn't entirely eradicated which meant her prognosis could be terminal, but it still looked promising.

On a gradual basis the side effects of the radio and chemotherapy took hold, which primarily were tiredness and loss of appetite. To start with Caroline was her normal self but in the weeks and months which followed she became increasingly tired, spending much of the day in bed, and her weight loss was dramatic.

The turning point

God bless her, now perhaps two thirds of her original weight, maybe less even, her clothes were hanging off her, she was frightened, and her thoughts day and night were consumed with fear.

Hoping the treatment would work, hoping to pull through it.

She had become tired, quiet and cut down her drinking and smoking.

By this time she looked ill, she looked weak, and she looked anorexic.

On my part I did the best I could to try to support her in every way.

There were times when she thanked me for staying with her now that she had cancer.

Ever since I told her that I wanted to split up, she had become less violent, less aggressive and less controlling. She no longer had the upper hand in the relationship, none the less she couldn't help reverting to type every once in a while.

I remember on one of our visits to the hospital the treatment had taken longer than we'd expected and when we got back to the car, we had a parking ticket.

Caroline proceeded to give the parking inspector, an enforcement officer, a piece of her mind, albeit he was purely doing his job. I don't blame her for feeling this way, it wasn't about the money, more a matter of principle. We could afford the parking ticket but what about those less well off than us? Some things in life really are ridiculous… I'm referring to the system not the parking attendant.

On one of our journeys back home from the hospital, she hit me in the face whilst I was driving. I think she mistakenly thought I was looking at a girl in another car, but I was just watching traffic lights, checking rights of way, traffic flows, what cars were where etc, in the interests of driving safely.

Caroline didn't drive, so was somewhat unfamiliar with the need to constantly be alert when driving, to know what was going on, what was likely to happen next and to anticipate the unexpected.

Perhaps she was taking out her frustrations on me.

Whilst my feelings about Caroline had softened during her illness, her ongoing

The turning point

behaviour only served to re-enforce that I wanted out of the relationship. However, in the here and now I simply wanted her to get better, and this was something I wanted more than anything else in the world.

A few weeks later… summer, towards end of July and a Sunday, I remember this well:

For many of the people I knew in the polo world, the biggest UK event of the year was taking place. "The Cartier Cup at Guards Polo Club" in Windsor Great Park was one of the biggest events in the summer season, the social calendar. Some of my friends and many acquaintances would be there for what would for them be a glorious day.

In contrast Caroline and I had to go to yet another hospital for Caroline to have a final blast of radiotherapy… something known as "brachytherapy".

It's when the clinicians treat the cancer very aggressively by inserting radioactive material directly into your body, into Caroline's body.

We were thinking this should kill off any final remaining cancer.

So we checked into the hospital. Caroline was in her own room and I was allowed to stay with her overnight. I tried to support Caroline in every way I could, practically and emotionally. I sat in the visitor's chair and whilst I got next to no sleep, I was so pleased to be able to stay with her and support her.

This now marked the end of the scheduled chemo and radiotherapy programme.

The treatment was now over. Caroline was tired, weak and thin, perhaps 60% of her original weight!

She felt a little bit more positive; we knew the tumour had significantly shrunk, the treatment had been working and so we felt the chances were on our side, that we'd got a reasonable chance the tumour would continue to shrink and be destroyed.

The treatment she had been given could be expected to continue to work over the next few weeks.

Caroline slowly started to put on just a little bit of the weight she had lost and regained some of her energy.

We wouldn't know for sure the outcome of the treatment for another four weeks…

The turning point

"Can we go on holiday?" Caroline asked.

We'd been to the West Indies several times before and so Caroline decided it would be good to go somewhere different, why not the East Indies, the Indian Ocean?

And so we went to Mauritius, stopping over en route in Dubai.

We flew out club class which had become routine for us but nonetheless special each time, and none more so than this one.

We'd seen Dubai featured in magazines and newspapers. We were curious to stop over and see for ourselves what it was like.

The baking heat was little surprise to me, I'd been to hot places before, but I didn't realise that swimming in the sea would be like taking a hot bath and that when you turned on the cold taps hot water would come out.

Caroline, being Caroline, came up with what was a good idea. As I said before, she loved history and there was an ancient palace which we were able to tour.

The Middle East is hot, its dry and Arabic, so the palace was built out of sand and clay.

What impressed me most was their use of what I'd describe as towers topped off with chimneys. These chimneys were air vents, they captured the wind and channelled it down into the rooms below. An ingenious cooling method which created a modest freshness and more bearable temperature, somewhat akin to today's air conditioning.

It was good to go to Dubai and I'm impressed with what the Emiratis have achieved but I think some of the other Middle Eastern cities are considerably more beautiful, for example Beirut.

On arrival in Mauritius, we took a helicopter from the airport to the hotel, landing on the adjacent golf course and then walking over to the hotel reception.

The Mauritian beeches are beautiful, and Caroline very much enjoyed trying to chill, relax and recover. However, of course, she was still worried, as was I. Had the treatment worked?

I remember some of the good times, I can picture them in my mind.

Caroline was able to enjoy several spa treatments, bathing in the lush warm

The turning point

sea, she was even able to buy a red "sari" and we spent the evenings together chatting, reminiscing and hoping… Our mood was very much subdued, with a potential death sentence still hanging over her head.

We returned home, flying back to London.

Shortly after our return we went to a clinic for Caroline to have a scan.

This was the big day. The day we'd been waiting for. The day in which it would be either good news or potentially terminal news.

The process was that after the scan the radiographer would send her report to the consultant and then he'd tell us if she would live or die. However, as soon as the scan had been completed Caroline asked the radiographer what, if anything, could she see.

Great news. Her tumour which previously had shrunk massively, was no longer visible.

The first thought which went through my mind was one of delight. I was so happy, so relieved, much more, of course, for Caroline than for me.

When someone is undergoing treatment for a deadly condition it's not just the patient who suffers, it's also their loved ones and those who care about them.

I was elated but now, every once in a while, at the back of my mind, in an occasional moment, I remembered that I had promised myself that once she had got through the cancer I would leave.

Which meant sooner or later I'd need to tell her, as I had done prior to the cancer, that I wanted out of the relationship. The thought of this terrified me; whilst I no longer loved her as a wife, I did have love for her.

The thoughts which went through my mind were contradictory ones: I wanted out of the relationship, I felt she'd abused me over the years, I'd promised myself I would leave her once the treatment was successful.

And now, from her perspective, she had had the most awful time of her life and now what? Her husband was going to tell her he wanted to leave.

My feelings for her were somewhat like a pendulum; a fondness for someone I cared about more than any other person. We had been a team; we'd lived and worked together. We'd been apart for just two days in more than 13 years.

The turning point

On the other hand, she was a difficult, controlling character and someone who had been abusive to me for many years. This was going to be very difficult. When should I tell her? And what if, in the future, her cancer was to come back? I'd feel even more guilty than I was feeling now. I'd become an emotional wreck.

I think if a father is faced with separating from his wife and leaving his children behind, he would be faced with a similar level of magnitude of worry and guilt that I was facing.

Ever since I told Caroline, prior to her getting cancer, that I wanted out of the relationship, it had become more balanced. She no longer had the same power over me.

But pretty much immediately after being told the treatment had worked, Caroline returned to her old ways, drinking heavily and becoming increasingly aggressive once again.

In the evenings she would get drunk, put the music on full volume and I would go to bed to get away from her and the noise.

She'd then subsequently come up to the bedroom and become verbally and physically abusive.

Hitting me, kicking me and trying to bite me.

The bedroom was adjacent to the landing area in the hallway. On these nights, I was always worried that, in her drunken state she might fall over the bannisters and onto the wooden floor some 20 feet below, and accidentally kill herself.

I think this routine may have persisted for perhaps three to four weeks.

The challenges we were facing seemed never ending, one after another, one trauma after another.

Timber, Caroline's favourite dog, had lost a lot of weight fast. We took him to the vet and he was diagnosed with cancer. The vet said it didn't look good and suggested he put Timber under anaesthetic in order to examine his insides. If it was appropriate to treat him, he would do so, otherwise he would put him to sleep permanently.

And that's what happened. Caroline's favourite dog had to be put to sleep, put down.

The turning point

Our dogs were like our children. Many dog owners say they prefer dogs to humans, they're always happy and give unconditional love.

God bless Caroline, she adored Timber. We were taking a real hammering in life.

How can life be so cruel? I'm numbed with silence writing these words.

I'm struggling to find words powerful enough to share with you how sorry I felt for Caroline. She was distraught and she wanted another dog immediately, and so we got 'Maybe', another husky, this one a predominantly white girl.

This girl husky was very different to the boy huskies we had, much softer, much more loving.

Whilst Caroline was violent towards me, she was rarely violent towards others and never violent towards the dogs. Caroline was an animal lover; in addition to having a hard side, she had a soft side as well.

She was like my right hand and her mine. We lived and worked together. We'd achieved so much together. We had been apart just two nights in 13 years. We spent most hours of every day together.

I appreciate I've just repeated myself but few people would experience the kind of togetherness that Caroline and I experienced.

We had been a team, albeit in many ways Caroline was very dependent on me. Everything was in my name: the house, bank accounts, credit cards, tax, business, everything… and Caroline never used a computer, mobile phone nor the internet. And Caroline didn't drive.

It wasn't that she couldn't have or do these things, she'd chosen not to.

As I say she was a complex character.

And in many ways, she leaned on me.

In some respects, particularly when Caroline had cancer, I felt very much like her carer.

Prior to Caroline getting cancer, I had told her I wanted out of the relationship.

Ever since we had received the news that the treatment had been successful, she frequently asked me: "When are you going to leave me?"

When we'd been told the news that she had cancer I had promised myself that

147

The turning point

I would leave once her treatment had been successful and if not, I'd live with her till the end. Now, post treatment and with her tumour eliminated, there was never going to be a good or easy time to break the news.

And Caroline was a very difficult, stubborn person who bore grudges.

However, living with her violent ways was intolerable.

It was about three weeks after she got the supposed all clear that I told her I wanted to leave, then did so. This was the hardest thing I have ever had to do in my life.

I remember it well.

It had come to the end of the working day.

December 1st.

She'd been difficult during the day and now I was facing another night, likely a repetition of those which had preceded it: she would get drunk, put the music on full volume and become abusive.

I had no plan.

How could I tell her?

How could I get out of this abusive relationship?

How could she cope without me?

I felt unbelievably anxious about telling her, knowing it would set her off in a rage, light a fuse. How could she manage without me? And after all these problems how could life be so unfair to her?

I was aware this would represent the start of a nightmare. I'd be swapping one nightmare for another.

The thought of telling her was terrifying.

I felt I was letting her down, I felt as though I had failed her. "Till death do us part" were the words in our wedding vows and I believed in the principle of them. I felt like I was giving her yet another crushing blow, but at the same time I felt as though I couldn't continue and what about me, what about my happiness?

Whilst Caroline no longer had the upper hand, she still had a controlling manner about her... she'd often ask me what I was doing.

The turning point

I called the Samaritans and had perhaps a 10-minute call. Rather than call them from my mobile, I called from a phone box.

I was worried she might see the call to the Samaritans registered on my phone, so I had gone out of the house and called them from the local village phone kiosk. Prior to calling them I knew it wouldn't solve anything, this was my problem not someone else's; no kind or good way to break the news and with no perfect outcome.

Having spoken to them, my thoughts reverted to what I'd concluded: there was no ideal time nor way in which to tell her. I returned home.

I told her at about 6.30 at night; she was in the living room.

I told her I was so sorry that she had had cancer but that I wasn't happy in the relationship, couldn't tolerate the abuse and that, as I'd said before she got cancer, I wanted out of the relationship, that I was leaving, and that I would do my best to support her.

I then left the house. All very short and sharp. I didn't want to get into any long discussion or argument leading to her likely associated behaviour of aggression, abuse...

And I didn't want a conversation which went around in circles, nor one in which she might try to persuade or coerce me into changing my mind.

I told her, then walked out of the house wearing the clothes on my back, car keys in hand, nothing else except a great sadness for Caroline, heavyweight guilt and concern for her welfare.

I had no plan.

I had little idea of where I was going other than I'd check myself into a hotel where I could get away from Caroline and the world.

Caroline was extremely resourceful, determined and vindictive. It went through my mind that she might try to track me down and that perhaps she'd realise I'd gone to a hotel. I deliberately checked into one which was not in our immediate area, where I was confident she wouldn't try to track me down.

She was the sort of person who would find out where you were, would find out which hotel room you were in and come knocking, banging on the door, shouting... if she were to see me, I'm sure she'd get violent. I wanted to get

The turning point

away from her. At first, I didn't want to tell my parents. I felt embarrassed about the fact that I'd split up from Caroline. They knew Caroline was difficult, troublesome, but were unaware of her abusive, manipulating and controlling manner.

My Mum and Dad are great but they're not touchy-feely types, it's not in their generation. I didn't open up to them about my feelings nor did they to me, we were not a family which was open about emotions… stiff upper lip and all that stuff.

Caroline didn't want people to know that she had had cancer. We'd shut ourselves away from people and the world for some 6 months, we'd, or shall I say she'd, told perhaps just a handful of people.

She wasn't close to my Mum and Dad, so we hadn't told them. They were unaware Caroline had had cancer. Mum had been worried about Caroline's severe weight loss in recent months because she'd popped over to see us at our house every once in a while, but we'd kept the news of cancer from them.

Caroline didn't want people to know she had had cancer; she was adamant about this. We only told a handful of people whom Caroline trusted, felt close to and wanted to share this terrifying experience with.

My feelings of guilt were spectacular.

I felt concerned for Caroline, worried about how she would cope and felt guilty leaving her so soon after suffering from cancer.

The first few nights following the split, and indeed the weeks and months which followed, were sleepless ones or at best disturbed. My mind was full of guilt and worry. I was worried sick about her, felt so sorry for her.

I spent the first two nights following the split at one hotel; I was worried she would find me and so moved to a different hotel.

Why was I worried she'd find me? I guess it was because she had such a resourceful manner, and I knew how nasty she could be.

A couple Caroline and I knew well insisted that I stay with them which I did, which was great, and then with great reluctance I told my mum and dad and subsequently moved in with them.

The turning point

"I'm going to Argentina in two days' time, why don't you come?" That's what Mark, one of the polo professionals I knew, said. It was early in December, work was about to go quiet, not that I had any tools with which to do my job! And after all the mental turmoil I'd been through over the years, I thought why not?

I called Caroline and explained what I was doing, and she was supportive. I think that was the first time I spoke to her following the split. She'd been speaking to mutual friends and I think they'd calmed her down somewhat. Furthermore, they probably said words to the effect of: "You can't blame him, you need to blame yourself."

I remember on the flight over to Buenos Aires I was in a club class seat, the one by the window. I'd been stressed for many months; Caroline had been abusive for so many years that I'd developed a nervous twitch which manifested itself in the slightest of movements duting the day when I was awake… just a little nervous twitch.

But when I slept it was a much bigger movement… on the plane I'd fallen asleep and I woke myself up with one of these sudden, big nervous twitches, and I remember the man sitting next to me must have thought what's all that about – what's wrong with this guy?

On the other side of the world in Argentina, Caroline couldn't easily jump in a taxi and pop round. I'd told her where I was staying.

So this was my second trip to Argentina. I stayed in the Alvear Palace, the Buenos Aires equivalent of The Ritz, although given the weak Argentine currency, the cost was more like that of a good Hilton.

It was palatial in its style but for me very lonely, I'd been with Caroline every day for some 13 years.

I'd joined Mark and a group of people. Hopefully I wasn't too miserable, we played polo a few times and the big event was going to see the most anticipated day on the international polo calendar, "The Campeonato Argentino Abierto de Polo" aka the Argentine Open, like the equivalent of the Superbowl, or Wimbledon.

Two teams, 8 players, this is like having a team of players all of the same quality

The turning point

as Roger Federer or Novak Djokovic, all on the field at the same time.

These players all had a handicap of 10. You need to appreciate that in a normal year in England, our highest handicapped player would be a 7 goal.

Watching the best of the best, it takes place in Palermo, right in the heart and heat of Buenos Aires.

Being away from Caroline I felt liberated.

During my time in BA, Caroline sent a message to me via fax, a handwritten letter, it was perhaps 10 pages long.

Over the years I had had enough of Caroline.

I had had enough of her manipulative manner and in some ways didn't believe things she said. Not that she was a liar, but it's difficult when you've lost trust in people. I thought the letter was likely to be full of rubbish, and how could she apologise for all the abuse over the years?

I didn't want back in the relationship; everything was very sore.

I destroyed the letter without reading it. This is one of the biggest regrets of my entire life. What did she say in it?

One of my greatest worries was around the consequences of her drinking too much and endangering herself.

I was worried she would get drunk and, in a swaying state, perhaps fall through the bannisters on the first floor of our house and onto the wooden floor some 20 feet below.

Whilst I still had feelings for Caroline, when I told people they were invariably very sympathetic towards me. In fact, a lot of people told me that they did not like her, and they were not slow in saying so.

One of the most frequent words used to describe her was "difficult".

On hearing of our break-up even Caroline's closest friends immediately said: "We couldn't believe you put up with her for so long."

And someone in another group of friends said that when they had heard the news of our split, they punched the air with joy.

They felt Caroline had got her comeuppance. Not really, the second person did

The turning point

not know Caroline had had cancer.

Despite her flaws, she had some very admirable qualities such as her vibrant personality and her love of animals.

Caroline was a difficult personality; splitting up with her was never going to be easy.

And so, from one dreadful chapter there followed another... I knew Caroline would be an unpleasant piece of work; I'd observed her nasty behaviour with strangers, acquaintances and, to a lesser extent, friends.

Now out of the marital home, I felt I had lost everything I had ever worked for.

When I split from Caroline, to say I was tremendously worried about her and riddled with guilt is an understatement.

Whilst the cancer treatment had been successful, no-one would wish cancer on anyone. And then for me to leave her. She didn't drive, didn't have a bank account, couldn't use a computer and could barely use a mobile phone. I used to do all of these things and more for her.

And following our separation I always made sure she had money.

You'll appreciate I'd been under a lot of pressure and was constantly in an anxious state. I had been for a long time.

Around this time, I was playing in a polo game, which is more exhausting than you'd imagine, and one of the pro players said to me: "You're not breathing properly".

In the days leading up to the game, I'd probably been in my stressed-out state, dwelling on negative thoughts and at times like this I would be taking shallow breaths. And I reckon you can, as I did at this time, develop bad habits.

Stress can cause shortness of breath.

His comments made me more conscious of my state.

Of course, this is something which is easily fixed. You've just got to become more self-conscious and disciplined to breathe properly, which means taking full, deep breaths.

This served as a warning sign to me, as something to be aware of.

The turning point

I had been subject to high levels of stress for a prolonged period of time.

In reality I was overwhelmed with my life, the various crises and complications and, most significantly, worrying about Caroline.

One of my friends recognised my state and suggested I meet with a counsellor, who I saw in the months that followed.

When I met with Erin, the counsellor, it proved to be a really calming and relieving session. What Erin did was largely to simply listen, and because she didn't know any of the people I knew, I could tell her anything.

Not judgemental, purely a great listener and sympathetic, she got me to relax.

I remember in my first session with her she said:

"Caroline is responsible for her own happiness; you are responsible for your own."

This is one of the most powerful expressions I've come across in my life.

I had been in a state of hyper anxiety and had been constantly worrying about Caroline.

However, I'd been abused by her, I didn't cause the cancer and I had been a very good husband, caring, committed and loving, nonetheless I worried about her welfare.

Once Erin had given me this very powerful expression, when I subsequently worried about Caroline, I was often able to reflect on this statement which helped calm me down. However, my concern about Caroline's welfare would be a lasting one.

I do believe this simple statement helped me to cope and it's one I remember vividly to this day.

The concept of seeing a counsellor is something which I believe as a society we should look upon much more positively. In the past it's been tagged with some negativity or as a sign of weakness.

However, I don't think anyone should be ashamed of seeing a counsellor. I was in such a state before seeing her, I wonder if otherwise I would have had a full mental breakdown.

Erin's counselling was reassuring, somewhat settling and was a building block for me to maintain self-belief and somewhat of a positive mindset.

The turning point

I think having counselling support is a smart thing to do, most people will experience some sort of trauma in their lives, and it can help most people navigate a better way through it.

❉ ❉ ❉

Chapter 5
The aftermath

Following the split with Caroline I expected to find Miss Right, I expected to find this ideal girl, get married and perhaps have a child.

I thought it would be straightforward.

However, it wasn't that simple.

Single life wasn't that easy to navigate and finding Miss Right wasn't as easy as I had hoped.

I wanted to love and be loved.

Having had several traumatic years in my relationship with Caroline, I thought I could expect an easier life, and some positive breaks in life. I expected to enter a period of stability, success and satisfaction.

However, what I experienced were the biggest mental health challenges in my life and one disaster after another.

I had it all and lost it.

Caroline and I had worked hard, taken risks and been under a lot of pressure, which had paid off. We had our own business, an 11-bedroom house with park-like gardens, horses to ride and a string of polo ponies.

When I look back on it, because there were two of us producing high incomes, this resulted in us enjoying sky-high earnings and it flattened out any peaks and troughs. This was a better business model than working by myself, as I would start finding out.

Obvious as it may seem, I'm optimistic and thought I'd be able to elevate my income without her… Would this prove the case? Or would the opposite apply?

I had it all but was slowly going to start losing it all, and my life was going to become an emotional rollercoaster: drifting, out of control and in a state of turmoil.

What followed was a very difficult and drawn-out three-year period.

It was a nightmare for both financial and personal issues.

The aftermath

Caroline was living in the house, complete with a costly contingent of secretary, gardener, cleaner and dog walker.

Everything I had worked for was in that house and, some 18 months into the separation, she'd got herself a boyfriend and he'd moved in. So she was living in the house with her boyfriend, and I was paying for it.

Our costs were sky high, and our income on the floor.

I had taken to living in a small modest flat. I could handle this but having to sell my Range Rover, give up polo and sell my horses was a bitter pill to swallow.

Much of the world of polo is flashy, extravagant and showy: have it, flaunt it. The wealthy polo community of which I had become part would clearly have seen I could no longer afford it. When you're spending and participating, you're part of an in-crowd, but once you've lost it, you feel more like an outsider. I felt it was difficult to hold my head up high, I felt like I'd lost my status!

It's surprising how quickly you can go from having so much to having so little.

In life you have your real friends and acquaintances. They're both important and provide for a social outlet; in reality my polo friends were more like acquaintances.

I'm not saying these people were not great people, just that most were not close friends.

I was losing the things in life which I prized most; in hindsight too many of which were materialistic, and status-fuelled.

I was working but work wasn't working.

One of the biggest issues I experienced was loneliness.

I'd lived and worked with Caroline 24/7, 365. We were apart just two days in 14 years.

Through the majority of those 13-14 years, we'd worked together. We were with one another during the working day, at nights and at weekends.

Now I was completely by myself both during the working day and outside of work; I was feeling spaced out!

I'd previously worked from 8.00 till 6.00, and then a bit at the weekends.

The aftermath

I was now working 9 till 5.30, 5 days a week but I was in a zombie-like state.

I failed to apply myself properly, I failed to focus, and I failed to generate enough activity.

Consequently, I had too few clients, too few vacancies and too few candidates out at interview.

And I wasn't getting the breaks either. For example, one of the big-name business process outsourcing companies wanted to enter new markets. They retained me to find them a managing director and sales director. Then they cancelled the expansion initiative and with it their plans to hire.

I'd spent two months working on this and the modest retainer they paid me didn't really cover in two months what I would ordinarily expect to bill in weeks.

Aside of the money, cancellations always feel like a setback when you've put your heart and soul into a headhunting assignment, and I'd got some really talented, quite amazing people lined up on my shortlists.

When a project is not going to go ahead it's a bit embarrassing going back to people who have invested time in meeting with me, talking to me and, after all, having got their hopes up.

For all of us, we want to feel like our work is worthwhile, like we're doing something good and winning.

Real success was temporarily eluding me.

My life at work and outside of it was unsettled.

The reality is that our professional and personal lives are inter-connected, they're inter-dependent.

I was kind of looking for love. I wanted to love and to be loved.

But I wasn't ready for it.

Although I was single, this wasn't the exciting chapter it had the potential to be because throughout this period I had this mixed set of emotions…

Whilst I had a deep resentment towards Caroline, I also still cared about her; I cared more for her than anyone else in the world.

I was working 9 till 5.30, five days a week but my fees were under 50% of what they had previously been.

The aftermath

Why was this?

I was using the same approach, doing largely the same things, in many cases talking to people I had dealt with before, and prospecting for new ones. Of course, some of the previous clients and candidates were either Caroline's or people to whom she had bad mouthed me and therefore were no longer contacts I could leverage.

Overwhelmed with concern for her, I felt guilty and anxious about all manner of things. I felt I had no control over anything. I was trying to get her to agree to a divorce, a financial settlement, the sale of the house, antiques and our various assets.

Whilst all this was going on, I wanted to move my life on. However, I was going around in circles, both in my work and in my life outside of work.

I was trying to work but not getting the results. To perform well at work, your mind must be in the right place otherwise you lack focus, your attention span is minimal, you don't get as much done, don't do things as well and overlook things.

In many jobs you need a certain edge, you might call it a killer instinct, where you push others to take a course of action and proactively drive through a set of events. I guess at that time I became less assertive.

In recruitment there's also a need to quickly cover a lot of ground, to communicate and speak to a lot of relevant people. The greater the number of important activities you get done, the greater your chances of success. Recruitment requires a relentless work rate, an intensity, and throughout this time I failed to maintain it.

I was living in a mist, my mind clouded and confused, lacking concentration, and my activity rate was lower than it should have been. Unbeknown to me hiring activity had picked up and I had missed out.

I was slow to catch on.

And I was acutely lonely. I was working by myself, living by myself and in a very unfamiliar environment.

Caroline had been verbally and physically aggressive to me over a long period of time and after years of abuse and put downs I not only lacked confidence

The aftermath

but would also flinch when people around me made a sudden movement.

My tendency to flinch was something I'd previously overlooked but now separated, I became more conscious of the effect Caroline had had on me. And not just Caroline, but also my broader set of traumas.

I had been and was living in a heightened sense of insecurity.

Was I having, or did I have, a nervous breakdown?

Here's Wikipedia description…

"A nervous breakdown is defined by its temporary nature and often closely tied to psychological burnout, severe overwork, sleep deprivation, and similar stressors, which may combine to temporarily overwhelm an individual with otherwise sound mental functions."

I wasn't sleeping at all well; each night I'd worry about Caroline. I was stressed about all manner of things… Did I have a nervous breakdown? I didn't collapse but, on many occasions, felt very close to doing so.

What I believe I had was chronic stress, and I'd got it really bad.

My symptoms were ones commonly associated with chronic stress:

i) Depression or general unhappiness, ii) Anxiety and agitation, iii) Moodiness, irritability or anger, iv) Feeling overwhelmed and v) Loneliness and isolation.

I reckon I qualified well on all five counts, a full strike.

Your emotional stability is dependent on three foundations: Your home, your relationship and your work.

When any one of these three is compromised, your emotional stability is threatened and if two or more are compromised at the same time your emotional state is exposed, and you are vulnerable…

For me all three were changed simultaneously.

And were compounded by money worries.

This really was a very difficult time in my life, full of great sadness, anxiety and a feeling of being lost. And not only being lost. In hindsight I was working by myself, isolated and extremely lonely.

On a personal basis I wanted to re-build a meaningful life, a good social life and romance. However, this was compromised by sleepless nights, feeling

The aftermath

that what belonged to me had been taken away and by an ongoing emotional rollercoaster; my mind was constantly unsettled.

In the preceding 13-14 years I'd been very affected by Caroline's behaviour. Constantly criticised, I lacked self-confidence. As I said earlier, I used to flinch whenever someone close to me raised an arm; it would take some five years before this went away.

I didn't handle the split with Caroline well, I was emotionally very upset, at times almost shaky, and lacked focus and concentration.

Handling the emotional trauma and being really upset and lonely was challenging. There were times when I wanted to feel sorry for myself, when I wanted to be alone and to blame the world, blame anything but me. Conversely, I wanted good things in life, wanted to overcome my situation, feel good, positive and move my life forward.

Following my split with Caroline my mother and father helped me tremendously. Whilst absent in my younger years they were now very much there for me, on side and a real pillar of support.

I was exercising a lot, going to the gym and playing tennis regularly, which helped alleviate some of my loneliness and uplifted my mood somewhat.

Depending on how down I was feeling, I found playing mood music a great instant pick-up, and also recognised that drinking alcohol in anything other than small amounts was counter-productive, but didn't always act on it. I found if I wanted to feel good, I needed to avoid late nights and next day hangovers.

Sadly, the reality is that when you split up, you compromise your mutual friendships, it can be awkward for everyone and you can find it difficult to maintain friendships; there can come into effect a conflict of allegiances.

Some friendships are impacted more than others, and you lose some close friendships.

At this point in time, I was beginning to socialise with new single friends.

There's always someone bigger than you, brighter than you, richer than you and funnier than you.

And there's always someone in a worse position than you.

For a while I was one of three musketeers; three of us were going out most of the time, most weekends, perhaps one or two nights a week.

The aftermath

That's how one person described us. Socially we'd go to the same places together. Three very different characters.

I'll mention Big Rich first.

A gentle giant, standing six foot five. A natural networker, a social "Mr Fix It" and one of those guys who is happy to be silly, happy to make fun of himself, not take himself too seriously… girls really love this quality.

I'm not short, I'm of above average height but Richard was the first friend I've ever had who's a giant.

When you stand next to another guy who's significantly taller than you it can take a while to get used to it. When you're in the company of others, you can feel small in comparison and you may need to, as I did, just get used to it.

Shake off any inferiority complexes, and just be big yourself, and accept who you are.

My friend Ian…

What can I say, one of those guys with a straight jaw line which often draws the interest of ladies? The brainy guy in the pack. An entrepreneur, seriously bright, he'd been successful, had his own company and was one of those people you expect to be the next James Dyson. In the here and now, dry sense of humour, jazz player and lots of fun.

And me. There was more than one time when I was likened to Charlotte in the TV series Sex and the City, I guess in so far as I was quite reserved, quite conservative and not one to have lots of girlfriends.

I was living life in reverse: I got married very early, had never been on the singles scene and now, into my 40s, was in unfamiliar, nervy but quite fun territory. The experiences I was having at this time with this group of friends were exciting, unpredictable and somewhat counter balanced some of the trauma I was facing.

Beyond the three of us, who were quite close for some time, there were other guys in this singles circle, one of whom, despite being in his 40s, managed to carry off a boy band image. Another was a pilot, who in another life should have been a comedian, and two multi-millionaire divorcees.

And there were others in the gang as well, who came and went over time.

The aftermath

Each of the people in this group had his little story: guys who lost their homes to wives who'd been unfaithful, left them and left them with nothing.

You hear of divorced women whose husbands played away and left them for younger models, which of course happens, but it is sad too to hear of guys whose wives were unfaithful. Everyone knew but them!

I came across one guy whose wife had gone back to her first love… lots of people had back stories.

Of course, these were people in my age group. I was largely mixing with singles people 40+ years old.

Similarly, many of the ladies on the singles scene had their stories.

And I came across people who'd been single, never lived with a partner nor married, the occasional guy on a continual pursuit of that perfect girl, and vice versa.

Lots of different backgrounds… there were some guys who now single, self-made millionaires, were able to do what they wanted, whenever they wanted and spent it large.

At the other end of the scale, I became re-acquainted with someone I knew from work and we became friends. His story was that he'd developed a cocaine habit which had got on top of him. His life slowly fell apart, his marriage fell apart and subsequently he became an every-other-weekend dad.

In his work life he lost his way; his employment track record lacked stability and success.

He lost everything but here's the good news. He attended Alcoholics Anonymous. Apparently, the group and approach work as well for drug addicts as it does for alcoholics. He re-built his career.

One of the things I most admired about him was that he managed to maintain a happy disposition, kept his focus on re-building his life and made it happen. Without doubt the times when I was single and spent time with these friends, were some of the most enjoyable of my life.

Whilst these were activities of people on the singles scene, they weren't just about meeting girls; it was broader, we were having lots of fun. Sometimes the best laughs were when we were meeting up in a car or going somewhere.

The aftermath

Often a highlight of an evening out in London was to pop in to Maroush, in Beauchamp Place, stopping by at three in the morning on our way home.

You don't get any more upmarket streets in London than this; Maroush is a Lebanese restaurant famous for its classy kebabs and clientele. A treat no matter how hip, rich or talented you are, even Paris Hilton has been known to go there.

The reality was that this group of friends was single, mingling in singles scenes, going to single person venues and I guess to an extent, singles bars/pick up joints.

Having great friends can help pull you through challenging times such as those I was facing. There were many reasons for this, including that simply spending time with them enables you to be more occupied by your social interactions and less consumed by your own thoughts, which happens when you are isolated and alone.

I'd always try to switch on my happy side.

You don't want to burden your friends with your problems nor bring a miserable personality to the party.

You've got to switch on your positive side and need to be conscious not to make the time they spend with you that which compromises their own enjoyment when socialising.

There were, of course, times when people open up to you about issues they have faced or their own problems, predicaments… and at times like this we'd swap stories.

Having developed new friendships with single people enabled me to go out socialising on a weekly basis, and gave me the opportunity to meet single girls, and whilst I didn't date much, these nights out were unpredictable and fun.

And not just evenings out but other events like country walks, playing tennis and boating on the River Thames.

Being single and mixing in singles circles was interesting, at this point in time something quite unfamiliar to me. In a mixed group you've got an element of guys pushing their chests out… trying to be funny, interesting. There's an element of competition and pressure to be entertaining.

The aftermath

Whilst I had been continuing to see the counsellor, I had begun to feel less hyper-stressed and more settled, or so I thought.

I wanted to be out there dating. But I had no libido. What was wrong with me?

I saw a new counsellor at a mental and sexual health clinic, thinking I had a physical problem or mental block. I saw the counsellor perhaps six times but in the end it became clear my problem was simply one of stress.

And on reflection there is no doubt I had "chronic stress"; it is the response to emotional pressure suffered over a prolonged period.

This translates into elevated cortisol levels and low libido, which meant that whilst I felt I should have been out there dating and playing the field, I wasn't ready. And not just that, in hindsight I guess I was thinking I wasn't that kind of person anyway.

I wanted to love and be loved. This may have originated from my childhood when I was sent away to boarding school and wasn't in a close family set-up.

Of course, different people want different things out of relationships, and these may change at different times.

Some, like me, simply had an underlying motivation to find a wife, the right one, of course. Others wanted to have fun, enjoy the moment and not take life too seriously.

I just needed to find Miss Right.

A near miss.

I met an interior designer with whom I had several dates, and a romance developed.

This lady had everything I was looking for, she was fun, intelligent, well-spoken, sophisticated and elegant.

Tall slim, long straight hair, delicate features, very feminine, a class act…

I think we all have a physical type of person we're attracted to and she was my type, and I liked her manner.

If you had a checklist, this girl had it all, and a great personality to go with it. I don't know if I messed it up, probably my fault, the timing wasn't right, I wasn't mentally in the right place. She dated someone else, and life moved on.

The aftermath

This isn't unique to me. One of the observations I was soon to make was that for people to form a meaningful relationship they both need to be in the right place.

By which I mean they need to be mentally settled and ready for a relationship.

Or perhaps that a couple can be so right for each other, they can get through awkward or difficult situations well.

Whilst I never had the opportunity to get to know her fully, I wonder what would have happened if we had got together properly.

I should have met Alex then.

At the time I was in my forties and I wasn't alone in having issues; many people were carrying baggage of some form or another which made them either unsettled or simply not ready to commit.

Most people have plenty of romances and relationships in their teens and early/late twenties before settling down and getting married. Not for me. I'd been to boarding school and my experience of girls was limited; they were a mystery. When I got together with Caroline, she was pretty much my first real girlfriend, and I married her.

Now, 15 years on I was single and swimming with the sharks.

I was in unfamiliar territory and although I had a dozen or so dates, I was an emotional wreck and in a constant state of anxiety.

Single life didn't suit me.

I wanted love, not sex, and wasn't interested in romances which didn't have serious potential to result in marriage and a life-long partnership.

I found dating somewhat daunting. Real life isn't like the movies. It's not one where the perfect guy meets the perfect girl, where the perfect chat up lines are exchanged, and it's not one where dates are dreamy.

But I think people's expectations are high, particularly for older people who know what they want. The problem is that perfection doesn't exist. For example, if a guy or girl is a six and a half out of ten in the looks department, they want a nine out of ten in their partner.

Apart from looks, I felt a pressure to be perfect company, to ask the right

The aftermath

questions in the right way, to entertain, and to be an entertaining and funny man on a date.

I thought and still think that a lot of girls want an Adonis. And it seemed to me that girls had high expectations in the bedroom department. I remember one girl saying to me: "you'd better be good in bed." I didn't go to bed with her, so it didn't matter, but it went through my mind that I'm not a magician.

I think she may have taken cocaine that night because ordinarily she was a class act, probably why she liked me.

I was too serious at the time, I should have been more relaxed, maybe I should have taken cocaine but I'm too straight for that, I don't do drugs.

You'd be forgiven for thinking this guy, me, must be mad.

I wasn't completely exited from my marriage; I was divorced but didn't have a financial settlement.

Here am I saying I wanted love and marriage, and if you've got half a brain, you're probably thinking just chill out. The last thing you want is a serious relationship.

I didn't trust women, and my view of romance was based on committed relationships and marriage, not casual sex.

The singles social and dating scene for the forty-somethings I was now participating in was dominated by forever single types, and the mixed up newly single types. The majority of people on the singles scene slept around.

You could place these single people into three categories:

Firstly, men who had never been in a committed long-term relationship, playing the girls and never able to settle down; there was always the chance of the perfect girl!

Secondly, in addition to the player guys there were also the player girls. These were the girls who'd also played around and were now childless, some of whom were hanging on in a last chance saloon, losing hope and their looks.

Thirdly, those men and women who had had children and whose marriages had failed.

What I observed was a singles scene of people jumping into bed together

The aftermath

shortly or immediately after meeting, and then either getting to know one another afterwards or moving on to the next person.

A large proportion of these people were unsettled and troubled personalities, like me! I felt out of my depth, had significant trust issues and the romances (dates) I had were compromised by my lack of trust, anxiety and lack of confidence.

Life wasn't working out that well during this seemingly never-ending sequence of catastrophes in my life. After living out of the married home for ages, our third husky "Snowy" died. We'd had him since he was a pup.

Snowy had remained with Caroline after our separation and he'd reached an age and stage in life where he'd become arthritic; the simple act of lying down or getting back up from lying down had become painful.

Clearly, he must have maintained some spirit and ability to run, because it seems that he died chasing a deer in the garden, which resulted in him falling in the pond and drowning.

He'd had his life; it was in reality a blessing. Perhaps I'd worn him out… two dog walks a day, 365 days a year, that's approaching 10,000 dog walks!

Meanwhile my divorce agreement was going nowhere fast and I wanted my share of the assets I'd accumulated with Caroline, I wanted my share of our wealth, I wanted the money which I'd earned.

Everything I had worked for was in that house and, some 18 months into the separation, she'd got herself a boyfriend and he'd moved in. So she was living in the house with her boyfriend, and I was paying for it.

The two years following my separation from Caroline were like an emotional roller coaster, full of emotional highs and lows.

There were many times when I enjoyed socialising, playing tennis and occasionally playing polo on rented horses.

I was living in Windsor, which was a great place to live as a single person in the period following my split with Caroline. I had some local friends and was able to walk into town on evenings out, go to pubs and bars… and walk home. Whenever I felt lonely or low, I was able to simply walk out of the front door and walk around the streets of Windsor, by the river, the castle and into Eton.

The aftermath

One evening I was walking in town with one of my closest friends and bumped into an acquaintance of Caroline's and mine. She was accompanied by two good looking girls, one a British blonde, the other a Turkish brunette. They were out for the evening and on their way to a bar. She asked if we would like to join them for a drink. Of course.

Later in the evening my acquaintance asked: "Which one do you like?" I replied, "the tall slim blonde".

I fell for this girl. In her earlier years she'd been a model and was now an accountant.

We started seeing each other but the early stages of the relationship were compromised. Caroline, who was by now living with a boyfriend, knew this girl; in fact, she'd suggested her as a girlfriend for me and had gone so far as to say she'd introduce us.

Which was ironic because when Caroline heard we'd got together she'd go out of her way to bump into her, and then proceed to be unpleasant.

Meanwhile, financially things were at rock bottom.

Whilst solicitors had issued paperwork and instructions for a financial settlement, technically I was divorced but financially we were still wedded, and Caroline kept dragging her feet.

The whole process wasn't proceeding at all and it felt like an eternity.

I felt as though everything I had ever worked for had been taken away from me and, having invested all the hard work and taken the risks, and taken pressure, that I had nothing to show for it.

Caroline was living in the house, had an administrator, a cleaner, a gardener, dog walker and horses on livery... Our costs were sky high; our income was on the floor.

I'd cut my costs, but our outgoings were still unsustainably high, these being predominantly attributable to Caroline's refusal to move on and make changes. So I moved out of my rented flat into my Mum and Dad's place whilst Caroline continued living in our 11 bedroomed house with her boyfriend.

She was making no effort to move on, no effort to agree to a divorce or to sell up and share our assets.

The aftermath

Exasperated, I went around to the house and kicked up a fuss. Banging on the doors and hooting the horn of my car in the driveway.

The police came around and told me to leave.

I returned the following day and a similar scenario unfolded. This time the police arrested me, placed me in a little box in the back of a police van, and I was taken off to the police station.

This isn't the stuff for middle class upstanding citizens like me. I was fingerprinted! And then placed in a cell. OMG. The place was cold, my watch and belongings had been taken away.

It was a stark reality; I had hit rock bottom. For several hours I did a lot of thinking, and I was then released.

I had no light bulb moment in the prison cell, just a sense of a lack of any control in my life. I knew there would be an end but not knowing when was mentally challenging.

In hindsight, I think the police hate domestic issues; they find them uncomfortable, awkward, upsetting, and importantly, they present highest risk outcomes. They probably bang up the guys to shut them up and calm them down. If I were in their shoes, I'd probably do the same.

However, you feel affronted. I am genuinely a decent person; someone once said of me that I didn't have a bad bone in my body, and I was released from the prison cell a few hours later.

It was around this time that LinkedIn started to have a meaningful effect on recruitment; it was to prove both disruptive and an enabler.

The tech sector, which is the sector I have been primarily focused on and which represents my core customer type, was an early adopter of LinkedIn.

In addition to being the first sector to exploit LinkedIn as a hiring tool, tech companies were advocates of the use of internal hiring capabilities, the in-house recruitment model of recommend-a-friend schemes etc.

These sea changes in the way in which recruitment was being undertaken represented a turning point for me; the value we could add as external recruiters and headhunters had been marginalised, or so I thought. More about that later.

I was continuing to struggle at work, with low/no billings. I was consumed with

The aftermath

problems, lacked a clarity of focus, lacked an edge and I felt like everything I'd worked for had been taken away from me.

In my confused, distracted and somewhat lost state I was ineffective in my work, and I was completing very few deals.

With little or no money coming in I was forced to give up my flat, but I knew there was an end in sight: my divorce proceedings were now coming towards an end.

I can't remember the exact circumstances but on two occasions I had no alternative but to sleep in my car.

The divorce proceedings and financial settlement were dragged out over several years, but it eventually came. I think the legal system here is prehistoric.

I took a gigantic financial hit when the divorce was eventually finalised, and the house sold.

Caroline received a considerably larger proportion of the assets than me, a greater proportion of the equity in the house, all our antiques and fine art (c.£250k), plus an additional amount of cash. Solicitors' fees came to some £100k.

I got around a third of our assets which was disappointing, but the relief was spectacular.

For me everything was now on an upturn, I'd got engaged to the former model and I proceeded to buy a new house.

I felt a weight lifted from my shoulders, as though I was able to get on with my life again.

There is a relationship between mood and performance.

Shortly after the settlement, I took up new offices and was able to re-focus and get back to my winning ways.

Re-energised and now with a sense of purpose, I was better able to apply myself, and to be proactive, confident and do more of the right things more of the time. I started winning an ever-increasing number of deals again.

Life was on the up again, I was enjoying exceptional billings and was recruiting into more senior roles than ever before, with bigger fees and some record

The aftermath

fee values. I was able to capitalise on what I'd learned several years earlier, largely through honing the headhunting experiences and skills I'd learned in my significant dealings with IBM.

I picked up two significant projects.

One was acting on behalf of an investment management company. They wanted to install a new leadership team in a company they'd acquired and hired an MD, Chief Operating Officer, sales & marketing director and head of customer services from me.

The second was with a business process outsourcing vendor who wanted two key hires in their senior leadership team (CxO level) to drive their public sector business, which had a billion pound revenue.

Successfully recruiting into these six senior executive roles was a real high point for me; not only was I back at the top of my game but I was also doing new things, bigger impact ones. So what next?

Some two years after the finalisation of the divorce.

Sunday 11.00, 23rd March 2008.

I was working in the office on a Sunday morning and my mobile phone rang. It was Charlie, one of my old friends. I'd not spoken to him for perhaps six to nine months and wondered why he was calling. Something specific perhaps, touching base or perhaps to fix up to get together?

He sounded all serious. "I've got some bad news about Caroline. Are you sitting down?"

I was thinking perhaps she had been in a car accident or got drunk and had an accident, or perhaps one of her new dogs had been run over.

He told me had Caroline died at 3.00 am that morning.

I had not heard from or heard about her; I had not had anything to do with her for perhaps 17-24 months.

Thoughts ran quickly through my mind: has she died in a car accident, of liver disease or did the cancer come back? Charlie proceeded to say Caroline's cancer had come back and was the cause of her death. I was completely shocked.

Devastating news. Caroline had been the closest person to me in my life, we had

The aftermath

done so much together, experienced and achieved so much together. Despite being separated I was still so fond of her.

This was the worst moment in my entire life. It's impossible for me to express the sadness and grief I experienced.

It was so unfair!

She was the first in our age group to die.

So cruel, I would have given all my money to have her back in the world, back in the world but not with me.

When someone who is close to you dies you replay what you recall of them.

Your first night, you think about the person all night long and you don't sleep. And this goes on, you remember things and you replay what you knew or experienced with the person, for many nights.

In the early days and weeks, memories came back to me randomly. Uppermost in my mind were thoughts about Caroline, my experiences with her and everything I knew about her. Thinking about my life with her, her feelings, and her life before and after her time with me.

I found myself thinking about her in a sequential order, playing forward in my mind from the time I met her, and backward from when I last saw her. Back and forth. Thinking about her over and over.

All intermingled with sadness and compassion for her. And that how cruel it was that her life had been cut short.

Eventually I had replayed most things.

This was an ongoing emotional nightmare. I felt guilty. I had spent so much of my time with her, pretty much 24/7/365. We lived and worked together, she didn't drive, and it is difficult to describe the extent to which we had spent so much time together.

I guess less than 1% of the population would have lived together as we did, so rarely apart.

I felt guilty that I was still alive, and she was dead.

No one deserves to die young. I suppose at 48, technically she was early middle aged. However, Caroline was the first in our age group to die.

The aftermath

On an ongoing basis I was in a state of emotional turmoil.

And this is one of the biggest issues I wish to share with you in this book: if you think you are going to travel through life without encountering crisis, think again.

I felt an ongoing sense of guilt and loss. Having lived with Caroline for 14 years and spent more or less every hour together, we'd been like peas in a pod. We lived together, worked together, I drove her everywhere.... I think when you have spent so much time with someone you feel guilty to be the one who is still alive.

Whilst Caroline getting cancer wasn't of my making nor fault, I felt a kind of responsibility towards her.

This was how I was feeling: riddled with guilt for leaving after she had had cancer, following what for her must have been an agonizing period with an uncertain future...

I didn't know the cancer would come back, but I felt bad for leaving her following such a traumatic experience. And intermingled with this was a sense of guilt, having spent some 14 years with her, 24/7/365, that I was the one still alive and not her.

I suffered survivor's guilt.

There is a term "survivor's guilt" also called survivor's syndrome, a mental condition that occurs when a person believes they have done something wrong by surviving a traumatic event when others did not.

I felt so guilty, so bad and that I'd let her down. I felt a loss, it was so unfair, I felt so sorry for her. At nights I'd think where was she, what is death, how could this have happened and how would she have felt? Why her? And my feelings of loss and guilt were not only heavy and consuming, but also a cross which I would have to carry for many years to come.

Some people say grief doesn't go away; nor did my survivor's guilt.

I'm not alone in suffering from this. If it doesn't apply to you, the likelihood is it will apply to someone you love or know.

In the years leading up to Caroline's illness I was stressed. When her illness struck, I was even more so. Throughout her treatment I felt anxious, worried

The aftermath

about her and, even when we thought she had got through it, I still felt worried about her.

After we split I felt guilty, and in the years following her death she was very much on my mind and a variety of thoughts would go through my head.

I wasn't there in the final years of her life. What did she think during the last six months of her life when the cancer had returned, knowing it was stage four cancer, terminal?

Ever since I first met Caroline, she had always been scared of dying of cancer. When it got to this stage, she must have been terrified. What was she thinking? How did she feel? Who was there to support her?

Some of her friends had shared with me some of their final experiences with Caroline before she died. She'd gone into a hospice in the weeks leading up to her death. Suffering pain, she was put on morphine and, as is usual, the dose was gradually increased.

Apparently, she didn't really want the morphine; she was afraid to go to sleep in case she never woke up.

I'm sure she must have felt petrified and would have been thinking: "Is death going to hurt?"

She'd have had so many thoughts going through her head….

Can you imagine what someone would be feeling, faced with pending death?

Caroline now in a hospice, she would have known she'd gone there to die.

It's over… That's what would be going through my mind. I wondered what would have been the overriding thoughts going through hers.

Aged 48, I reckon she would have been feeling short changed. Why me? How cruel for me to go before my time.

This is so unfair. Why me? The first in our age group to die.

She would have been thinking… What have I done to deserve this?

Sure, I've shouted at a few people, but I've not stolen, not killed, I've not taken drugs and I've worked hard, paid considerable sums of tax, why did it have to be me?

Caroline would have known she'd be injected with morphine.

The aftermath

She was smart, had a great memory, was well read, she'd have known that as the pain of cancer increased they'd increase the dose of morphine. Slowly becoming increasingly less conscious, she'd be aware that at some point she'd go to sleep and not wake up.

If I close my eyes, I may never wake up.

When you're young you feel invincible, old age and death seem so far away, you don't have to worry about it.

I reckon Caroline would have thought it's over and, reflecting on her life, be thinking it's felt so short…

If you put yourself in her shoes, I believe she would have re-played her life in her mind. I could imagine her thinking back to her earliest memories of her childhood, where she had grown up, her mother and father, friends.

How she'd lived in Taunton, Salisbury, London.

Her first boyfriend, her subsequent boyfriends, how she'd inherited money from her aunt and spent it all, on numerous holidays to the Caribbean, Canaries and on cruises, and on clothes. She told me she'd walk into shops and buy items of clothing in every colour.

She'd inherited perhaps £100,000 in today's money and blew it all in a matter of years. She went to the bank one day and there was £300 left in it.

This is before she met me.

She moved to South Africa with one of her boyfriends. He, Peter, turned out to be gay! I met him in subsequent years; charming guy, great company, they split up when he came out.

Married twice before she met me.

One was a marriage of convenience to get the money from her aunt, the inheritance I just mentioned, and her second marriage was to a guy called Jim, who moved to Singapore. I think he worked for the Financial Times.

She would have been playing through her mind her times living in London in Stoke Newington, and of her first dog Sherlock.

And of her early years in recruitment prior to meeting me, when working in the West End of London. She'd go out in the evenings, it was the 80s, the time

The aftermath

of lively pop music. The things she loved most were our dogs, animal welfare and history.

One of the biggest loves of her life would have been our 11-bedroom house, she would have been playing this all back through her mind.

I guess she'd have been thinking about family and friends. I know one of her best friends, Kate, went to visit her in the hospice daily.

And no doubt she'd be thinking about her boyfriend.

I don't have a clue how strong or poor their relationship was.

So her thoughts about him may have been good, bad or indifferent.

However, I do think Caroline would have been thinking of me. I think Caroline would have wanted me at her side, I am so sorry this happened to her, her shortcomings were outweighed by her strengths. I hope she realised we had such great times.

In the weeks and then days leading up to her death, you could envisage she would have re-played her life story over and over again.

I knew from her previous behaviour she would have been terrified. If I were her, I'd be thinking "Is there a life after death?", although I know she didn't really believe in the afterlife.

If I were her, I'd feel some bitterness towards me.

In her shoes, I probably would think how long will the people whom I know and care about live. How will their lives unfold?

And what about the things I could have done in the next 20+ years?

It's difficult to imagine the fear and absolute cruelty to be facing death at the age of 48; we all expect to live into our 70s and 80s.

Imagine being in a hospice, knowing you have just 7-14 days to live.

Each day, being one closer to the end.

And her thoughts must have included: "When are the lights going to go out?" Caroline didn't believe in life after death.

My intuition suggests she would have known the lights were going to go out and never come back on, that this was the end.

God bless Caroline.

The aftermath

I am so sorry for her, and that this happened.

As I inferred previously, in the weeks and months following Caroline's death, I probably thought of her every hour of the day.

In addition to grieving and feeling guilty about Caroline, other thoughts were going through my mind, I had other things to worry about.

Trying to make work work. The recruitment market had moved on, it was becoming more difficult, my income was unpredictable and variable, with huge peaks and lows.

How could I make it really rock as I had done before?

Where had all my money gone? I'd lost a massive chunk of my net worth through the course of my divorce.

Let me be honest; I admit there were times when it went through my mind that had I stuck around with Caroline I would have ended up with all of the money, and all of the assets, rather than a fraction of it. Of course, hanging around was never an option, given her aggressive and controlling manner.

Back to my life.

I'd been working hard, as I always do, I'm a workaholic, so some months later I decided that I needed a break.

I'd become somewhat exhausted, having taken a battering over the recent years. It was December, which can be quiet in recruitment, and I decided to go on a polo holiday to Argentina. I went by myself.

At the time my fiancée was consumed with supporting one of her friends who had sadly lost her son in a freak accident at school, so she was OK with me popping off for a week.

This was the second time I'd been to Argentina by myself and I quite liked doing so. Upwards of 14 hours, it's a long flight, giving me lots of time for reflection.

I was excited. I'd been to Argentina twice before, loved the place and the relaxed way of the people.

I'd been doing enough business simply to get by, no more than that; in fact, I shouldn't really have been going on this holiday because I hadn't earned the

The aftermath

extra money during the year to afford it. However, I'd always come up trumps, I'd always been able to work hard and to make money. And I'd got a big deal up my sleeve.

Fingers crossed, the following day I had someone at a fourth and final interview stage, with an exciting quite early-stage US company called Concur; the role was to head up Europe/EMEA. The global head was flying into the UK to meet him; this was the final stage and both the employer and candidate expected to progress to an offer, accept and start.

And for me this would be a significant fee.

I'd invested a lot of time in finding this person; recruitment and headhunting is considerably more time consuming that you'd ever imagine. I was fatigued with the long hours I'd been working on this and other assignments.

Tomorrow I'd be waking up in Argentina.

To enjoy their summertime, feasting on the best meat in the world, cooked gaucho style Asado, jumping in the pool in the baking heat and playing polo. And a highlight of my trip: the Argentine Open. I'd be seeing the highest standard of polo in the world, the biggest match of the year, in just three days' time.

I arrived at Buenos Aires airport around 9 at night and was met by Mariano. We jumped in his pick-up truck and off we went.

Heading away from central BA, driving through the country on largely single carriageway roads in the hot evening air…

Mariano is a polo professional. I'd met him over here and he was running polo holidays (four to six people would go over to his place at any one time).

Midnight, we arrived at his estancia (farm) and he showed me to my room, which was a converted stable, farmhouse, gaucho in style, windows with shutters, ceiling fan, terracotta tiled floors, en suite bathroom, great, all good… very much what I expected.

I jumped into bed and was out for the count. I slept like a log.

Buzz, buzz, buzz.

I was woken by my mobile phone; a text message had arrived.

The aftermath

6.00 in the morning, the first day of my holiday.

"Sorry, I won't be attending final interview with Concur, I've changed my mind and will be staying where I am".

I was presented with a fait accompli.

Argentina is three hours behind; this candidate was expected in 30 minutes by the chap who's flown in from the US to see him. The candidate was more than two hours away; even if I persuaded him to go after all, he wouldn't be able to make it.

The employer client was not impressed. As a headhunter, recruiter, when things like this happen it marks your score card, your client relationship is compromised, your credibility lost.

I called both sides, but this was not something which could be recovered.

This is the reality of recruitment: people are not like products; they have choices, preferences, influences and changes of circumstance; people are unpredictable.

I felt let down by this candidate, especially as it was at the last minute. Why could he not have let me know sooner?

However, there's the need to respect people. I bit my lip, was understanding; in recruitment you need to keep people on side. You never know, the people you deal with today may be tomorrow's prime customer or candidate!

In the here and now, not a great start to my holiday.

Up till this point in my life this was the best holiday I had ever had.

I love riding horses and playing polo. Mariano has lots of horses, perhaps 70 of them; he had a breeding programme and when I played polo at his farm the horses which I rode were powerful, well trained in the discipline of polo, his polo grounds were flat and had fantastic high-quality well-kept grass playing surfaces.

The polo was of a good quality, fast, and it was perfect for me, in the hot dry Argentine summer.

The group of which I was part comprised 6 people with whom I socialised day and night; they were great company, and at the end when it came to leaving, I really didn't want to.

The aftermath

Back to my life in the UK. My fiancée had somewhat of a loathing of Caroline, which meant she couldn't understand why I was distraught over her death and grieving. Not only was she not empathetic, but she also took offence to it.

And she was costing me a fortune. Tens of thousands of pounds a year. Was she with me just for my money? Which was rapidly diminishing.

She had a genuinely nice personality. We spent four years together, we got engaged and moved in together. As an accountant she may have been good with numbers but was costly to run.

I was continually wondering how I could recover my financial position once again.

I was now working by myself.

Following the separation and the death of Caroline, I largely worked by myself, and the loneliness was significant.

It felt like me against all the troubles of the world, including financial pressures.

Previously, with two sets of billings, my down periods and dry spots would be offset by Caroline's, and vice versa. This cushioned the bad times.

Now, as a solo operator, the bad times were more severe, more painful, more worrying, all adding up to a mental double whammy.

Caroline and I had billed pretty evenly; over a period of upwards of 12 years there was not more than 10% to separate us, except in one of my IBM years in which I hit the jackpot.

A couple of years on, I encountered challenges yet again!

When I got together with the model, we decided to have a child, and looked for a house in which we could settle down and build our little family.

I bought an amazing house at the top end of the property market; the market had been buoyant, and I was buying at a peak. Our idea was to get the best house possible; I would put in my money and she would sell her place as soon as possible and put in her money.

I was able to secure and afford a massive mortgage, which I'd be able to fund by myself for a reasonable amount of time until she had sold her flat and put her money in. The new mortgage would then be more manageable, especially

The aftermath

in the case of a market slow-down or collapse.

She had previously been working part-time for her former boyfriend (life's complex, isn't it?) And he'd been paying her for more hours than she was working. When she wasn't working for her ex-boyfriend, she worked part-time in a boutique.

I didn't think this was right or fair for her ex-boyfriend to be paying her for more hours than she was working and so I said to her: "Why not just work part-time in the boutique and I'll make up the difference?"

Furthermore, bearing in mind our plan was to have a baby without delay, after all, we weren't getting any younger; I'd anticipated she'd ultimately give up work anyway.

Despite having many flaws, one of my strengths is that I'm hard working and relentless. At this time, I was working six days a week, which isn't unusual for me. In fact, there have been many times when I've worked seven days a week, sometimes for months on end.

I've always been an early starter; I wake up and I'm ready to get on it. It would be very unusual for me to start work any later than 8am and often I'll start as early as 6.30am. I was doing well, and my outlook was positive.

For perhaps two or three years I was paying a large mortgage and giving my girlfriend tens of thousands of pounds a year to cover her lost income and costs associated with her flat. In previous years, with a substantial income, these extraordinarily high costs were ones I was capable of covering.

Short term, these costs would be sustainable, but they wouldn't be long term in the event of a massive drop in income.

However, life didn't quite unfold as I had hoped. She had mixed feelings about having a child; it seemed she would have liked a baby girl but not a baby boy, which I found strange.

I felt somewhat let down and compromised by her failure to sell her flat; in hindsight I wonder if she felt it gave her independence or perhaps she was not so sure about me. Had she sold her flat and put her equity into the house, I would have been paying for one home not two, and it would have brought the remaining large mortgage down to a realistic amount.

The aftermath

My outgoings would have been manageable.

However, a crash was about to happen.

If you'd been reading the news around that time (as I had) you could see an economic slowdown or recession was coming. 2008 depression, and biggest financial crisis in living memory happens.

The great recession. To say this was a career impacting event is an understatement.

The crisis was largely driven by what was happening in the USA, and this directly impacted the UK and the rest of the global economy.

With the UK economy in decline there were widespread job losses which massively outnumbered new job gains. There were fewer jobs than the number of people available.

For me the impact was severe. The majority of my clients were US tech firms; with the US market on the floor, they were cost cutting because of problems in their home markets and spending in the UK was low down in their priorities.

Losing my driving licence was the last thing I needed. 12 penalty points and you lose your licence, and I'd accumulated four sets of three. These points were all for the same kind of office, driving at 39mph in 30mph areas on roads which I thought had limits of 40mph.

I went to court to appeal and explained that I needed to be able to drive to do my job: to get into the office early, leave late and work weekends. And to have the flexibility to easily meet candidates and clients at short notice. Without being able to drive I would be less effective; I stated that the economy was on a downward spiral, going into recession and the hiring market was poised to crash.

The pending recession, which was about to wreck the economy and people's lives, had been widely projected and reported in the news.

My billings would drop and not being able to drive would be catastrophic; my billings would collapse, and the bottom line was that my income would be marginalised. And I wouldn't be able to afford to pay my mortgage and would likely need to sell my house.

They didn't buy it. I lost my driving licence.

The biggest recession in living memory took hold and my earnings fell to

The aftermath

the floor. Although I was right in anticipating the recession, I made some stupid choices.

Around this time, I had a business idea which was to prove costly and a distraction.

People were losing their jobs, there were few jobs to go after, and finding a new job was becoming an acute problem.

My idea was to create some engaging videos giving people a winning platform for their job search, supported by comprehensive information and insights on a portal (website). My aim was to help people "find a better job faster".

I called it "mycareercoach.com"

However, getting this right and getting people interested was to prove a nightmare.

At this time internet streaming was beginning to work well and YouTube etc was becoming popular.

So I created some videos: how to write a better CV, how to find a better job faster and how to ace the interview.

But I failed to make a success of this, due to some of my own shortcomings, naivety and stupidity.

One of my biggest mistakes was failing to acknowledge that people did not see a need for this kind of help.

Failing to differentiate between need and desire. I could see there was a need but the people these guides were aimed at didn't really want them.

I didn't take proper notice of what people were telling me about the idea.

Although I could see how people were failing in their approach to job search and looking after their career interests, when starting out in the world of work, after school and university, not once they were established into their careers.

They weren't buying into it.

The feedback was that people needed advice about job search at the onset and in the early stages of their careers, not mid-career.

However, what I had observed over many years, and was observing all the time,

The aftermath

was that people who were mid-career had a problem; their approach to job search, managing and developing their career interests was poor.

I was convinced there was a market, but the market was clearly far from convinced about what I had to say. If only I could get people to buy into these themes and their benefits!

How to find a better job faster. How to negotiate a better salary package. How to better manage their career interests; surely people would be interested in these areas.

After all, they spend money on personal trainers, on the latest trainers, phones, the biggest and flattest TVs, German cars….

I didn't give up.

I had not got all the content at the time, so was having to develop it as I went along and underestimated the size of the project.

Beyond my own shortcomings, the people I worked with to help me package the content, create the videos and construct an engaging website had their limitations too.

At the time, all things web, digital and e-commerce were pretty embryonic. A lot of people claimed to have expertise but had skills gaps.

I failed to work with the right people. There's a difference between a copywriter and web engineer, and a video engineer and a voice-over artist.

The people I was working with were good in their own silos, but I needed to make these joined up, and packaged correctly.

Some people could do the mechanics but not the design, some could do the design but not the mechanics and some could do 90% of what was required in an area of what for them was supposed to be a competency.

But not the remaining 10%.

At the time, much of this was new; it hadn't been done before.

I have a short attention span which, if I had better recognised this, I would have more precisely mapped out my requirements and expectations.

Perhaps in hindsight I could have been better organised and more precisely mapped out my requirements, expectations and approach to my suppliers, but

The aftermath

at every hurdle I stumbled, from the quality of the content through to failing to appreciate budget nor to properly manage the cost.

However, I wasted upwards of £100k. And there's only one person to blame for that, and it's me.

My only consolation being that at least I tried. However, I didn't give up and, in the years to come, continued to spend even more money on it and, equally significantly, time.

Just to put this in perspective, this was happening in 2008/2009, during the biggest recession in living history.

At this time there were very few jobs available, and companies didn´t want to pay a recruitment/headhunting fee when they could easily find people themselves. Which meant that for a period of a year or so I had few vacancies to work on and, though I prospected and networked to pick up vacancies, I did so without 100% effort nor belief.

My ability to bill recruiting fees and earn was very limited by the depressed hiring market, so why spend much of my time on this initiative?

I did have a conviction that there were lots of people who had lost their jobs and that for them job search was unfamiliar.

In a growing economy, companies don't let their best people go, while in this shrinking economy, a state of recession, even good people were being let go.

People were struggling to find new jobs, struggling to get interviews and struggling to get a job offer. In a depressed hiring market, people in between jobs will take any suitable job. However, for many of these unemployed people, even getting one of these was proving difficult.

And it was taking people longer to find a new job than they expected; it was proving costly, and people were becoming anxious.

I was observing this on an ongoing basis, and I thought my coaching products were just the answer: how to look for a job, write a winning CV and ace the interview process.

People spend 99% of their working lives working and 1% in job search mode.

Job search is not a core competency which people possess.

The aftermath

Yet job search is one of those subjects about which everyone has a view, and many people think they are an expert, despite spending only 1% of their time looking for a job.

What works well for one person, in one situation and at one point in time, may not work for another.

People with biased or limited experience of job search will often offer guidance to job seekers. Such guidance may be flawed, narrow or outdated, perhaps applicable to one field or level of seniority and not another.

There exists a widespread scenario of the blind leading the blind!

Unconscious incompetence is something not all people recognise, in particular older folk, many of whom are too arrogant, have outdated perspectives, are too set in their ways and burnt out.

This applies more to men than it does to women.

I ran a series of job search workshops attended by directors, sales managers, consultants and project managers. Whilst these people were bright and showed initiative, they were not familiar with job search. Their CVs were generally OK but not good, they had few ideas about how and where to look for new jobs, how to apply for them and how to best approach an interview.

These workshops proved really successful, resulting in people going away with a job search action plan, being better prepared in their job search, their job seeking efforts were more productive, and each of them secured job offers inside 6 weeks.

All but one!

He was an older guy, slightly arrogant, somewhat set in his ways and somewhat burnt out.

As your level of seniority rises, the number of available openings for you to pursue shrinks. And this chap was a senior director. During the workshop he was more interested in offering up advice than listening and discovering new ideas or techniques.

He did not apply the best practice guidelines outlined in the workshop and nor did he listen to what other people in the group had to contribute.

His own approach to job search was restricted to tapping into his limited people

The aftermath

network at a time when very few jobs were available. The job he subsequently found was a level below that which he had previously enjoyed and was not one he really wanted. Without being fully motivated to perform in the job, which was quite a high risk one, he ultimately failed.

Having had several jobs in short succession prior to this, what he really needed was something more secure, more long term, in which he could re-establish a strong track record and credentials.

Failure in this job was the final nail in the coffin of his career and contributed to his decision to give up and run a small country house hotel instead.

Had he applied himself better to his job search in the first place, then he could have been expected to land himself a good job, perform well in it and keep it.

I'd enjoyed creating the job search frameworks, CV templates, LinkedIn tips and running the job search guidance workshops. However, I wanted to get back to what I love… headhunting.

This was a tough time at work, and I needed to get back to my winning ways, to what I did best and what worked.

I love headhunting and wanted to put my foot flat down on the pedal.

The hiring market had pretty much ground to a halt and my billings were minimal.

By this time the companies in the marketplace I served were software firms (mainly US owned). They brought more recruitment in-house, i.e. recruiting directly to the exclusion of sourcing from external recruitment firms.

And LinkedIn had opened up a new way to hire. This was to prove the most disruptive event during my time in recruitment and headhunting.

The candidate database and people network that headhunters like me had to offer clients were no longer as valuable, and seemed to be becoming obsolete.

The tech community (my clients) were early adopters of LinkedIn. They embraced it with open arms, it empowered them to more easily recruit direct, and better leverage their own people networks.

At this point in time, there was little or no need for them to find people through us, when they could quite easily find people themselves without paying a fee. In fact, most companies had a regular stream of reasonably qualified people

The aftermath

applying direct. I'd put all my money in a property at a peak time, 2007/2008, there was an economic crash taking place, I lost my driving licence, and I was paying for two houses, the one I had bought and my fiancées apartment.

The economic crash of 2008/2009 was the biggest depression in living memory and my billings had crashed; recovery would not be overnight and at its very worst I had no billings whatsoever for several months. My outgoings were higher than my income after tax, finding new clients was difficult, few companies were hiring and most of those that were, were able to source good candidates without having to pay recruiter/headhunter fees.

I was running out of money; I was going to have to sell my house to release cash!

I sold my house.

The stamp duty tax which I had paid on the purchase of my property just 18 months earlier and the difference between what I had paid for the property at the peak of the market and its value now in a crash, translated into a net loss of over £100k.

I have suffered some really big setbacks in life, one after another and these have had an effect on my success at work and in my home life.

However, I started to realise I was continually blaming some of my failures, faults and flaws on circumstances and other people.

Blaming anyone and anything else but me for my own mistakes.

In reality some of my setbacks and shortcomings were a result of my own poor decisions and the way I chose to look at things, the poor application of my own emotional intelligence.

I'd lost £100k on my property, and as my income had plummeted, I'd been spending more than I was earning, perhaps as much as £50k, and by this time I'd invested perhaps £100k in coaching products and portal business initiatives. That's £250k I had wasted away. And now my income was on the floor.

❈ ❈ ❈

Chapter 6

The pursuit of happiness

Life had been throwing me one set of challenges after another.

So, to recap, here's what had happened in the last 3-4 years!

My ex-wife, whom I still cared about, had died, I'd been put in a prison cell overnight, I'd lost my driving licence, I'd lost £100k having been forced to sell my house, my billings were on the floor, and I'd wasted tons of time and money on a failed business venture.

It didn't stop there!

The economy had collapsed and my outlook was not good.

I wanted to love and be loved. I wanted to be successful, secure and happy.

My journey to finding happiness would be a long one.

It was the time of the most significant economic crisis in living memory, and my work had imploded. Around this time I had few or no vacancies to work on, which meant my income was minimal, and something needed to change.

The type of companies I'd been recruiting into in the last few years had now reached a peak; at best, they'd reached a plateau. At worst, they were in a state of decline; they had little or no need for headhunting services.

I needed to adjust my focus and secure new clients.

Out with the old and in with the new.

The lessons of history apply in the business world.

They illustrate constant change, the expected and unexpected.

It applies to me and it applies to you too.

Ruling dynasties come and go, for example: the Ottoman, Egyptian, Roman and British Empires!

And in more recent times, the 20th Century was dominated by the rise of the US powerhouse and its economy.

Now in the 21st Century, it's the Chinese who have become the dominant global economy, and there are the well-educated, hard-working Indians everywhere.

The pursuit of happiness

The world does not stand still, it evolves.

And, of course, there were also natural disasters.

We live and work in an ever-changing environment.

Economic cycles of growth and depression – history shows us there's a recession every ten years. I've worked through three of them in my recruitment career/business.

Innovation: the wheel, the horse and cart, the steam engine, train, car, aeroplane, wireless, phone, computer, artificial intelligence and machine learning, handheld devices…

We can learn from history the need for us to evolve, think ahead, and think about the future.

And this relates to people's jobs and sustaining employment, a need for us all to acquire new knowledge and sought-after skills, to think to the future about things like working in growth sectors of the economy rather than those in decline. Being in the right place at the right time, moving to where the best opportunity lies.

This applies to me in my work and to my outlook, and it applies to you and those you care about.

Because of the economic crisis, established tech companies were not recruiting. However, I did identify the next wave.

A disruptive change was about to happen in the tech sector; a new way of delivering business application software was coming to market: Software as a Service (SaaS).

Innovative companies were emerging, delivering SaaS. The highest profile was salesforce.com, with a handful of others coming into focus, and I managed to develop relationships and do business with two of these: NetSuite and Concur.

Together with customers in other areas, these new SaaS clients gave me the platform to start winning again and making a reasonable income.

I'd pulled it back together.

It was around this time I split up with the girl to whom I'd got engaged.

The pursuit of happiness

She had a lovely disposition, a happy personality, a wonderful smile, but I didn't feel that she was 100% committed.

One of the things which troubled me was that she was incredibly shy, which meant we rarely socialised. This was ironic because not only did she have a striking look, but she was one of those girls who dressed to impress.

There was a lot to like about her. I loved her.

Perhaps we'd both made some mistakes, and there were some shortcomings in the relationship.

Most importantly, I felt she had taken advantage of me big time financially. I'd been paying her mortgage, for her apartment's costs, her lifestyle and her penchant for boutique clothes, designer handbags, and jewellery.

She was no stranger to Cartier, Harrods or Prada.

At my expense.

In hindsight I should have been firmer with her.

I felt let down by her; I'd put my money into the house I purchased, but she failed to do the same.

I don't think she'd wanted to sell her place and had dragged her feet on it.

We'd been together for upwards of 3 years, and I felt she wasn't committed to the relationship. I thought she wasn't committed to me. I was worried that she was with me for my money, as a meal ticket which by now, with her excessive spending and some of my own mistakes, had dwindled.

She wasn't 100% about the relationship either, and of course, I had my shortcomings too.

I wanted to draw a line under it. In hindsight, I may have misjudged her and her behaviour; I have a lot of respect for her, she is a very special person.

I thought, no more. Caroline had taken advantage of my good nature, so no more, never again.

We split up. And so I was single again.

When I reflect on my previous life with Caroline and, to an extent, some of my interactions with other people, I realise that I allowed myself to be pushed around, but ever since my split with Caroline, I had become a stronger character,

The pursuit of happiness

more inclined to hold my ground and with a tendency to overcompensate.

Returning to the work side of my life, something outstanding was about to happen.

I got a lucky break.

One of the people I knew, who rated me, joined salesforce.com.

He had various responsibilities for hiring in Europe and choose to work with me.

This was a fantastic opportunity; at the time, they were pioneering and were displacing the established computing and software vendors.

Salesforce.com hired 24 people through me, three of whom stand out in my mind:

They asked me to find them someone to spearhead their drive to become EMEA (Europe, the Middle East and Africa) market leader in a new line of business.

I investigated the market sector, and there were about ten primary vendors – five of which were the most relevant, and one was the most directly related competitor.

Guess what?

Earlier in the book, I told the story about how when I was on holiday in Argentina, I got a text from someone who had decided to withdraw from the recruitment process for a GM position. And how he'd pulled out just two hours before the final interview was due to take place with the US global exec who had flown into the UK specially to conduct the last interview.

In situations such as this, it's easy to get upset and annoyed, but if you do, you'll shut yourself off from ever being able to deal with the person again.

Fortunately, I had kept my head at the time, was understanding, polite and professional, despite being blamed by the client who took out their frustration on me.

It was a good job I didn't get annoyed with the candidate and kept the door open to come back to him in the future.

He was the head of the #1 company in the market sector salesforce.com

The pursuit of happiness

wanted to move into, build-out and ultimately dominate. Salesforce was known for CRM (Customer Relationship Management), and they wanted to expand out into other areas.

Of course, I'd met this guy before, I knew he was right, and this opening at salesforce.com was genuinely exceptional.

I called him.

After exchanging a few pleasantries, I asked how things were going for him at his employer company, on the professional side of his life.

He said that salesforce.com had called him directly three weeks ago asking if he would like to work for them, but he had said NO.

We'd only been on the phone for two minutes; I'd not even mentioned salesforce.

"Would you like to work for us"?

I thought that's interesting. His choice of words was interesting.

Perhaps his interpretation of their approach was, "Would he like to work for them?" it struck me that this might have been too strong a question to ask, too much to ask…

A bit like going up to a stranger and saying can I have a French kiss.

Perhaps they'd asked too much of a big question.

A play with words, what he had said to me was that they had said:

"Would you like to work for us?"

So, I flipped the wording.

I explained to him that I was tasked by salesforce with headhunting someone into this position.

He said he wasn't sure if the opportunity would be a big enough challenge for him, and that he couldn't see how it would be worthwhile giving up his existing employment for, and that he was happily employed.

I responded by saying clearly, it's an exciting opportunity, it's relevant to you and the scope for impact in the role is massive.

I went on to say that Salesforce have the potential to dominate this market.

"Would you be happy to have an exploratory meeting with them?"

He said "Yes".

The pursuit of happiness

The courtship began. I fixed up an exploratory meeting, explaining to salesforce that the guy is happy, not intending to move and that perhaps if they and the candidate had a meeting, and subsequent meetings, it could result in a relationship and trust being developed, and a meeting of the minds.

Appreciate in this instance, the candidate was a 5 Star candidate, working for the pre-eminent company in the market niche Salesforce wanted to move into; hiring him would be a coup.

It's not unusual for a senior person to say NO to a direct approach from a competitor, but to say YES when engaged with and presented by a headhunter.

The reason being that people at this level don't want to be exposed as being open to a move, or interested in making one.

There can be many reasons for this which include the fact that it can jeopardise the way in which they are seen with respect to their commitment to their existing employer, boss or business owners, and similarly be viewed in a negative context regarding competitive positioning in the market. If they're open to a move does it mean their business is weak?

This is one of the reasons headhunting services are so highly valued.

I fixed for him to meet with them, and he was ultimately offered, accepted and joined in the role.

AVP (Area Vice President), EMEA. He was on a good package including lucrative stock options. Inside two years, he grew his business area revenues 10 times over.

I'm not going to publicly state what a particular person might have earned or how much money specific companies pay these types of people but I will say that it wouldn't be unusual for someone in this kind of role to earn over half a million a year, and then add in some stock, with a gain perhaps of another million or two.

Someone like this may not have previously earned more than 250k and may not have gained from stock.

I have headhunted quite a few people into roles in which they've made a million, or indeed several.

The second great hire which I'm really pleased about was of someone whose

The pursuit of happiness

move to salesforce.com would prove life changing.

Again, salesforce.com wanted to enter new markets, to sell broader offerings to big global companies, and win mega-sized deals. Up till this time they'd been landing in companies with a small footprint and building out sales from one department to another, but they had few seven figure UK deals.

They wanted to push out a strategic programme to sign multi-million deals with the largest UK-owned firms and to hire someone to trailblaze a pathway to success.

Having identified a prime target for the role, I approached him, and his immediate response was: "NO, I'm not interested, and I'm not interested in salesforce."

However, I persuaded him to meet with me, tuned into his motivations and positioned the opportunity to him. I subsequently presented him, he was offered the job and accepted.

This was a life changing move; he more than doubled his income, benefited from stock and enjoyed career acceleration; today he is a member of the senior leadership team.

I love the best parts of my job as a headhunter, but it can be subject to crushing blows as well as exhilarating highs.

People are unpredictable and sometimes their behaviour can be brutal.

The third significant hire which stands out in my memory is one which came with a kick in the teeth.

One of the areas which salesforce.com wanted to break into was what would become known as Platform as a Service.

At the time someone not familiar with salesforce.com nor its strategy nor the merits of it, would be unclear as to why this would be a great opportunity.

I identified a number of suitable candidates and went about approaching them.

One had an ideal profile for the job.

When I approached him, his immediate response was to say NO, I'm not interested.

He couldn't see how salesforce could be successful in this line of business.

The pursuit of happiness

I knew that as long as I could get 15 minutes with him, I'd be able to tune into his motivations and way of thinking, and most likely position this as a genuinely amazing opportunity.

I got him to agree to grabbing a coffee in Starbucks, established some rapport, tuned into his interests and perspectives then positioned the opportunity, raised his interest level, and persuaded him to meet with them. He was offered and started in the job.

Here's the brutal twist in the story.

One of his first, most pressing tasks was to hire people. But instead of asking HR to work with me to find them, he asked to work with a tall, slim, brunette recruitment consultant in another company.

It was quite amazing.

I had been the catalyst for him to take up an exceptional opportunity, I'd done a good job and I could have recommended others.

Recruitment is one of those jobs in which people's behaviour can be quite brutal.

Nearly every day you get rejected, and sometimes the rejections are bigger and hurt more than others.

And when someone behaves like the guy I've just mentioned I feel insulted and unappreciated. And it was at times like this that I still felt really down, not only as a result of the crises I was experiencing at work, but I was also so sad about the death of Caroline; I was somewhat haunted by my memories of her.

I think when you've suffered big traumas, minor issues can potentially trigger anxiety and sadness, and I'd often feel like I was battling against the world.

Throughout this time, I was doing well at work but it was full of these ups and downs which could be mentally draining.

Financially I was earning well, but I had a constant craving to get back the significant wealth I'd enjoyed several years before. I wanted the status, a big house, first-class, long-distance holidays, the unlimited spending power and the personal pride of being so successful.

However, whilst I was doing well, achieving something commensurate with

The pursuit of happiness

what I'd accomplished before seemed increasingly unrealistic.

In fact, I often wondered whether it would have been better never to have had the riches I'd enjoyed, rather than to have had them and lost them.

In the social side of my life, I had friends whom I could go out with. We'd most often go out locally into Windsor, which was great; you can walk from one bar to another, take in the beauty of what is a very historic town and cruise around having fun.

Normally we'd go to places which had an older clientele, given that we were all in our forties, and some of the places were too young for us.

It was on one of our nights out that I was briefly introduced to a hot fitness instructor who apparently had been seeing one of my friends.

A few weeks later I bumped into her again at what I guess you would call a singles bar. She was on a singles night out, and at the same time my friend who'd supposedly been seeing her, had gone to London, also on a singles night out, with one of his single friends: they'd gone to a pick-up joint, they'd gone out pulling. So it didn't seem to me like they were seeing each other.

Big mistake.

If I could have turned back time, I would choose not to make this mistake. However, I did…

I was immediately attracted to this girl, and every other man was too.

Several things drew me towards this girl.

Firstly, she was extremely attractive; secondly, she had quite a magnetic personality; and thirdly, like me, she said she was ready, completely committed to getting married and having a baby now.

And that was exactly what I wanted, and I also wanted it now.

Both of us had reached a stage in life, and an age in life, when time was running out to have a child.

It was now or never.

This girl and her friend joined me and one of my friends as we went on to another bar. Afterwards my friend dropped me and the two girls off at my place, where we had a few drinks.

The pursuit of happiness

This fitness instructor was really quite bewitching, and wearing a black, silk slip of a dress, perhaps better described as lingerie; and when she leant in to kiss me, the temptation was too much.

My friend got to know about it, and to say it didn't go down well is an understatement. So I avoided meeting up with her again, at least temporarily.

In the weeks which followed she invited me to connect on Facebook and I accepted. By this time, she and my friend had supposedly moved on and a couple of months later she messaged me on Facebook, and we hooked up.

One of the things we had in common was a desire to have a child, and with a sense of urgency; time was running out.

However, had I applied my common sense, I would have kept my head and resisted the temptation in front of me. As I understand it, with the exception of the last 9 months, she'd been in a long-term relationship of some eight years. In fact, she'd been married and was now separated, was taking the opportunity to party, enjoy her newly found single status and play the field.

I don't think she was ready for a serious relationship and if she was, probably not with me.

Flashy, flirty and fast. This sexy, slim brunette had a vibrant personality and wore revealing clothes. I fell into the honey trap.

When I started seeing this girl, I knew I was playing with fire. If I am honest with myself, I realised at the back of my mind that she had a colourful past; I never really trusted her.

No longer young, we were both fast approaching the last chance saloon to have a child, so both of us were broody.

Now in my late 40s, if I wanted to have a child I really needed to do so very quickly. Likewise, she was 39, and time was running out for her too.

In hindsight, although I was keen for a committed long-term relationship, I don't think she was mentally settled, or in the right place.

Four very exciting months.

The word exciting can be applied to both positive and negative feelings. Our first two months were quite dreamy, but the second two months were more of a nightmare. I found her behaviour erratic, strange and wondered if perhaps

The pursuit of happiness

she had been taking cocaine. I remember her seeing one of her friends a few times, whom she said was regularly taking cocaine.

One minute she'd want to be with me and the next she'd be telling me she was having second thoughts. I should have said: "No problem, let's go our separate ways." Instead, I hung on to her, I found her personality engaging and manner sexy.

Lust not love. How could I have been so stupid?

So it should not have come as a surprise to me when one night she told me she'd slept with her ex that afternoon.

OMG. I was taken aback. What a blow!

Various thoughts ran through my mind…

I felt so let down. Was our relationship so meaningless? Was I so meaningless? Are relationships meaningless to you? Who are you? I really don't know you.

What have you done to me? How could you possibly have done this to me? How dare you do this to me?

At the time I felt so let down, so betrayed, it made me feel small, lacking and inadequate.

For several weeks I felt belittled, completely betrayed and embarrassed.

Not good enough to keep a girl?

When I look back and reflect on it, this was only a short relationship: four months, two really amazing months and two which were disappointing.

On reflection, what I liked about her most was her sassy look and manner; I liked her looks but there wasn´t any deeper connection. Silly me. I should have looked beyond the eye candy.

I'd confused lust with love.

Nonetheless a bitter pill to swallow.

At the time I felt crushed, and consequently I lost faith and trust in girls, and the concept of being in a relationship. However, it was the best thing that could have happened.

Not only did I dodge a bullet but in the fullness of time it would free me up to meet an angel.

The pursuit of happiness

The highs and lows which I was continually experiencing were spectacular.

I now accepted the fact that I was too old to father a child, although this wasn't the end of the world. There are other pleasures in life to pursue, it was just that being a dad wouldn't be one of them.

At the back of my mind, I had a burning desire to get back the wealth I'd lost. However, I'd earned big money when the market had been more buoyant, and conditions were very much in my favour and prior to the impact of LinkedIn.

I was becoming ever increasingly self-aware that the real thing I should be pursuing was happiness.

On the domestic side of my life, things were quite good. I had some very good friends and a great social life.

Single again, I didn't go in for Tinder, Match.com etc and although I had a few dates, at the back of my mind I wondered where was Miss Right?

I was keeping fit, in good shape and my polo skills were progressing nicely.

Having taken a two-year break from polo a few years earlier, I started playing again and quickly bought two horses, followed by a third and a fourth.

These were flown over from Argentina and were quite hardy horses, their manner more tranquil than many other types.

I was playing most of my polo at a private club, playing what's known as low goal polo or farm polo.

At the top end of the game, the sport is funded primarily by the super-rich who sponsor high goal teams. This team will typically comprise three professionals and what's known as a patron or "the money", the person who pays for it all.

And in high goal polo, running a team may cost tens of millions! Paid for by some of the world's elite and billionaire types. This is the best polo to watch, fast and well played.

There's a middle ground: medium goal polo, where patrons may be spending hundreds of thousands.

And then there's the low goal – where people are spending more like tens of thousands. People like me. This is not the best polo to watch, not the fastest and not often played well!

The pursuit of happiness

Low goal polo is often referred to as the grassroots of the game.

By this time I had developed into a reasonable amateur player and subsequently quite a good one.

I played rugby during my school years which is a tough sport; when you take a knock, suffer a body blow or get stamped on, the pain can be excruciating. Polo is similarly dangerous, perhaps more so, with horses travelling at 30 miles per hour and hard polo balls reaching perhaps 110 miles an hour. You can get knocked unconscious, break a limb, have your teeth knocked out or, at worst, get killed.

I've played polo for upwards of 10 years and sadly know of two people who I have met in my polo career who have died whilst riding.

For me the ever-present danger adds to the excitement of it. There's a certain edginess about polo.

It's physically demanding and difficult.

It's a complex game, you need to be able to anticipate what is going to happen next, there is no point in going to where the play is… it will move.

You've got to go to where the play will be next… and know who is entitled to do what; it's all moving lightning fast; there's you, your horse and other people, constant change.

I love it. It's an exhilarating game to play. Lots happening, very quickly, with constant change, it is an absorbing and enthralling game.

Most summer weekends I was playing in tournaments as part of a team of four, wearing white polo jeans and team shirts. This was a lot of fun, I loved it and I felt very privileged.

Polo boosted my ego and gave me an outlet for my appetite for social and sports interests.

It's difficult for me to explain how uplifting I find polo, and in particular why.

There are three aspects to it which I find so exciting, engaging and all consuming.

Firstly, riding a horse is such a beautiful experience. It's a double act, the horse and me. My job to give direction to the horse, which is unbelievably complex; you can give one instruction with one body movement and a conflicting one

The pursuit of happiness

with another, simultaneously. What I like most is synching with the horse, moving together in a kind of unison, like ballet, a powerful unified force.

Secondly, the game. It is so complex, fast changing and the rules are difficult.

It's physically demanding. There's so much to think about, what you should be doing at any one time, what can be expected to happen next, where you need to be, what you need to do next, why, and what other people are doing.

Of course, horses run a lot faster than people and, as I just said, polo balls can travel at speeds of up to 110mph, which means reading such a quick game isn't easy.

I love playing it, I like making an impact and I want to be the best I can be. I always want to be improving, not just in polo, but in everything.

And thirdly, and I find this embarrassing, there's a certain kind of kudos involved in playing the game; I felt my status in life elevated by being a polo player. It's often referred to as the Game of Kings, the sport enjoys a certain cachet and elitism.

For several years I was practising during the week and playing tournaments every summer weekend.

I'm surprised I didn't hook up with one of the many girls in the polo community.

They fell into categories; those who loved horses, those who loved riding and those who loved the glamour. Some loved all three.

There are hundreds, possibly thousands of Argentinians in the UK who play polo as professionals and who look after horses.

They are a wonderful type of people.

Invariably many of them loved the looks of the Argentine guys, characterised by their dark, olive coloured skin. Polo professionals or grooms, they were working with horses every day which meant that they were strong, athletic and macho. Many have those strong square jaw lines girls adore, others with angelic faces.

Many have a certain charm and swagger.

A prime example is Nacho Figueras, a top Argentine player and global male supermodel, the David Beckham of the polo world.

The pursuit of happiness

Like any other community, word gets around and people can develop a reputation.

Rightly or wrongly, some of the girls had a reputation, and the same applied to the guys.

I'd like to think I'm quite an eligible guy but finding Miss Right was not quite as easy as it might seem, and something I wouldn't expect to find in the polo world.

In the polo scene some women are independently wealthy, others want to bag a rich man, and all seemingly have high expectations.

No longer rich, you could count me out; I wouldn't have met some of these girls' expectations.

I was wary of many of them, not knowing what may lay behind their looks and initial impressions, and life isn't quite like it is in the movies. Occasionally I'd find myself interested in getting to know a girl but failing to find the right moment in which to have a meaningful or leading conversation.

To meet me, you might not realise that I'm shy. On the outside I can come across as outgoing and confident, but that tends to be when I'm in the right mood…

Which isn't 100% of the time and often, when faced with various traumas in my life, I have felt insecure.

I was shy, wary and whilst many of my single mates were happy playing the field, I wanted a permanent relationship and, at the back of my mind, if possible, to have a child; but I was getting older, and time was running out.

Being single had its upsides and downsides, a major downside being by yourself, at times feeling lonely.

Otherwise, on the domestic side of my life things were quite good; I had some very good friends and a great social life.

However, on an ongoing basis I was trying to come to terms with my loss of status.

The work I'd done with salesforce.com had been uplifting for me, I'd come to understand a new market and they had paid me several hundred thousand pounds in fees. However, as salesforce.com grew and matured, they had less

The pursuit of happiness

need for headhunters. Some of the best talents were knocking on their door. A new head of EMEA chose to bring recruitment totally in-house and decreed no budget to pay headhunter recruiter fees, and so my winning streak with them was terminated.

In the very short term this presented no immediate problem, but I'd need to find a big client and/or several others to replace them.

For the past year or two I'd been happy, work had been going well, I'd been enjoying socialising, going to the gym and playing lots of polo.

I'd been on a high.

Socially, I had my friends, enjoyed some great nights out, including amazing dates with girls including Miss World, Miss Campanologist and Miss Ideal.

One of my friends fixed me up a date with Miss World. She wasn't actually Miss World, but she looked something like Catherine Zeta Jones and Katy Perry. It was the worst date I ever had, there was no chemistry and probably one of her worst dates: me! I was trying to be engaging, interesting and fun, but nothing resonated. I've had better times at the dentist and reckon she'd say something similar too.

Whilst Miss World was stunning, but we didn't click.

I met Miss Campanologist (campanology meaning church bell ringing) in a bar. She was a natural beauty, one of those girls who looks great without any make-up, intelligent, cultured, and we had several dates. However, she'd lost a close family member during the past year, and from what she'd said it seemed she'd been seeing a married man.

Her behaviour suggested to me that she was still seeing him, and I let it drift.

And after that I met Miss Ideal, from my perspective the best of these three by far, with whom I had some fantastic dates and times. A PR girl, blonde with looks every man would love, just as good looking as Miss World, she was intelligent, easy to be with and had a sincere manner.

But she was 15 years younger than me.

I held back from developing a full relationship with her.

I thought if I fell in love with her and we got together permanently, that in the years to come the age gap would be just too great.

The pursuit of happiness

So, finding Miss Right would at least for the time being elude me.

Although I'd got this ongoing desire to love and to be loved, I didn't just want romance, I wanted to be happily married and I was feeling somewhat broody.

Late 40s, and time was running out. I didn't want to be a 70-year-old dad at his son or daughter's 21st birthday nor the deceased dad absent from his son or daughter's wedding.

Together with some of my single friends, we would sometimes go up to London where there are some great venues and people to match.

I remember on one occasion going speed dating, which was exciting and a lot of fun.

On either side of the table, a man and a woman, just two or three minutes of talking and you instantly know there's either a chemistry or there isn't. Put on the spot, having to rapidly engage in a chat with girls whether I liked them or not, I felt obliged to be fun, polite.

However, what was a real eye opener was being asked for your number by a girl.

Naturally, if I liked the girl, I was going to be delighted to give her my number and take hers, and to follow up with a call and hook up.

However, if I was not interested, I wondered how to respond? By saying "thanks but no thanks" or "I'm not interested"? I can't remember what I said but it struck me that when girls are asked for their number or for a date, it must also feel so awkward saying no.

My situation now, working solo and living in a flat.

If you compare this with the lifestyle and status I enjoyed several years ago, with a team of people working for me, and living in the 11-bedroom house, it was a stark contrast.

I was trying to come to terms with loss of status.

I wanted to get back what I'd lost.

Many things in life are about choices, particularly concerning time and money.

At work I was facing an ongoing dilemma; there was a dream at the back of my mind, and the day-to-day reality. My dream was to create a popular, successful

The pursuit of happiness

and profitable career coaching portal to include a directory of career coaches. I'd believed in this dream for many years, but my first attempt to create this had failed.

As a recruiter and headhunter, when I met with candidates, I assessed their careers, and I noticed how many people failed to exploit their potential and their career interests.

The failure of people to fully exploit their career potential in the absence of guidelines and support led me to be convinced that there was a need for career planning, development and performance solutions.

Some employers offer this kind of support; the majority do not, and those who do have a bias towards supporting their own best interests, not necessarily being independent.

I refused to give up on my conviction, self-belief and passion.

Trying to create this portal was a Herculean task. But I needed to make money on an ongoing basis.

I found a thinking partner.

As a result of developing my career coaching contacts and listing of coaches, I'd had discussions with several types of coaches in the areas of CV writing, personality profiling, career coaching, out-placement, executive and performance coaching.

One of these was an executive coach who was aware I was struggling to find the time for my portal, was challenged in respect of how to spend my time and, in hindsight, the reality was that I was getting too distracted from what produced my income.

The executive coach said: "Why don't I give you a complimentary coaching session, and you can see what you think?"

I thought.

Why not?

On an ongoing basis, I was faced with dilemmas about how to best spend my time, with my recruitment headhunting activities a priority. However, at the same time, I was still developing my own career coaching concepts,

The pursuit of happiness

materials and trying to market them. My priorities and interests in these areas compromised one another. However, it was recruitment that worked and produced a reasonable income in the here and now.

At this point, I was working by myself and didn't have anyone to talk to.

One of the advantages of working with a coach is that you can tell them anything, whereas with your family, friends and business associates, you may not wish to open up about everything. What you talk about with a coach stays between you unless you agree otherwise.

I came to realise that a coach can be an ideal thinking partner.

Many coaches undertake their coaching on the phone, and that's just what the executive coach did with me. It cost around £150 per one-hour session, based on a block booking of 10 sessions and, depending on what opportunities, issues and problems I was facing. I'd have a call with her every fortnight or once a month.

The loneliness of leaders.

During these calls, I realised from what she was saying about her work with other people that one of the most significant reasons business owners, leaders, and entrepreneurs use executive coaches is the loneliness of leadership. While people in middle management roles can talk things through with their superiors, there are limited choices for senior managers in respect of who they can speak to as a thinking partner.

Often they will face issues regarding their dealings with other senior leadership team members – how do they best handle problems or dilemmas with their peers?

Leaders of businesses are regularly making decisions, ones which have implications for other people. For some, positives, for others, there are often no ideal solutions; talking things through with a coach is empowering and liberating.

My challenges were different. Mine were that of establishing priorities and time management. And working with her gave me a certain sense of accountability. This sense of accountability is essential to anyone ambitious, goal-oriented, and standing still is not an option.

The pursuit of happiness

She encouraged me to develop a greater focus on my work-life balance. I'm one of those people who live to work rather than work to live.

This coaching was worthwhile and helped keep me grounded; my coach acted as a thinking partner, challenged my ideas, and prioritised what I was doing and shaped my thinking.

The starting point was determining my strategic goals.

What did I want to make happen?

In what timescales did I want to make these happen?

What were my short-, mid- and long-term goals?

What did I want to accomplish over the next year, two years, three years, five years?

This is ironic! This goal setting concept is one I espouse in my own career planning frameworks, the ones I've developed…

Practice what you preach. Heh!

My own goals were ones I'd set some time ago. I'd lost some discipline about focusing on them and breaking them down into tasks.

Although I had clear headline goals, they became more specific when I wrote them down, which prompted me to better prioritise them.

When you work with a coach, they can help you better frame your goals and think through your choices and priorities. However, it's not them who's got to do the hard work.

It's you who's got to make the change happen, not them.

In this case me.

I didn't execute well on my career coaching portal business ideas, or perhaps I was unlucky. More likely, the former.

I was trying to take on a big project requiring time and money.

Time which I didn't have. Money which I didn't have either.

And no surprise for you here. Trying to perform well in my day job as a headhunter compromised my ability to get my career portal and coaching initiatives successfully launched, and vice versa.

The pursuit of happiness

This was my second attempt to develop this business idea. I was trying to build content and to package it up attractively and market it.

I made one mistake after another.

I spent time and money creating videos that people didn't watch, creating web content, which was not sufficiently engaging or adequately set up, sending emails to people which they didn't read, and advertising to people who didn't click to discover more.

In hindsight, I should have stopped wasting time, money and energy on this failing initiative, but I didn't, and it cost me hundreds of thousands of pounds in direct costs and lost income.

When I first started having coaching sessions, my billings had dropped off, and my coach helped me focus and better allocate my time.

The benefits of coaching didn't come to me overnight; my fees at this time were low, and things would get worse before they got better.

What I gained from working with this coach were two things.

Firstly, I got to experience first-hand the benefit of working with a coach, as a coachee; this helped me to better understand how a coach can help people, by being on the receiving end of it myself.

Secondly, I benefited from the encouragement that a coach was able to give me, at a time when my billings had dropped, and I wasn't 100% focused.

And of course, for me; I was working by myself which can be lonely, sometimes you have obstacles to face and no one to talk to.

Sometimes there are things you don't want to speak about with people in your network or your friends.

Working by yourself is easy when things are good, but when you encounter a series of problems one after another, it can be a lonely place, and you can feel it's you against the world.

I'd always realised there was a relationship between our success and happiness, in both our work and home lives. However, when I was coached, this really cemented my understanding of this inter-dependence.

My return to my winning ways wasn't attributable to the coach, but she certainly

The pursuit of happiness

helped me. For a while I wasn't getting the breaks, and I experienced some costly mistakes.

In recruitment, it can take time to recover from a low or no billing period.

When recruiting people into reasonably senior levels, a hiring cycle can be upwards of four to eight weeks.

You've then got a potential notice period of four to twelve weeks, and it can take eight weeks to be paid – that can mean a five-month plus cycle from spending your time on something to being paid the complete fee.

This means that if I experienced a run of bad luck, I could be faced with the prospect of running out of money.

A not so Happy Christmas…

Fingers crossed; I'd be in my new house for Christmas.

I'd found a great house to buy, mortgage approved, the solicitors were dragging their feet… I'd been living in a rented property for a few years and wanted to get back on the housing ladder.

I picked up a vacancy to recruit a sales director to build out a public sector business for a big data software vendor. This was a type of vacancy for which I was very well connected to fulfil, and so more than happy to engage with the client on a success only basis, i.e. they'd only pay a fee if they hired from me.

There's more work to recruitment than some might think. Generating the candidates is more time consuming than you might appreciate; I spent perhaps two to three weeks on this vacancy; often the investment in time is much longer.

I identified a handful of strong, relevant people who were interested. The company interviewed three stand out candidates, one of which progressed to an offer and acceptance.

The successful candidate had told me early in the recruitment and interview process that he'd worked with the general manager of EMEA previously and that this person was a hard taskmaster.

However, he proceeded to say that he had handled this before and would handle it again, albeit that such a heavy, pressured leadership behaviour wasn't ideal.

The pursuit of happiness

However, he said that the upsides of the job were extremely positive. It was a senior position, there was significant scope to impact the role, the company had a formidable offering, strong market opportunity, and it was well paid with tremendous upside earnings potential.

The candidate accepted the job, started and I submitted my invoice.

I then called both sides to check how things were going in the first week and again 2-3 weeks later; feedback was good, great company, great hire…

Three to four weeks later I called to check the status of the invoice, reminded them that payment would be due soon etc.

I repeatedly called the employer company client, chasing for payment and got the answer, "It's up for payment approval", so I called again seven days later: "It's up for final approval", and that I should be paid within the next seven days.

It was ten days before Christmas and eight weeks after the person had joined.

Once again I called, chasing the company for payment, and was told the person had resigned the previous day, that the bill had not been paid and was not going to be paid!

His elderly father had suddenly died of a heart attack, he'd inherited money and no longer needed an income, and he didn't need to work for an aggressive boss.

Ahh.

Not only had I lost fee income, but also lost much of the goodwill of the client.

Having opened a door into a new prospective customer, if the first person hired through you leaves, your record is tarred from the outset. It can be difficult to recover from this situation, and unfortunately I didn't.

I felt floored. That was my only deal, my pipeline was weak and my outlook poor.

From what I recall, my billing was low or zeroed in the two or three months preceding this.

Regretfully, I decided to pull out of my house purchase in the knowledge that

The pursuit of happiness

my cashflow in the months to come could run close to the wire!

I appreciate you may think this extreme but in recruitment it can be like a roller coaster of a ride. With an income subject to so many peaks and troughs. You're probably thinking, Robert, you should spend less and save more! You'd be right but it's not that easy, recruitment is unbelievably unpredictable.

I do try to set aside money for a rainy day but it's not always possible, nor easy to do so.

I wanted to put down a reasonable deposit on the place and, with other expenses, I was worried I was over-extending myself.

I always try to work with a buffer because frequently in recruitment you can have a period in which you have low or no billings and so have no income. Therefore, it's possible to run out of money!

This is a constant worry.

In the last 2 years I'd benefited from having a good flow of work from salesforce.

But without an ongoing set of vacancies at salesforce.com, I was beginning to struggle.

You could say I'd put too many eggs in one basket with salesforce and therefore had too few other clients; I'm not complaining.

However, I'd got some assignments and plugged away at my network looking for more.

I got a break, or shall I say what I thought was a break.

One of the people I'd dealt with at salesforce.com had been asked about how to best approach hiring a GM across EMEA. The company wanting to make the hire was one of the top five SaaS vendors. I was recommended as the "go-to person" to find the best person for the job.

Following several calls with their folk in the USA, I was retained to undertake the search.

The company paid me a modest retainer. In hindsight, I should have pressed for more.

I spent around five full weeks identifying suitable candidates, engaging in a dialogue with them, interviewing and shortlisting people. Eventually, the

The pursuit of happiness

company chose not to go ahead with the hire.

The terms I'd agreed to didn't cover payment of any additional fees if they were not proceeding. I'd spent five weeks working on this and had been paid what I'd expect to earn in two.

This is something which happens in the headhunting world, not all assignments end up with happy endings.

Some like this one are completed and then something goes wrong; it's just as likely to be an employer side problem as it is to do with the candidate.

Successful completion rates are c. 80-90%.

Not all searches result in a hire being made.

Those searches which are not completed are often attributable to a change in circumstances at the employer such as restructuring, a decision to promote someone or simply a U-turn on a hiring initiative.

Sometimes it's because a company makes an acquisition, or is sold to another company, or merges with another company.

If a job is a good one, then the absolute majority of them can be filled with a strong candidate, but if an employer's expectations are high, and what they have to offer is very average, it obviously presents difficulties… average company, average job, average salary!

Success was temporarily eluding me.

So my struggle continued.

Head up high. Think positive. Act positive.

I persevered. It's unlikely you'll get external recruiters or headhunters to tell you that they're struggling.

We all need to project an image of success.

Who wants to work with a struggling headhunter? You want to work with someone who is in demand, successful and who gets results.

In recruitment and headhunting, we smile and act cheerful, even when we feel beaten down.

We've all got our shortcomings and I have mine. However, one of the things I like about myself is that I am persistent, I have a high work rate and ethics.

The pursuit of happiness

I always return to my winning form, I'm proactive, hardworking and never give up.

I managed to pick up and successfully close out a few deals and had a few projects cancelled.

Recruitment can be very unpredictable.

I persevered and got a more significant project.

One of the investors I had previously worked with had bought a company that they wanted to take through a period of aggressive growth. They wanted to strengthen the leadership team with critical appointments of a new managing director, sales director and marketing director.

I was briefed on the background to the acquisition of the company, their objectives for it and at a headline level, what they wanted these three new leaders to achieve. Often, investors like this simply want to give me the task or problem to get on with to avoid getting distracted themselves.

They also tend to value another person's point of view.

This is my job at its best, and it's doing this kind of work which I enjoy most.

The investor looked to me to precis the challenges at hand, outline the roles' remits, and determine the person criteria.

He asked me to write up the job specs, which I was happy to do, to which he made some tweaks, and we were good to go.

When working on openings of this nature, I feel a great sense of responsibility and my sense of purpose elevated. The investor was relying on me, and I felt an incredible duty to get it right.

The process of assessing candidates and co-ordinating progress, feedbacks and maintaining momentum requires patience, persistence and diplomacy, particularly at the most senior levels.

People are busier than ever before. Getting hold of people who are heads down and happily employed isn't easy when they have other demands on their time.

Identifying and engaging with the right people is far more complicated than people appreciate.

The pursuit of happiness

And there's the need for me to be selling the opportunity to the prospective candidate whilst simultaneously looking to qualify their abilities, requiring a balancing act. Most of the people I headhunt are employed and, in many cases, heads down and happy.

I do believe if you want to perform the role of a headhunter properly and genuinely, then one of the most important things to do, is to:

Persuade the right people to move to the right jobs for the right reasons.

This serves the best interests of both the employer and candidate, and it's not just about short-term interests being met but also taking into account longer term considerations.

From the employer perspective, this persuading the right people to move to the right jobs for the right reasons is integral to maximising chances of hiring success. Candidate side, you can be impacting people's livelihoods… you've got to be responsible.

When I embark on any search, I'm determined to make it happen; I have a fear of failure and a determination to succeed.

Some of the things I like about myself are my focus, persistence and work rate.

I'm pleased to say that I completed these hiring requirements.

These openings kept me busy for two to three months, and I closed out several other assignments.

At its best, this is a job that I love, but very few recruiting assignments at senior and specialist levels are straightforward.

I see the good, the bad and the ugly.

When I'm interviewing candidates for senior level positions, I'm assessing people's motivations, the scope, scale and significance of people's track records, capabilities, emotional intelligence and executive presence.

Because I meet with a considerable breadth and depth of people, if you were in my shoes, you'd observe and assess people, draw comparisons between people, and benefit from feedback from both the client and candidate side.

One of my observations is that many people ignore small, seemingly unimportant

The pursuit of happiness

things, which collectively add up to the difference between success and failure. Too few people correctly apply themselves to their career interests, acquire new knowledge, develop new approaches, or update and elevate how they present themselves and their ideas.

This will apply to people you care about, such as your mother, father, son, daughter, husband, wife, brother, sister, nephew, niece and possibly someone very familiar to you as you look in the mirror.

On a wholesale basis, people are failing to exploit their work opportunity.

The resultant effects are that you could be passed over for a promotion and miss out on job offers you should otherwise have got. There are no prizes for coming in second; being paid 10% less than what you could have been if you had negotiated your salary package properly.

Some people fail to manage their career and end up bouncing from one lousy job to another in a state of decline.

Why wouldn't you want to invest in yourself?

A high proportion of the people I meet with don't know the adjustments they need to make to be the best, most successful and happiest they can be. They don't know what to do, nor how to acquire skills, experience and credentials to move them to where they want to be.

Without taking the right initiatives, they will fail to excel in their jobs or careers.

It's for these reasons I've been so keen to develop a career coaching initiative, but my ideas about how I go about this are in some respects very different to others. Mine is an online initiative (some app capabilities, templates, insights, guidelines, frameworks); most coaching is in person, one to one stuff.

So, thus far I've not been able to make it happen. However, I'm like a dog with a bone, and I don't want to give it up.

I'm fascinated with the whole area of career management and career mobility. People often ask me, "How can I build new skills and advance my career?"

As I see it there are three ways.

Firstly, leveraging marginal gains. Doing little things which collectively add up to a marked improvement.

The pursuit of happiness

Secondly, making changes happen of a breakthrough nature; this would, for example, be studying for a new qualification which will massively transform your career prospects, like an MBA. Another example would be to proactively seek out a project which you can undertake, which would give you additional credentials to accelerate your skills and career.

The third one, you get lucky.

I'm not the biggest believer in luck; I believe if we apply ourselves well we create our own luck, which means initiative and hard work.

When it comes to making the most of yourself in your working life, there are opportunities to be capitalised upon or missed out on in respect of marginal gains, as well as ones of a breakthrough nature.

This applies as much to me as it does to you.

Marginal gains would include, for example, developing new habits or acquiring new skills which help you to stay on top of your game, or better still, improve yourself.

Too many people overlook seemingly simple initiatives such as developing and maintaining an exercise routine, so that you become more energised and have better posture.

Other obvious actions that people can take to maintain and develop their employability and value include attending a training course, which adds value or refreshes what you do.

For example, a change of a breakthrough nature would be moving up from being an individual contributor to a team leader, moving from one occupational area to another, studying for and gaining an MBA.

Marginal gains come with little or no risk.

Breakthrough changes often carry a risk but, by definition, they offer scope for gains on a whole new scale, perhaps even life-changing ones.

One of the great things about being a headhunter is having the privilege to observe people.

Younger people, with their whole lives ahead of them, tend to over-estimate themselves, often lack an understanding of what they don't know and tend to have an optimistic bias. In their 20s and 30s, with no health concerns to worry

The pursuit of happiness

about, no financial security worries, lots of opportunities and a runway in the years to come, they are full of optimism.

However, if you think you can travel through life without encountering setbacks, trauma and crises, you're mistaken.

As I look around me, I see many people aged 50+ who've suffered divorce, lost loved ones and, once on top of their game, are now struggling with expectations not fulfilled. Their time is running out.

Most are subject to considerable obstacles standing in the way of them re-building their lives and re-establishing successful careers. With egos and expectations to be satisfied, and stubborn, sometimes awkward personality types, there's a lot of emotional issues I encounter, challenging, time-consuming, and tiring.

This is one of my biggest observations as a headhunter. Some people enjoy careers in which success is sustained, their career trajectories being progressive and without gaps in employment. For some, their careers fall off the rails.

The world is a dynamic place, you shouldn't take your career interests for granted.

My task is to find the best people, to maximise the chances of hiring success, which also means de-risking. I have to be brutal in deciding who to include and exclude.

I'm not here to help people find jobs. My mission is to find the best of the best, to the exclusion of the rest.

It's not an easy job.

There are many variable parts in recruitment cycles, and people's motivations can change from one day to the next on both sides of the interview table.

Interruptions to progress include customer priorities to attend sales opportunities or prioritise sales bids, emergency customer or operational/back-office problems, holidays, sickness, family issues, transport blockages, and changing minds or preferences.

At its best headhunting is a fantastic job. The nature of the hiring challenge and complexity of successfully completing the search is varied; there are those which are difficult to navigate, those which take more time than you'd hope or budget for, and there are those which are straightforward.

The pursuit of happiness

So back to my timeline.

Here's an example:

Around this time I got a break and completed what I'd refer to as the perfect assignment.

This break was a surprise, another recommendation due to the work I'd done a year or so earlier with salesforce.com. Another one of the Top 10 SaaS software vendors wanted to hire a GM in the UK to run Europe.

California-based, they wanted me to identify the best-suited people, approach them, sell them the opportunity, and then comprehensively interview them. Then to report back to them with recommendations to fly someone over, interview the people I rated as being the top three recommendations, and offer their preferred choice.

That's just what happened, resulting in an offer and an acceptance.

This kind of work makes me feel proud, influential, empowered and engaged. I loved it, applying everything I have come to know at a high level.

Some of the highs I enjoy don't just come from the satisfaction of meeting employers' needs but also from being the catalyst for great things to happen in people's lives, and such events don't get any bigger than this one.

I was recruiting into roles where a vendor was taking to market new innovative SaaS apps, and one of the people I approached initially said "NO".

However, I persuaded him to go for the job.

Like me, he had suffered some real setbacks in life.

Following a divorce, he'd lost much of the wealth he'd worked so hard to create.

His separation circumstances were brutal; in fact, I remember him saying how his father had told him how proud he was that he had kept things together. He responded to his father saying:

"You didn't see me crying in the shower."

This is the reality of life, men have feelings, but we don't want to open up about them.

You've heard the stories about the happily married man, aged 50+, wife, two

The pursuit of happiness

grown-up/teenage children, big house, his mortgage nearly paid off and a good pension.

He's worked hard through his life, long hours, high pressure, puts his family first and…

He comes home one day to find his wife in bed with the builder. He then loses his house in the divorce, has to pay maintenance to his wife and children, and now rents a studio, everything he's worked for lost. He's now got zilch!

I'd persuaded him of the enormous potential of this job opportunity, so he agreed to interview with my client, interviewed with them and got the job offer, accepted and started.

Within 12 months of joining the company I'd recruited him into, he had won a $200m deal, and rumour had it that he earned perhaps £3m from it.

So, what next for me?

"Best run businesses run SAP."

I got a break into SAP, the Global #1 enterprise business applications vendor.

It's often said that 60-70% of the world's biggest businesses, as well as governments, run their operations on SAP.

Hence one of SAP's straplines is "Best run businesses run SAP".

A campaign designed by Ogilvy & Mather - simple message, leveraging the most aspirational brands of SAP's existing customer base, communicating how critical SAP is to their customers' businesses.

Their portfolio of offerings is awe-inspiring in its breadth and class; most SAP offerings are the best in category.

Not only does SAP have the most formidable offerings, but it also has a high-performance culture, and when it comes to hiring, SAP understandably sets a very high bar.

I proceeded to recruit some 40 people in sales, management and project management roles. Over perhaps 2-3 years this represented a real high point for me, both in terms of enjoyment and income.

It's never just about the money.

Entering the zone!

The pursuit of happiness

In the headhunting world there are two types of people: consultants and researchers.

The consultants engage with the employer clients, they agree fee rates and terms of business, take the briefing...

The process of finding the candidates is often done by dedicated researchers, who'll find the people and then pass them back to the consultant.

The consultant will then interview and appraise the candidates, shortlist them, submit them and do the follow-up work to make great hires happen.

My belief is that achieving great hiring outcomes is very much dependent on finding the right people in the first place, which means I like to do this work myself, and I like to approach consulting and research myself, all of it, a 360 degree approach.

I find it a challenging and exciting profession, I love it.

Once I've taken a briefing from a client and embarked on a search most of my time is spent sourcing candidates.

When I headhunt for a company, I feel like I'm representing their brand, like I'm part of their mission, part of their team and the challenge is to get it right, each time, every time.

The key challenges are to deliver well and do so on time.

This keeps me mentally alert.

Whenever I headhunt for a company, I enter into a zone of absolute conviction that my client company and its role is a prized one. I develop a self-belief, confidence about the opportunity for the right candidate. I develop a genuine interest in it, I become a man on a mission, and this motivation drives my focus, persistence and success.

I go into overdrive.

This doesn't just apply to me, it's universal, and it applies to everyone.

"Motivations drive behaviour."

You've got to understand this, if you're hiring, managing or coaching people to be the best they can be.

If someone is interested and motivated, this translates into the potential for high performance.

The pursuit of happiness

In recent years most of my work has been at the other end of the spectrum to big companies such as SAP, with early-stage and first-to-market small companies in AI, ML, digital healthcare, EdTech, infotainment, innovation and compliance.

Big companies have large workforces, which means they're familiar with hiring. Invariably, and understandably, they'll have HR and in-house recruitment teams. Much of the time they'll want to turn to their inhouse specialists rather than external recruiters and headhunters.

New hires augment their already successful business models so the risks employer and candidate side are marginalised.

In contrast, start-up and small companies don't have such a depth of hiring experience to draw on. Each hire's impact is critical to success or failure, and ordinarily, the founders will have limited hiring experience.

There's more at stake.

Many of these entrepreneurs will be keen to seek out the insights, experience and know-how of people like me, which means that they will often value my opinion highly and seek my guidance and recommendations.

The impact of hires on their side is massive, stakes are high, and for me, this is headhunting at its most engaging and fulfilling…

Identifying, engaging with and developing the interest of prospective candidates is an exciting challenge.

Often target candidates are unlikely to be aware of my client's company name. Sometimes they may even have no understanding of the nature of my client's business…

If my client is a market maker, prospective candidates may be unaware of the value the company and the solutions they bring to business, consumers and society… they may have little or no concept of the opportunity.

Opening their eyes is an art, a rewarding one…

The majority of the best people are employed, head down and happy.

Connecting with and capturing the interest of these people is challenging. Often I need to do so in micro-moments because we're working in a non-stop world.

The pursuit of happiness

There's a lot at stake when someone is employed. Often they'll be happily and securely employed, they don't want to risk what they've already got: earnings, employment stability, respect of their colleagues and possibly a promising career ahead in their employer organisation.

And what you say has got to be hyper-relevant in order to command and maintain their attention.

Once I've developed the interest of candidates, the next step is shortlisting…

Sometimes I play God.

I'm often the one determining.

Who should they choose to meet?

Who are the best candidates?

Which is the best candidate, and what do I think a job offer should be?

I have an expression of my own, "The balance of power"; sometimes an employer has it, sometimes a candidate and there are times when I have it.

This balance of power is something which can be subject to change and which the employer, candidate and I may misinterpret when headhunting.

I, however, will ordinarily have a greater awareness of it.

Much of my job is fascinating. There are times when I love it, although it is one of those jobs which requires a demanding, relentless high work rate, so I make energising and exercising a priority; I try to be religious about it.

A few years of big success followed, I was doing well again, my life was rocking.

Work good, social life good, but where was Miss Right?

The best things come in small packages.

Meeting the right one…

The first time I saw Alex I remember thinking: "Who's that girl?"

I worked in a large business centre located within an enormous, grand mansion house, and I first spotted her in the café.

Besides being very pretty, slim and elegant, she was the most beautifully dressed girl in the building. She was wearing a flattering knee-length dress.

Short, petite and blonde.

Who was she?

The pursuit of happiness

A few days later, one of the people in the business centre whom I knew, called Stuart, knew Alex and he introduced us. He told me Alex was single and rode horses. This girl had the cutest smile, a happy disposition and was tiny. The saying that the best things come in small packages immediately sprung to mind.

Whilst I had had quite a few dates and romances, I was actually shy and reserved when it came to meeting girls.

It just so happened that on the day we met, the tower in this mansion was open. It had never previously been open while I had been there, perhaps a year. So I said to Alex: "The tower's open – why not come and walk up to the top and see the panoramic views with me?"

It was my lucky day. When we had finished the next step, of course, was to ask her out…

I asked her if she'd like to come horse riding with me.

And so, a few days later we hacked out on two of my polo ponies in the Berkshire countryside on our first date.

What a perfect first date.

She rocked up, looking all petite and adorable in her jodhpurs. If you're not familiar with the horse world, these are tight, figure-hugging trousers, and wow, Alex has an amazingly slim, well-toned figure.

With long blonde curly hair, she looked stunning.

And off we went riding through parks and country lanes to a pub called "The Bell", a medieval building, predominantly wood in construction with white walls and black beams.

It was an idyllic day; hot, dry weather and, with us riding the horses, it took the pressure off what was a date; albeit, in reality, we'd immediately clicked.

After which Alex took me to see her horses, a promising sign; I thought perhaps she likes me!

Our next date was like one of those really romantic ones you see in the movies.

It was a hot summer night, and I picked Alex up from her cottage in the park. If you recall Cameron Diaz and Jude Law in the film "The Holiday", Alex's

The pursuit of happiness

house was like the cottage Diaz stayed in.

Tucked away in the countryside all by itself at the end of a lane, it was a quarter of a mile from the nearest house and in the middle of the woods.

I knew Alex had a big Bernese mountain dog, Paddington, which meant that I felt apprehensive as I approached her house's gates: would her massive dog like or loathe me? I needed to pass the dog test. If Paddington liked me it was going to be a good start.

Of course, big powerful dogs can be intimidating and scary, and as I walked to the gates, Paddington trotted over with a big, deep bark. Being a dog person and having had dogs before, I was fluent in doggy language and started talking to him. He was fine. I'm one of those who talk to animals, and undoubtedly sound stupid in my tone and content.

I took Alex to dinner at one of the best restaurants in the area, and certainly the prettiest, called "The Winning Post", located off the beaten track, some 10 minutes' drive from Ascot Racecourse, hence the name of the place!

It is tucked away from the world, in the picturesque village of Winkfield, with no traffic, no road lights, and no noise.

Set back from the road behind wooden fences, shrubs and with a gravel driveway, the place is very tranquil.

A single storey, 18th century cottage with a veranda at the front, red brick walls with wooden structures and inside, exposed beams, brick walls, stone floor, open fireplaces and well-worn wooden tables.

It's a relaxed, dreamy and ever so slightly up-market place.

It was a hot summer evening, and I'd booked a table outside; it was gorgeous, a white tablecloth draped over our table, covered by a white parasol and with a candle glowing in a hurricane lamp, a truly romantic setting.

I was dressed casual smart, wearing navy jeans, a pressed white shirt and sporting a navy blazer; I like classical styles. I'd dressed to impress, and with it being summer, my face was slightly bronzed.

Alex looked stunning.

Clearly, she'd dressed for the occasion, and I was taken with her.

The pursuit of happiness

Alex has long, slightly curly blonde hair, a pretty face; she's one of those people who lights up the room, she smiles easily, often, and has a very natural smile. Much of her beauty is in her manner but she has a very striking figure. She's well-toned, slim, size 8, she's a really petite girl.

She'd chosen to wear a blue poodle skirt and white blouse.

In case you're not familiar with them, a poodle skirt is tight around the waist and expands out as it goes down, a bit like an ice cream cone upside down. She is the first girl who I've ever been on a date with, who's worn a poodle skirt, and no doubt will be the last.

She looked amazing.

As we talked, it didn't take me long to realise this girl was beautiful on the inside as well as on the outside.

We had dinner outside by candlelight, under the stars; by the end of the evening, we'd held hands across the table a few times and kissed at the end of the evening.

And so, our romance blossomed.

Alex and I have similar interests. I find her mentally and physically challenging.

At the time she was the sales and marketing director for a niche market software vendor; she has a sharp mind around her work, good focus and is very determined.

Outdoors and active, she's like a Tonka toy with Duracell batteries, tough and non-stop.

Naturally pretty, with delicate, feminine features, but behind it hyperactive, I developed a nickname for her: "Dinkie".

I so wanted to be in a relationship. A good relationship. Fingers crossed. Hopefully, this one.

In our first winter as a couple, we were blessed with snow, and from Alex's cottage we were able to walk in the park and go sledging. A little family: Alex, her dog Paddington and me.

I loved him, there's something quintessentially dog-like about the Bernese mountain dog. Paddington typified all Bernese characteristics; he was

The pursuit of happiness

substantial, tough and sturdy, but with heaps of soft fur with distinctive black, red-brown and white markings. He was an ideal combination of robust and cuddly.

The three of us would go for long walks together and, on several occasions, walk for an hour in the early evening through Windsor Great Park, in the snow to a pub with a log fire and, as midnight approached, then walk back home.

On one of these occasions there was snow on the ground, the snow bringing light in the otherwise dark night. Simply magical.

Our first holiday together was on "Kefalonia", one of the Greek islands.

It's the island where the romantic film "Captain Correlli's Mandolin" was set and where Myrtos beach is located. It's one of the most photographed beaches and is featured on thousands of holiday websites and online brochures worldwide.

Kefalonia is a hilly and mountainous island, so much so that in the winter its majestic mountains are often snow-capped; in the summer they're green, giving a tranquillity and stunning backdrop against the Ionian Sea.

A stunning island, quiet, marked by sandy coves and dry rugged landscapes with an indented coastline, made up of limestone cliffs, bays and short strips of white sand. Many beaches are only accessible on foot, via narrow twisting roads or best accessed from the sea by boat.

Alex being Alex, the moment the mountains caught her eye, she thought there's a great walk.

My thoughts were, it's going to be hot and hard work walking up those hills.

Despite being small, Alex is strong and has limitless energy.

She had us walking up a mountain in the heat of the day. Genuinely exhausting, but it felt great, and the views at the top were simply amazing.

This was to set a precedent, a sign of things to come, good things to come.

I love walking, and so does Alex.

We'd take a trip every morning, usually involving a walk although, with Alex, it's more of a route march than a stroll; I don't mind that; I exercise a lot and quite enjoy a pacey, long, demanding walk.

The pursuit of happiness

On two of the days, we went to Assos, one of the most beautiful villages in Kefalonia. It has a castle on one side of the bay and a Venetian village on the other; we'd swim in the crystal blue waters from one side to the other. If Heaven is a place on earth, Assos is a contender… complete with Alex, my lover, best mate and companion.

Kefalonia is a quiet island with many sandy roads, not a lot of traffic and some very steep hills.

I suffer from vertigo; some of the roads were ones winding along the top of these steep mountain-like hills, in places on heights upwards of 300 feet, with almost vertical drops.

To get from one place to another there is no choice; you take the coastal road, high up, driving along the coastline, there's the road, and there's the drop. No barrier.

Eyes on the road, go slowly, keep focused, you don't want to skid here.

I quite liked driving around the island; it was tranquil, and the scenery was stunning. Most days, we'd take some sort of trip out, and I'd drive to a place of interest: a spectacular backdrop or one of those cute Greek villages with houses with whitewashed walls and blue shutters.

We all fantasise, don't we? And if this book was used as a story for a film, and I were the producer, it would end with the following incident, which would give it a happy ending.

One day, we went to Myrtos beach.

The beach is a big one, semi-circular in shape surrounded by towering, white, rocky cliffs with lush green vegetation on top of them leading down to the white pebble beach and the crystal sea, creating a spectacular setting.

It is so stunning that it enjoys international recognition. It's also one with strong currents, and you'll often see red danger flags.

It was a glorious summer day with clear blue skies, the sun was beating down on the land and the beach.

We were surrounded by beauty. The green cliffs and the sea, a magnificent azure, providing a unique backdrop as pretty as any picture.

The pursuit of happiness

It was away from the main road, accessible by a dirt track with perhaps 20 cars parked up. This was not a heavily populated beach, nor an unoccupied one either with perhaps 50 or so people scattered across a vast expanse. Men and women, young and old, in their costumes, men sporting trunks and women in bikinis.

Some swimming in the sea, others were playing ball games, or sunbathers were topping up their tans.

It was around 2pm, and we'd had our lunch and decided to swim in the sea. Wow! What a temperature; the sea was both warm and cool, that ideal temperature, so we swam.

Yeah. This is the life.

We swam out, perhaps 100 feet from the beach, swimming and fooling around.

When we swam back to the beach, we stood up at the shoreline, where you're still knee-deep in the water and where the waves can still be coming in high and heavy.

If you were looking, you'd have seen us smacked by a big wave, taken under by the current and out of sight for perhaps 10 seconds. You would have then seen me reappear, stand up, glance around, see Alex and grab her, pull her up, then looking into one another's eyes with surprise, excitement and big smiles.

It felt like a close call, a current beyond your control, so powerful, you knew it could drown you.

Only seconds later.

You'd then see a second, more enormous wave crash down on us, and we'd disappear, this time for longer, perhaps 15 seconds. This being much more dangerous, life-threatening.

Would we reappear? Would we be victims of a strong current? Would it be fatal?

Once again, you would have seen me come back into view, more slowly this time, stand up, looking around with urgency for Alex, spot her and grab her with all my strength, pull her up with such purpose; you'd then see her standing up, supported by me holding her arm.

Then again, looking into one another eyes with love, exhilaration and happiness.

The pursuit of happiness

We were then walking back onto the beach, hand in hand.

I find it hard to choose words powerful enough to describe how I felt: indeed in love, elated and rock-solid with Alex.

I'm still standing…

Despite all my setbacks in life, I've got endurance, I'm not giving up, I've got everything to live for, and I've found happiness with Alex.

However, Alex's real love in life isn't me, it's horses.

She's had horses since she was a little girl; in fact, she frequently went to the stables and rode horses instead of going to school in her childhood.

Alex first got involved with horses and riding aged just seven!

Rather than having the privilege of being given a made horse, one which has been schooled, trained and the finished article, her first horse and most of her horses have been novices.

Novice meaning new.

This means she's had to train or finish them.

In some cases, she has backed horses, meaning preparing a horse to be ridden for the first time and then training them, i.e. riding horses which have never been ridden before…. not an easy job.

A special, talented girl; I'm a lucky guy.

She is a marvellous rider; her particular interests in horse riding are dressage and jumping.

You'll know what horse jumping is, but you may not be familiar with dressage.

If I were to liken it to something you'd be easily able to relate to, I'd equate it to ballroom dancing.

Dressage is a refined way of riding a horse, showing it at its best and most elegant, with the rider and horse in sync, moving together with a calmness, showing off the horse at its prettiest, in a walk, trot and canter.

The actual word "dressage" is French and evolved from the verb dresseur, meaning to train.

Before meeting Alex, I had little knowledge of dressage.

The pursuit of happiness

There are many dressage competitions where riders and horses compete with one another, and it's often referred to as "stressage" it's not easy!

On a technical basis, dressage is described as "the highest expression of horse training" where "horse and rider are expected to perform from memory a series of predetermined movements".

You're thinking it sounds complex. It is.

Like most hobbies, interests and sports, riders who undertake dressage spend 95% of their time practising and less than 5% of it competing. Dressage is the horse-riding activity which you see on TV, in an arena with the riders wearing white breeches or jodhpurs (horse riding trousers) and navy jackets, and a smart matching hat.

They then do this kind of performance routine thing, like I say, like dancing.

It's complicated because it requires very subtle and precise movements.

It requires a lot of skill, patience and practice.

Had Alex had the opportunity in life, she could have been a top performing equestrian professional.

Sadly, we don't all have the chance to do what we love for a living.

I admire Alex's riding ability, and whilst my type of riding has its differences, she's guided me in my attempts to become a better rider.

She loves animals, and I love that about her; we appreciate many of the same things and share similar values: love for animals and respect for people.

I wish I had met her sooner.

Early on in our relationship, Alex had mentioned the Spanish Riding School in Vienna.

It's the pinnacle of riding schools, dressage and equestrian performance, featuring magnificent white Lipizzaner stallions performing in the Hofburg Palace in Vienna in the Winter Riding School. Alex had always dreamed of going there.

So I fixed for us to go to Vienna for the weekend.

Vienna is one of the most beautiful countries globally, and the Austrians

The pursuit of happiness

have such a sophisticated manner about them, you feel like you are walking among Royalty.

I had pre-booked tickets for the showcase dressage performance at the Spanish Riding School, and wow, what a treat, it completely surpassed our expectations.

It's one of those places and events which I'll remember forever.

I feel privileged to have been able to see such marvellous things; the hall in which it took place, simply magnificent, constructed c1750. When I entered it and sat down, I thought about all the people over hundreds of years who would have been here.

Able to see a performance, this is the best in the world, and its roots go back in time well before 1750.

People dedicate their lives to breeding these magnificent Lipizzaner horses, training them and performing with them.

If I'm honest, this was more for Alex than for me, to treat her, and as an expression of my love.

Afterwards, walking in the cold night back to the hotel through Vienna's historic streets was glorious.

You cannot get a better evening in life than that one.

The weekend, unexpectedly, had another treat in store!

Alex loves pandas; she'd never seen one before and guess what? We were able to see one in the zoo in Vienna.

Alex was and is so easy to be with. Elegant and sassy, she switches me on.

The saying "Behind every great man is a great woman" applies to Alex and me.

One of the things which impresses me about Alex is that she is very empathetic, she can tune into other people, she's socially very aware; this is one of the cornerstones of emotional intelligence. By the way, women tend to be more emotionally intelligent than men.

I'd got myself a new family: Alex, her dog Paddington, and me, plus all of our horses.

Having had some unsuccessful relationships, I was slow to commit, but there's

The pursuit of happiness

no stopping it when you love someone.

I'd decided I would marry Alex, and at the back of my mind I'd been thinking through some proposal plans; when, where, how?

I thought it would be respectful to ask her father for his approval, and so one day, when we were at his house, I asked him…

"Roy, I love Alex. May I have your approval to ask her to marry me?"

His response wasn't quite what I expected.

He was just looking at me blankly.

No response, just silent, didn't blink an eyelid for what seemed like 30 seconds, although perhaps it was just 10.

I quickly realised that Roy was hard of hearing, which meant he hadn't heard me properly. I had to ask him twice for his approval. He said YES, the second time I asked.

I'd been thinking about when, where and how to propose for a while.

Researching and buying the right engagement ring isn't something I could do overnight. I wanted to get it right, to buy one she'd love. After all, it would hopefully be on her finger forever. And I wanted to get the right size.

How could I do this without her knowing? I asked Alex's Mum about her finger size.

And where would be the best place to propose? After some thinking, "bingo", I had a great idea…

In May 2017 I took Alex to Florence in Italy.

She'd been there before in her teenage years with her father, mother and two sisters, and I knew she loved the place.

I'd got it all planned out: I would propose on the famous "Ponte Vecchio" bridge, a medieval stone segmental arch bridge over the Arno River.

It's noted for having shops along it: jewellers, art dealers and souvenir sellers.

So we set off on a walk around the city and I knew my destination: the bridge. I'd got it all worked out, ring in my pocket and what I was going to say.

However, having got there, I changed my mind. This wasn't the right place.

The pursuit of happiness

The bridge had very few Italians on it. Instead, it was packed full of people, mainly tourists and scores of African immigrants selling selfie-sticks and other rubbish. More cheap than chic, it wasn't romantic.

However, I could see other fabulous bridges, so we continued our walk, and I led us to the next one up. And in the middle of the bridge, with Florence all around us and the river below, I got down on one knee and said…

"Alex, I love you and will make every effort to make you happy; will you marry me?"

And she said:

"YES."

In my story, here in this book, I've been trying to explain how I've felt when at high points in my life, and also the low points; I've had a hard time of it, and I've explained how life has thrown all sorts of trauma at me, but I appreciate I'm not the only one.

Alex has also had a hard time of it.

She's had her own set of crises, although she's one of those people who is always there for other people, a good listener and supportive.

Often these caring types spend tons of time listening to and helping others, so much so that their own needs can become overlooked. So, I've got to be careful with Alex.

I've developed a consciousness about this.

Alex's father had been in a poor state of health for perhaps a year.

We got married in August the same year, but sadly Alex's dad died in the days leading up to our wedding. However, whilst I did not get the chance to get to know him well, I was fortunate to meet him several times and to get married with his blessing.

Our wedding ceremony was at the Windsor Guildhall, an old and beautiful building in the heart of historic Windsor, adjacent to the castle. Prince Charles got married to Camilla at the Guildhall, as did Elton John and David Furnish. If it was good enough Prince Charles and Elton John, it was good enough for us.

I remember standing in front of the desk in the ceremony room, facing the

The pursuit of happiness

registrar, waiting to hear of Alex's arrival.

When I turned around and saw her walking through the hall towards the ceremony room, she looked stunning. With a veil gently draped over the top of her head, I could see her pretty face.

She was wearing an elegant close-fitting off-white embroidered silk dress, classic yet contemporary, straight in its form from her shoulders to her feet, figure-hugging around her petite body and with a small train extending outwards on the floor from the bottom of her dress.

Alex looked stunning, I was proud, excited, and I felt on top of the world.

We had a small family ceremony followed by the usual wedding breakfast. Afterwards, we stayed in Great Fosters, a romantic luxury hotel, once a 16th-century royal hunting lodge set amongst 50 acres of stunning gardens.

The next day we flew out to the French island of Corsica for our honeymoon.

We stayed in a boutique hotel just over the mountains on the other side of the sea, so the beaches were only 10 minutes away, and the hotel we stayed in: wow!

Corsica is mountainous and all the rooms in the hotel were located such that you could see across the valley and the mountains to all sides.

The rooms were chalet-like, two to a block, partly set into the hill, none of the buildings more than two floors in height and spread over an expanse of gardens. It was truly magnificent.

Our room had floor to ceiling windows with far-reaching views across the valley to the mountains and was complete with an infinity pool.

Corsica has a rich history, being at times part of Italy and more recently France. Of course, it's a Catholic country, and each of the villages had churches and old cottages spread out over the hills and mountains.

In the hot baking summer, we were able to walk from one old village to another, through the fields and pathways, up steep hills on sand and stone pathways, and down again.

These were long, arduous walks but nonetheless romantic ones. Typically, two hours each way in the heat of the sun, which gave us a challenge and the reward

The pursuit of happiness

of food and cold drinks when we got to the village we were walking to, and back to our hotel.

So, I married the girl of my dreams and then what next?

Some 2 years later…

✱✱✱

Chapter 7

Covid

The last few years have been eventful.

In 2019 I had a routine: every day I'd go to the local coffee shop; it opened at 6am every day, which meant I was able to grab a coffee, read the news and then head off to the gym, and be exercised, showered and at my desk for 8.30am.

Each morning in the coffee shop I saw the same faces.

Over a process of weeks and months several of us got to know one another, and five of us guys clicked.

We talked about work and life, news, football and stuff. Slowly, we all started opening up to one another about some of the challenges we faced, and worries about money, security and stress.

When I think back on it, it's strange how we were prepared to open up to one another. I think that as guys, when we are younger, we are too proud to open up about our crises and anxieties, and what was evident in the coffee shop conversations was that we were all conscious that we were worried about stress.

It's the first time I've used this expression in this book. How about this as an expression and its meaning? Worrying about stress!

The other guys have kids, so they have children to worry about, whether they will pass exams, get into soccer school, what career path they will take up, and we all have our wives to keep happy.

No longer young, I'm over 50, and the four guys I got to know well were also over 50.

Guess what? Older, more mature, we were happy to talk about our feelings and emotions. In our younger lives, we men don't want to open up about issues. However, I'm increasingly noticing that, as we get older, people are more willing to open up about problems.

The point I am making here is that most of us guys (and women) have issues,

Covid

and opening up about them is a good thing.

One of the guys, the only one without any stress, is a yoga instructor and fanatic. He's 70, looks 60, formerly an executive coach; he became addicted to yoga perhaps 20 years ago.

He told me how he practices yoga and meditation, and how it brings him and everyone else who practices it a calmer, less stressed state of mind, a healthier mind and body. He told me yoga and meditation enable you to "live longer, healthier and happier".

A powerful expression.

My life has been full of stress, possibly too late to turn back the clock for me!

I started playing tennis with one of the other guys from the coffee shop; tall guy, big serve, our games are entirely unpredictable. Technically I'm better, I have all the shots, cover the court fast, I am fit, but he plays me with brainpower! He's super-intelligent, analytical…

When he beats me, it's because he reads my game and works out what I do well, so he avoids playing to my strengths and exposes my weaknesses. It's pretty even, and I win a little more than he does.

Whenever I beat him I find it's because I have stayed focused, calm, and therefore been able to bring out my "A" game.

It's strange; all five of us making up the coffee shop gang have anxieties, yet we're all reasonably intelligent, responsible, fun, good guys.

In the work side of my life 2019 was a good year, and I achieved some outstanding billings.

I was very much enjoying my work, I'd been fortunate to work on fab projects, and every week I'd be interviewing people in the City of London, Old Street and Paddington. London has become a hub for the tech sector, the one I headhunt within, and simply being in the City is uplifting. I find it vibrant, and it has such a buzz every time I'm there. It's exciting.

The tech sector used to be seen as one full of geeks and nerds.

No more.

It's now an incredible sector in which to work in. It attracts some of the

Covid

brightest, most ambitious and vibrant personalities.

There's a talent shortage in the sector. Companies can find ordinary people quite easily themselves, but it's the more senior and high impact/high performer types who are harder to identify, harder to bring to the interview table and harder to sign up whom I'm tasked with headhunting.

Upwards of 80% of the people I headhunt are employed…invariably I'm persuading people who are heads down and happy not to move.

But I love the challenge, and if I say so myself, I'm good at it.

Something happened in October 2019, which I didn't think about too much, but I came to reflect upon in the fullness of time.

I'm lucky now. I'm married to an angel.

If you believe that there are angels in life, Alex, my wife, is one of them. These angels go to great efforts to help other people, are generous with their time and love, rarely speak up when they have a problem, and often don't get much back.

She'd been working for a French company, and in October 2019 she had to go to their Paris office; during her visit she had to meet with someone who'd just flown in from Wuhan in China and who spent two days with her; in an office!

At the end of her trip, we'd agreed that I'd pick her up at Heathrow airport, and it was something I always liked doing. However, this time she'd texted me to say she'd be on an earlier flight back, she wasn't well.

During her trip she'd come down poorly, with a temperature higher than she could ever remember experiencing before. She had a cough, had collapsed the night before and had been sweating a lot. When she tried to book onto an earlier flight, they refused to check her in.

Alex is resourceful, which is one of the qualities I admire about her; she freshened up, returned to a different check-in desk, and managed to catch an earlier flight.

Our relationship is full of love; when we see one another, our eyes light up.

When I greeted her in the arrivals lounge, she was white as a sheet; I gave her a massive hug and kisses, picked up her bags and drove her home.

Covid

For several weeks she continued to be poorly, with a fever, high temperatures, splitting headaches, body aches and shortness of breath.

In the weeks which followed, I remember being poorly myself with severe headaches, fever, and some coughing. However, I didn't think about it, other than I stopped going to the gym for a couple of weeks.

I've always loved exercising. Every day I do something; around this time it was going to the gym. My favourite activity is working out on the cross-trainer or otherwise playing tennis.

In the last few years I'd stopped playing in polo tournaments but I continued to ride horses.

When my earnings are high, I can afford it. However, it is very costly, and if my billings are not high, I struggle to afford it.

In the years in which I have played polo, my billings income has gone down and my expenses have gone up! When I've not played, my billings have gone up and my costs come down.

I'm not sure if this has been bad luck, or perhaps I get distracted by it!

A couple of years earlier I'd reached a stage where my polo ponies had got older, I needed to refresh my string and, if I'm honest, I couldn't justify spending the money.

I should have bought one of those winning lottery tickets.

I now ride every week, and I often 'stick and ball'. This means riding a horse with a polo mallet and ball; you ride, tap, and hit the ball around, like practising. It's my salvation, I just love riding.

As I said at the start of the book, I'm the man who made a fortune and lost it.

When I worked with my ex-wife, there were two of us; it worked exceptionally well. I think the sum of the two added up to something more significant than the parts. When I started in the world of recruitment with my ex-wife, it was exciting, dynamic, and lucrative. However, it's become more challenging over time, more difficult every year…

Following the split with my ex-wife, I've primarily worked by myself. I've

Covid

employed one or two people here and there. I always have a little army of people doing things for me, accounts, marketing, IT/web and research/admin. However, I've primarily worked by myself in reality.

Recruitment is a hard job. I fell into it with my ex-wife; it's unpredictable and for me lonely; I would not have chosen this pathway nor to work solo.

However, I'm good at it; recruitment and headhunting is a profession whereby the more experience and observations you have, the greater your ability to identify what skills are most required to maximise hiring success and mitigate risk.

I'd like to think every year I get better at it.

Headhunting is a job I love. However, the low points can be brutal.

In most years I've enjoyed a good income from it but if I don't get the breaks I can experience a billings gap of 3-6 months which is stressful, to put it mildly. Then I'll typically enjoy a winning streak.

I've not beaten my record year in 2000! Whilst I have come close, I have not yet exceeded it. Incredible 20 years on! I have unfinished business.

I'm ambitious, determined and have aspirations to do new things, to accomplish more, and it's not just about money for me. I'd like one of my online coaching initiatives to prove successful, but not only that, I also intend to scale up my recruitment business once again.

To expand my business, I need money and motivation. At times I don't always have the funds available to hire people and invest in growth, and on the occasions when I do, I don't always have the motivation.

Training, coaching, and managing people is time-consuming.

Anyway, forgive me. I've just gone off track. Back in 2019, the year was working out well.

From November 2019 to January 2020 news of a virus (Covid-19) in Wuhan was making the headlines.

The last twelve months had been good ones; by January 2020 I'd had a financially terrific year.

Life was going pretty well up till Covid.

Covid

January through February 2020 it became apparent that Covid was a real significant threat to our society; there were recommendations to avoid unnecessary travel.

What initially sounded like just flu was something much more severe.

I remember one night in January driving back from Alex's mum, and we were listening to the radio; a reporter was recounting what she had seen in a hospital in the North of England.

She said that the condition was like nothing she'd ever seen before, nothing that the doctors and nurses had ever seen before, that people were dying; it sounded like something from a horror movie.

An epidemic like Covid isn't something we had ever envisaged nor imagined.

It came out of the blue.

For those of us in the UK, we've been part of a generation who have been lucky not to have lived through a war. However, this life-threatening epidemic struck what I presume would be a similar level of fear in society, and me.

In the work side of my life, things had been going well, and for the last 12 months I've been writing this book and had been developing an online career planning framework which I'd named bright-future.com.

This is a better version of what I'd created before.

Lots of people say I'm crazy, and I should give up on my dream. But this whole area of job search guidance, career planning, personal development and career mobility is something I'm passionate about.

By February 2020, bright-future had been a year in the making and ready for launch; all I needed to do next was give it some finishing touches, put it up online, give it some app-like features.

One of the challenges is to make this book something interesting to read, easy to navigate, and compulsive.

In the weeks leading up to lockdown, the economists were concerned about a recession. The headlines in the news were forecasting a downturn, job losses, and so the outlook was now a bleak one.

Many of the vacancies which I had, had been placed on hold. However, one

Covid

of my clients had solutions that improved workflows, teamwork, learning and process – I thought they'd excel through the lockdown. What they had to offer would help home working.

This client had appointed a new European MD, and he'd been told good things about me by his predecessor and two of their recent key hires who were people I'd introduced.

The briefing I had with him was most peculiar, though I've since found out that it was not completely unheard of.

After saying "Hello" to one another and some small talk.

He asked me: "What's your story?"

Of course, I had my back story, and for some reason I had a sixth sense he had his own.

So I told him in a very pacey manner.

How I'd had it all, had made and lost a fortune.

How my business had been the number 1 in its space.

How my ex-wife was abusive and an alcoholic.

How I'd told her I wanted to split up, how she'd been diagnosed with cancer just two weeks later.

How I'd stayed with her during her treatment and recovery.

How we'd then split up and how she'd then died 4 years later. And…

How this was the saddest thing in my entire life. I went on to say…

How I'm now happily re-married but scarred from my past.

I then asked, "What about you?"

He then told me his story; up till five years ago, he'd had a tremendously successful career, but his last five years of employment had been one with short tenures and employment gaps, things hadn't worked out.

Worst of all, some 18 months ago, he had lost his son to suicide.

I thought I'd had a tough time of it over the last 18 years. However, to have lost your son like that.

It was so easy for me to empathise with him. We bonded instantly.

Covid

On a professional basis, they wanted to scale up their EMEA business massively. He needed to hire a group sales director to build sales teams across Europe, and an operations director, so I got to work.

In the weeks that followed, I tabled two shortlists. He interviewed ten people from me but unfortunately the jobs went on hold. I wasn't entirely surprised.

More about him later.

23rd March 2020…

"From this evening I must give the British people a very simple instruction - you must stay at home." UK prime minister, Boris Johnson.

When Boris Johnson made his speech announcing the lockdown I remember thinking it's Armageddon; we'll run out of food, they'll be a loss of law and order, society will change completely.

How many people will die, will I be one of them, will my wife be OK?

Boris had said we would all lose people we know, love, care about. I'm not sure where I got this thought from, but if I recall correctly, the inference was that perhaps 1 in 10 people would die.

Will Alex and I live through this, will I ever see my Mum and Dad again, will my brothers, friends etc. be OK?

If 1 in 10 people will die, who'll draw the short straws?

Dig for victory.

March-April 2020 was a hot spring and after work on many an evening, Alex and I sat in the garden talking and sharing our thoughts…

It was a scary time; the supermarket shelves had been emptied by people in their panic.

With their need to buy lots of food came their need to buy lots of toilet paper.

Alex and I, on the other hand, had not stacked our kitchen full of tinned food nor essentials to keep us going for 6 months.

Everyone had been panic buying except us, we didn't think it was responsible.

However, we did go to the garden centre, bought compost, trays, fruit and veg

Covid

seeds to create our own little food factory.

Everyone was thinking...

Will we run out of food? Will food supplies stop? Will the farmers stop farming? Will the food producers stop producing? Will the supply chain break?

Will the streets become deserted and empty?

Our thoughts included: will people start stealing?

Will they raid our market garden?

Will there be riots in the cities and towns?

Will the government have to impose curfews?

Will the water and waste services cease?

Will the electricity and telephone networks break down or their services become intermittent?

So this virus had morphed out of Wuhan.

It was so strange; my wife and I had conversations about things such as "Is it chemical warfare?"

And on a few occasions, having had a few glasses of wine, we'd have some more extreme thoughts like, was this something sent to earth by aliens? Perhaps this was their first strike action, to disable our society and capabilities, and would they be landing soon, to take over Planet Earth, would they land on our street?

When Boris announced lockdown, he effectively shut down the economy; with this, you get a reduction in the size of the economy and the wholesale loss of jobs.

Having been through 3 previous recessions, I was aware of its likely impact, which led me to realise that what people will need most now is job-seeking advice. This would be an ideal time to bring mycareercoach ideas to market. However, what I'd been working on had been how people can better manage and develop their careers, not my job search guidance ones.

The ideas which I had for these were created in 2010 and now were somewhat out of date.

Covid

I've been through recessions before, so I knew what to expect. As a headhunter, the impact for me would be that employers would stop recruiting, my billings and income will crash down to low or zero!

Not good news for me. I realised financially I'd be going to be travelling backwards in life.

Two worries for me, not one. Firstly, will Alex and I survive? In other words, will we come out of this alive, and secondly, I'll probably lose a year's income!

Some people in some sectors of the economy, including all of those in the public sector, will continue to get paid; others, like my wife and me, would have no income.

However, the economy isn't something we can individually influence, there's nothing we can do about this, and many of us are in the same boat.

Frightening! Both on a financial basis and faced with the prospect of Death by Covid!

However, strangely March through June were some of the happiest times of my life. I may not have felt more content at any other time …

Against the backdrop of potential death…the material things which we buy and lifestyles to which we aspire to are no longer important.

When sitting in our garden with a cup of tea, hearing the birds' tweeting and seeing the beauty of our garden, and when walking in the countryside, I felt grateful for the simple things in life.

From April 2020 onwards, there seemed to be an increasing clarity about the Covid symptoms; the stand-out ones seemed to be a high temperature to an extreme which people had never experienced before, and coughing.

Alex and I came to wonder if she might have contracted Covid when she visited France some 6 months earlier. You may recall I mentioned earlier how she'd attended a business event in Paris and that she'd sat for two days next to a colleague who'd flown in from Wuhan, China.

Had Alex had Covid back in October 2019? And if she had had it, surely I must have had it too.

When I first heard about Covid, I was scared. However, from c. July 2019

Covid

onwards, I'd become more relaxed yet heavily respectful about it. Not everyone who gets it will die. The majority will survive.

It began to appear that some people are more vulnerable than others and that there is an aspect of luck and bad luck.

On the subject of luck, Covid has seen large sections of society continuing to enjoy employment and income, and others massively impacted with unemployment, low or no income. Somewhat of a lottery, it seems very unfair.

It seems unfair that the government has paid benefits to some people but not all, and for some people like me, no benefits, but I'll be one of those picking up the bill for it through increased taxes.

For me, it's been a costly year. From Lockdown 1 in March to October, I billed nothing.

When we first went into lockdown, the vacancies I was working on were placed on hold, in reality cancelled.

I was working but not earning.

However, it gave me a window of opportunity to bring my job search guidance framework bright-future up to date.

I had a lot of sleepless nights in 2020, worrying about money and producing an income. During the year, I probably lost 8 or 9 months' worth of income.

However, hiring activity picked up in October/November 2020.

Strangely, in the time that followed, it's seemed harder to recruit good people in the tech sector.

Possibly simply a demand/supply issue, otherwise perhaps a reluctance of people to move in this Covid era, or maybe a bit of both.

There still exists a talent shortage in the tech/digital sector. Finding the best people with specialist skills is taking more time than it was before Covid.

Following an initial slowdown, the tech sector has boomed because of Covid, with the world becoming more digitally-driven, i.e. mobile, online, personalisation, smarter supply chains etc

Before Lockdown 1, which began on March 16th 2020, I'd been going to the

Covid

gym every day. I'd done this for perhaps five years, every day before work.

Through the ups and downs of my life, I'd come to appreciate that exercising energises you, which helps you to perform at your best and stay there.

And if you're depressed or facing problems, it will help you elevate your mood and is a stress buster.

"I've done my daily exercise. What about you?"

That is the headline of a posting that I've pushed out on LinkedIn every day since March 16th 2020.

And in every posting, I've elaborated with a message about the merits of exercising, to raise awareness of how exercising can help us when faced with challenges and how it can help us be the best version of ourselves.

In the early stages of the pandemic, most people were frightened about their lives. Faced with the prospect of potential death, I felt like that.

How did you feel when it all started?

And sadly, we started to hear of deaths on an unimaginable scale. What we read in the news became closer to home.

I remember hearing of the first person in my network who had died of Covid.

Aged 60, he'd spent his life working in high-pressure jobs. His only crime drinking lots of whiskies and smoking lots of cigarettes.

In March, what I found really terrifying was the reports and pictures of an Italian convoy of military lorries in the dark of the night in Bergamo.

Reported to have been carrying out dead bodies because the local morgues couldn't cope with more coronavirus deaths, so the Italian army had been drafted in to take the dead to remote crematoriums.

This was frightening.

Now confined to our homes, it struck me that many people would be terrified for their lives, no longer able to socialise or see loved ones.

There were two sets of people: those who were scared that they'd die from Covid and those who were calm, who saw it as just the flu.

For lots of people, not just fearful for their lives but also their livelihood. And except for key workers, everyone now confined to homes.

Covid

I knew that exercising would help people overcome fear, anxiety, stress, and being confined, locked in and suffering cabin fever.

I'm now going to share some of my observations about how Covid impacted people and the postings about exercising, which I blogged out on LinkedIn.

"I've done my daily exercise. What about you?"

Job loss

Lockdown shut down lots of industries, put people out of work, and stopped people from earning; it was like a lottery!

Most people employed in the public sector were able to maintain their employment, security and income; but not so for the rest of the economy. The government terminated the incomes of a lot of people, and temporarily that included me.

Lots of people would feel like they've drawn the short straw.

You've lost your job, and now what?

What else could you do? Much of the economy has been shut down.

The number of job vacancies is going down, the number of jobless job seekers is going up.

And at the beginning of lockdown there was no end in sight.

I live near London, Heathrow. Thousands of pilots were furloughed. I know several pilots.

Imagine being a pilot, a well-paid, high-status job and being furloughed. That would be a frightening prospect.

No short-term prospect of returning to the skies? In fact, would you be able to fly again?

Not just pilots, other people were working at the airport in logistics and in import/export-related jobs.

If not, what other types of jobs could you take up? What salary and status would these jobs command?

In the first weeks and months following lockdown, there were no jobs, only job losses, except working in supermarkets and as delivery drivers for supermarkets.

Covid

A lot of people were in for a fall.

It's not just pilots, but all sorts of industries have furloughed people on a wholesale basis, in sectors like travel, hospitality, retail shopping, entertainment…

When people lose their jobs, they lose income, and they suffer a loss of status. A lot of people have deep-rooted industry or specific job skills that are not easily transferable.

At the beginning of the lockdown, it was all bad news. Most people who were unemployed or whose jobs were at risk would have had little self-belief that they'd find a new job.

This is what I posted:

"Exercising helps you to manage your mood.

It releases endorphins which give us the feel-good factor.

Getting out and about in the fresh air will help you to maintain self-belief and self-confidence.

If you are in job search mode, it'll help you develop and maintain a positive mindset, thus enabling you to better apply yourself to job search.

And ultimately find a better job faster."

Self-employed, freelancers and business owners

It's easy for most people to relate to people losing their jobs, but what about the self-employed, freelancers and business owners?

As much as people losing their jobs was an issue, there were the business owners and self-employed, many being unable to trade.

An endless list of restaurant owners, small business owners, hairdressers, bar owners, shop keepers, beauty technicians and personal trainers.

People like me. I knew from previous experience that hiring would grind to a halt. My vacancies and income would dry up.

How long would I be without an income? I wondered if it would be 6, 9, 12 or more months.

And I had ongoing business expenses, office contract; my LinkedIn contracts are £10k per year, plus accountant's fees and various software subscription

Covid

services. For people like me, not only no income, but my business costs are upwards of £2K per month.

Throughout the Covid chapter, I always had vacancies to work on. However, every one of them went on hold from April to October.

Having vacancies helped me maintain my positive outlook but I got calls every week from quite desperate and fearful job seekers.

I come across many people in my job and am socially well connected. I was very aware of the predicament many self-employed people are in.

Lots of them in obscure occupations, like actors and musicians. They're not all well paid. Some do it for job satisfaction, it's their vocation in life, and lots of these people have little or no savings to fall back on. Not all qualify for help or benefits.

Their businesses and livelihoods shut down, perhaps no longer with any sustainable sources of income, perhaps with ongoing business costs and overheads, now loss-making companies; hard-working people now building up debt, or being forced to close down their businesses.

It can't be easy for a couple with three kids living in London, earning £100k a year, now having to get by on £20-40k, living off benefits or furlough.

One of the people I know had a building firm, and his contracts were terminated, he was owed money, he quickly ran out of cash and ended up doing odd jobs, his earnings in the day putting the food on the table at night for him, his wife and three young kids.

I've got quite a high number of connections and followers on LinkedIn, and I knew many of them were facing trauma.

Feel-good factor

News reports stated the UK hospitals were full, death rates high.

It was in late April 2020 that the London Nightingale Hospital was opened up.

To me, this was scary. It looked more like a processing facility than a hospital.

Goods inwards at the front, it looked to me like the further a patient with Covid went into the building, the more likely they'd come out the other end. The dead

Covid

end. It looked to me like a mass morgue.

To me, it seemed obvious.

The sick with no or minimal hope would be brought to this hospital, located next to the Thames, and the dead could be ferried out of London on the Thames for cremation in the regions.

Covid had made the world a scary place.

Some of the messages which I pushed out on LinkedIn about the feel-good factor related to the predicaments we were all finding ourselves in… as I said, I always started them off with:

"I've done my daily exercise. What about you?"

And posted about things like:

"Exercising releases endorphins which give us the feel-good factor."

And how "Having exercised, we'd be better placed to handle problems, avoid going into a downward spiral of negativity and depression."

And how it would help us to "Maintain a positive outlook, we'll get through this."

"I know from my own experience that exercising lifted me up when I was down. It also gave me a purpose, structure and focus for my day and life." And…

"If you've been furloughed, lost your job or suffered a financial setback, exercising will help you to develop self-confidence, to maintain an upbeat manner and positivity. Exercising will give you a platform to enable you to return to your winning ways."

Relationship, family and loneliness issues

It must have been around July 2020 that society had been proven to be able to function under lockdown.

Whilst offices were closed and the economy shut down, the essential stuff was working, perhaps most importantly supermarkets and supply chains were working.

And things like electricity, water, gas, phone and internet services.

Covid

The bin men and waste disposal services were working.

Keeping society safe isn't just about health workers. It's dependent on other stuff like police, garbage collection, shelf stackers in supermarkets, farmers, lorry drivers... all sorts of heroes and heroines that make our lives possible.

Society wasn't going to break down as I initially thought not entirely impossible.

But we were all locked in.

I remember around this time going to see my Mum and Dad.

Not allowed to meet people, but I drove around and waved to them from outside their house; they were in the kitchen, and I was outside in the driveway.

Not allowed to meet in person, we waved and smiled at one another. Covid felt such a real threat to life. Would I ever see them again, would they ever see me again?

I nearly cried.

Covid was impacting people's family lives, particularly on households, putting pressure on couples and families.

Having personally experienced relationship issues in the past, I knew that a multitude of problems could emerge as a result of couples being locked in, in lockdown.

I'd lived and worked from home with my ex-wife Caroline in the past, so I knew that living and working together is not all that it's cracked up to be.

At its worst, people would be living in abusive relationships.

Not only are women abused by men, but women abuse one in five men... did you know that?

Abuse isn't just physical. It's also mental abuse, like put-downs and manipulative behaviour.

I know because I was one of them in my former relationship with my ex-wife.

It's easy for relationships to turn sour under the stress and strain that living and working together can place on them. It can cause people to start irritating one another, to fall out of love and for marriages to fall apart.

In my conversations with people, I picked up on the difficulties which people were experiencing...

Covid

Babies were crying whilst mum and dad were trying to work and do Zoom meetings.

One of my customers told me how he started going to a business centre so that he could have the privacy and tranquillity to get his work done.

No grandma nor grandpa to help with childcare, not giving mums or dads a night off, not a morning or afternoon off, not even an hour's break; grandma and grandpa no longer allowed to.

I remember speaking with one of my candidates, with a two-month-old crying on her lap, a four-year-old in the background, her husband at work and she was having a nightmare, day after day.

And she had a day job to do!

Mum and dads with young kids need the patience of a saint.

I'm lucky, my wife Alex is an absolute gem, but even we irritate one another once in a blue moon. Relationships do not get any better than the one I have with her.

I found that under lockdown I was able to run and get out of the house. Get away from the negativity of the predicament we were all in and do something which made me feel good.

Lockdown was like a pressure pot, reaching a boiling point for couples and families.

I posted things on LinkedIn about how:

Exercising provides solitude and an escape.

"It helps you to avoid getting cabin fever."

And that it's terrific for relationship issues.

"Exercising outside by yourself and without headphones allows you to escape from the people who matter most in your life at home and work!"

"Getting away from them, without distractions or immediate pressure, you can chew over niggles, frustrations, disputes, crises, predicaments and dilemmas."

"And think about the consequences of your actions, contemplate how you can

Covid

handle your interactions with loved ones, colleagues, bosses and friends, and make better choices about what you do, say and how you say it!"

"So that rather than kick off at those people who are most important in your life, you can ensure your interactions are more constructive than destructive, more enjoyable than destroying, more loving than loving."

"Chill and be a better husband, wife, boyfriend, girlfriend, mum or dad, boss, workmate or friend."

"And remain one."

"Sometimes you'll realise that problems which you thought were created by someone else may have been ones you created. Alternatively you may have misinterpreted a situation."

"In addition to exercising giving you a break from others, it gives them a break from you!"

"Exercising gives you time to contemplate your people issues, make better choices concerning how you interact with them and, in doing so, enables you to be the best version of yourself."

Zoom fatigue

Since March 2020, two of the most boring, overused words must be "Zoom" and "fatigue".

Employed people I was speaking to told me they were now having more meetings each day, their commute to work, now non-existent, replaced with a more extended working day.

To start off with, they felt that working from home was terrific; however, a few weeks on, or a few months on, and lots of people were telling me they were exhausted.

Working from home wasn't making everyone's lives easier. For many, it made lives more complex.

Add into this scenario a potentially toxic mix of relationship issues, kids suffering mental health, home-schooling distractions, an ongoing fear about Covid and the effect of being confined to home, cabin fever.

All stress-inducing.

Covid

It's a stress buster.

Exercising outside will help you avoid being lethargic, tired by Zoom fatigue. It will get you away from your desk, energise you to perform better, and work with a more positive attitude.

Every day I was posting out about the merits of exercising, and how it will help you manage your stress levels and mood.

Exercising is a stress buster which enables us to be happier and better people.

It allows you to work stress out of your system.

And to give yourself a break from the problems, anxieties and worries you're facing.

By mid-2020, I noticed a change in sentiment taking place on LinkedIn.

Everyone realised they were in the same boat.

People were increasingly opening up about personal issues, feelings and emotions in their postings, likes and comments.

I noticed as the months passed by that people became increasingly prepared to post on LinkedIn about their job search difficulties, lack of progress, failure to get interviews, rejections and how companies had gone silent on them.

Their applications had gone into a black hole.

Interviews they'd attended they'd not heard back on.

People were saying their confidence had taken a kicking. They were feeling stressed and depressed.

It became acceptable to talk about mental health.

Before Covid, statistics suggested one in five people suffered an issue.

Following the arrival of Covid, lockdown and its aftershocks, I wonder if it's now one in four people who suffer a mental health issue.

And everyone sympathised with those suffering.

Not just on an individual basis but also on a corporate one.

Big companies were now pushing out ads and social messaging, expressing understanding and support.

Corporations wanted to send out a message of care.

Covid

Energising

Sixteen years before Covid arrived, I'd switched on to the merits of exercising.

I was aware from my personal experience that exercising is a catalyst to energise and how being energised enabled you to be the best version of yourself, particularly for people in senior and high-performance roles.

I'd posted on LinkedIn about this before Covid. However, it was now even more pertinent. I posted things like:

"In the sweepstakes of life, you should never underestimate the importance of having a commanding physical presence."

"Which is dependent on several factors, including being in good shape and energised."

"Without being energised, you won't be able to energise others."

"Energising others is critical in leadership and high impact roles."

"Exercising is a catalyst to energise you, and this is powerful because it helps boost your cognitive performance, enabling you to work better longer. Being energised is a critical success factor for anyone ambitious, in a demanding or senior role."

"If you're a leader, manager or someone in a position in which influencing others is critical to your success, such as sales or project management, you've got to be energised yourself if you want to energise others."

"Your executive presence or personal brand is dependent on you being energised, and exercising is a catalyst to energise you."

"If you're unemployed, exercising will help you energise yourself, giving you a platform to approach your job search more effectively and find a better job faster."

In my capacity as a headhunter, I'm assessing people every day.

One of the observations I have made is that most people know what they need to do, know how to do it, and often know how to improve what they do. However...

The big obstacle standing in their way isn't knowing what to do.

It's actually being energised so that you can consistently apply yourself at 100%.

Covid

People get tired, lazy, slow down, distracted, and take shortcuts and postpone things.

They don't apply themselves 100% during the day. They do so between 50 and 100%.

If you want to be the best version of yourself…

You need to make managing your mood and managing your energy level a priority.

I'd say the worst Covid months were April to October.

Many people were placed on furlough during this time, others were made redundant, and there seemed no end in sight.

Vaccines were under development, but nothing advanced that we knew of.

The number of people getting Covid seemed to have reduced over time, but that was mainly because everyone was locked in.

Do you remember the chap whom I mentioned earlier, who had lost his son to suicide?

Whilst his vacancies had gone on hold, I stayed in touch with him and sadly, it turned out he lost his job. He was made redundant.

I reached out to him.

He opened up to me about how he felt down and had little confidence he'd get back into work.

I asked him about his daily routine and his approach to job search.

I was aware from my own experiences how life can crash down around you, how loneliness and grief and lack of self-belief can stop you getting better.

I knew how he felt. I was able to listen and empathise with him. Sometimes people want someone to talk to.

Often people who are in between jobs have few people to talk to.

And we guys have historically been reticent to open up to one another.

I knew his back story.

It was easy for him to open up to me.

And I gave him some tips and some leads.

Covid

One of my tips, of course, being about exercising.

And a few weeks later, he told me he'd been exercising every day and that his mood had picked up. He'd been better able to apply himself to job search.

He later started doing some work on a freelance basis for a company I suggested he reach out to, which eventually turned into full-time employment.

And he is now in a job he loves. Very much his dream job.

I do not think he would have got it had he not been exercising.

Exercising gives us the feel-good factor.

Employers want to hire positive, motivated people who add to their environment vs depressed ones who can turn a good one bad.

"The E"

One of the postings which I have made was about how different people are affected by the economy.

Economists refer to a "K" shaped recovery, meaning some industries are undergoing high growth and, conversely, others are in demise. However, I see it more like an "E", or the impact on people as more like an "E".

Those whose lives are rocking, they have it all; but there are those who are plodding along and those who've taken a hammering under lockdown, unemployed and incomes killed.

I wanted to send out a message of empathy.

I posted on LinkedIn about how I've made and lost a fortune. I once had an 11-bedroom house with park-like gardens, a string of polo ponies, took first-class holidays to the best locations, then life crashed down around me.

I've experienced the loss of loved ones, grief, anxiety, stress, isolation, loneliness, living with an alcoholic wife, abuse, divorce, being with a girlfriend who was unfaithful and financial collapse.

And I posted that I've always been able to return to my winning ways, and that exercising has been the platform on which I've been able to do so.

"It's worked for me, and it will work for you too."

I made the point that whatever category people fall into, Covid is likely to have impacted them.

Covid

The rich and successful are not immune to isolation, domestic problems at home, people issues with colleagues and employees.

Those in the middle can't afford to buy their way into a little bit of happiness; some felt like they were in a cage, like hamsters going round in the same cycle each day.

For those at the bottom, unemployed, furloughed and those self-employed or business owners who had their livelihoods crushed by the knock-on effects of Covid shutting down their business, the impacts are most significant: worry, stress, anxiety etc.

Many people were going to bed at night worrying about money, children, mums and dads, or relationship issues, having no sleep or uninterrupted poor-quality sleep.

I have always found that exercising first thing in the morning before work energises me and sharpens me up.

I'd be at my desk at 8.15 or earlier. Mentally switched on and good to go.

I am feeling good, feeling bright, feeling energised, feeling sharp and feeling confident.

Ready to excel in the day ahead.

My discoveries:

Before lockdown I was unaware of the merits of exercising outside.

However, running outside was very different to being inside. Before lockdown, I went to the gym every morning; I'd go there before work.

But being outside gave me something new, a new uplifting experience!

Staring at your computer, tablet and mobile screen all day is not good for you. It's stupid.

I found being outside gave me natural daylight… yeah, tell me something new, you may say. It gives us vitamin D, nothing new there for you either.

But you may not know vitamin D is known as the sunshine vitamin. Nor that it boosts your immune system, and it's a catalyst for fighting disease, reduces depression and is a weight loss booster.

What's not to like?

Covid

I found swapping the gym for being outside made me feel more of a human and less of a machine, less of a person trapped in a treadmill of life.

I found it helps my body clock, wakes me up naturally, refreshes me and makes me feel good.

When I start work, I'm all set to have a great day.

Emotional intelligence

A discovery for me was that exercising outside and without headphones helped me be more emotionally intelligent in my approach to my home and work life.

This was because it gave me thinking time.

Before, when I exercised in the gym, I had to drive there vs step out from my home into the natural daylight. And at the gym there was the noise and distraction of other people.

Whilst on the treadmill or whatever piece of kit I was using, always people and noise around me.

Getting outside by myself and running gave me a real escape from the world, and I love it.

I found it's given me time to think, reflect and consider options – all emotional intelligence stuff.

Our emotional intelligence is shaped by five dimensions: self-awareness, self-management/self-discipline, social awareness, social management and motivations.

I found exercising outside by myself enabled me to think through what I needed to do each day.

The trap for all of us is to do what is in front of us and fail to make time for what is most important.

It's the things that are most important but not urgent which really move our lives forward; all too often, we don't do them.

Exercising gives you time to think about what's most important and how you can make time for it in your schedule.

I don't know about you, but when faced with problems, I don't always solve them too quickly. Sometimes I'll keep trying to solve them with the same or

Covid

a similar approach... I find exercising and being away from distractions and pressure enables me to think more creatively and outside of the box.

My most significant discovery has been about how exercising gives you thinking time to contemplate your people issues, your relationships in your home and work life.

These are ones with high stakes, and they are time-consuming.

Get them right, and you're a star; people love you, and of course, the opposite applies.

Exercising is a stress buster. Being outside by yourself, you can chill out and give yourself a break from other people and them a break from you.

Being outside by yourself and without distractions, you can think through....

What if the problem is you, not them?

What if you've overlooked something?

How might the other people be feeling?

What are your options? One of which is doing nothing.

What are the likely consequences of your choices?

Your people issues are often your most time-consuming, distracting and the ones with the most significant paybacks and most significant penalties.

Exercising does help you to develop a better self-awareness in respect of your mood and how you can best manage yourself; I'm talking about "Managing your mood".

Thank you

The postings which I've just been alluding to making on LinkedIn only had a modest number of viewers but on a weekly basis people were saying to me how much they appreciated them.

For some they just liked the postings and it put a smile on their faces, but for others, who clearly had had a really tough time of it, largely through loss of incomes, domestic/relationship or mental health issues, they said it really helped keep them going.

Enabling them to maintain their self-motivation.

Covid

Many people have said that my words of encouragement helped them to more positively apply themselves to making the most of their lives despite challenges brought about by Covid, and for those in job search mode how it helped them in their journey back into work.

In my postings often my penultimate sentence would be…

"It works for me and it will work well for you."

Clearly for some it did, and my comments were based on my personal experiences of life.

The theme of this book is about the ups and downs of life, and the emotions of a man (me). Much of it is about my time with my ex-wife Caroline.

Right now, it's 12 years on from Caroline's death and it still hurts.

However, I can think of her fondly, with positive memories and most of the time no longer shedding a tear.

We all want to be loved and I've now found that with my wife Alex, we've been together 8 years, she's the best thing that ever happened to me.

So, there you have it.

I started writing this book before Covid and at the time thought the highs and lows in my life were behind me.

Now, whilst I've lost 9 months' income in the last year (2020) I'm now rocking again in 2021.

In 2020 I could have been completely stressed out. However, I was able to manage my mood much better than I had in my previous crises, and I was able to do so applying the initiatives which I've mentioned in the book and have chosen to precis in the appendix.

What next?

For each and every one of us, only time will tell.

✵ ✵ ✵

Appendix 1
Underneath the iceberg

If you've read this book, you'll realise that I've experienced spectacular peaks and troughs in my life... including feeling abandoned, how I made and lost a fortune, suffered loss of loved ones/grief, betrayal, enjoyed sky-high earnings, interspersed with financial collapse.

I've experienced stress, chronic stress, depression and possibly a nervous breakdown. However, I've repeatedly returned to my winning ways.

In this appendix, I'm going to share with you what I have done to recover and some of the things I've noticed about other people...

I hope that some of my observations, and what I have learned, may help you or help you to help people you love.

One of my friends recently shared with me an expression I'd not heard before which said a lot in a few words:

- If you're depressed, you're living in the past.
- If you're anxious you're living in the future.
- If you're at peace you're living in the present.

One in five people suffer from a mental health condition; the reality is that most of the time we don't recognise it.

We don't see their problems, we don't recognise their hurt, we may see a surface level issue but this may only be the tip of the iceberg.

And, of course, some people don't recognise that they have a problem.

For me, many of my issues have been money related ones, my expectations have been high.

I wish I'd appreciated much earlier in my life that it's not wealth and materialistic things which counts most, but the pursuit of happiness.

When I reflect on this book and what I've written, one of my self-observations is that much of my behaviour and the feelings I experienced were derived from simply wanting to be loved.

Underneath the iceberg

Something absent in many chapters of my life… but not now.

I think this is something which is universal. It applies to me; it applies to you and it applies to the people all around us. We should never underestimate the need we all have to feel loved, wanted and respected… easy to give in our daily interactions with those whom we love, care about and whose lives we touch, but something we often overlook.

I didn't realise it then but when I reflect back on my difficult years, I now have a clarity about the fuzziness I experienced in my work.

At times, for months on end, I wasn't able to focus properly.

So much so, that in reality I couldn't even read a book!

This is not unique to me.

One of the consequences of people suffering mental health issues is that they struggle to concentrate, so much so that they cannot read a book.

I have spoken with people who have also experienced this.

That's a pretty unsettled state of mind in your time outside of work, so imagine what it does to your performance at work, if you're a knowledge worker (having a job which uses your brain)?

When I think back to certain times when I was working, I was thinking I was working flat out. However, in fact my productivity at work had fallen off a cliff.

I couldn't concentrate properly; I would be constantly distracted by my problems.

Why was I billing big one year and not in others? At times my performance at work was crushed, in some years I billed 30% of what I should have done… because my mind was confused, compromised by disasters, disappointments and distractions, which had happened and were happening in my life.

My decision making was compromised.

I made some bad, very costly work decisions and big domestic ones, like choosing the wrong girlfriend/s because my decision making was impaired.

I didn't sleep properly.

Three foundations in your life form the basis of your emotional stability, these being your relationship, your home and your work.

Underneath the iceberg

Off and on, over a period of 10 years, my life lacked a stability... the split from my wife, subsequent on/off relationships or lack of one, moving house several times, and my work – being the kind which was unpredictable, subject to highs, lows and dry periods!

On an ongoing basis I felt guilty and grief about the death of my ex-wife... and not just the loss of my ex-wife; I felt grief about the loss of my status, financial net worth and my home... my 11-bedroom house was what I had been most proud of in my life.

Where had it all gone? I felt crushed... I was constantly playing all these issues through my troubled and unsettled mind.

My income rocked up and down, which meant much of the time I was worried about money.

I found myself in an almost constant state of heightened anxiety.

Sometimes, when I was sleeping, I'd accidentally wake myself up with a sudden, significant and rapid movement of my arm... this was, I believe, both a consequence of chronic stress and years of mental and physical abuse I'd got from my ex-wife Caroline.

Because I wasn't settled mentally, I suffered sleep deprivation.

It also ruined my opportunities to have romance and a relationship until I met Alex, my second wife, and love of my life.

One of the things I'm most proud of is that I'm always cheerful, I have a happy disposition and I'm an optimist... I'm a fighter and whenever I'm down I always return to my winning ways.

When I reflect on the hardest of times, I'm convinced that because I have always made exercising and energising a priority, I have been able to maintain my energy levels and to put on a brave face... exercising is a stress buster.

However, I believe other people would be much harder hit by the consequence of stress and sleep deprivation on energy levels.

Despite my energising routines and discipline, there were times when I was fatigued, down and feeling depressed. My confidence level took a real hammering, which was bad news when interacting with people at work, when I was single and wanting to be charming, funny and good company on dates.

Underneath the iceberg

In my earlier years, I experienced stress but it wasn't until my 40s, when all these traumas and crises struck, that I came to experience chronic stress…

I came to realise there's stress and chronic stress!

Stress isn't necessarily bad. It can be positive.

But stress suffered over a prolonged period of time (chronic stress) is not good news.

For me, I encountered one problem after another, being stressed by one crisis after another, some coming simultaneously.

Stresses resulting from the dot com bust (recession/economic crash), collapse of my marriage, my wife's cancer, separation from my wife, loss of a fortune, nasty divorce, isolation, working by myself, financial difficulties, then my wife's death (confusing and conflicting emotions) and following this a similar set of traumas/crises.

In this book I've been talking about my own perspectives of mental health, most notably stress and anxiety; in severe forms these are crushing.

I wouldn't choose it nor wish it on anyone, and I do appreciate that they are just one form of mental health illness.

I'm older rather than younger now; one of the benefits of getting older is that you see more of life, and as you do so, you observe others and you develop a broader perspective.

What I've come to learn is that for most people, if you think that you can travel through life without encountering some crisis in your work and/or home life you are mistaken.

The kind of problems I experienced resulted in sleep deprivation, anxiety, sadness, grief and a fuzziness of my focus.

Issues which are quite commonplace among the people you interact with in your home and work life.

Ones which arise from critical concerns such as relationship problems, job insecurity, unemployment, debt, divorce, grief, anxiety over elderly parents with dementia or Parkinson's disease, or children issues.

My own experiences of mental health illness are limited to stress, anxiety and

Underneath the iceberg

sadness. However, there are more than 200 classified forms of them. Some of the more common disorders are depression, bipolar disorder, dementia, schizophrenia and anxiety disorders.

When it comes to mental health conditions, they can be mild, moderate or severe.

- Mild… when a person has a small number of symptoms that can make their daily life more difficult than usual.
- Moderate … when a person has more symptoms that can make their daily life much more difficult than usual.
- Severe … when a person has many symptoms that can make their daily life extremely difficult.

And you can experience different levels at different times.

If you have a severe mental health disorder you should seek professional advice, i.e. consult a doctor, otherwise if your issues are more anxiety, stress or burnout related there are actions which you can take yourself – more about that later.

I'd like to share with you some of my observations and realisations…

Recognising your feelings

My own experience tells me that we need to recognise our feelings and mental state.

This is something I quite like about myself; I like to think I'm good at recognising my strengths and weaknesses, and as a man – facing up to the reality that we have feelings and being prepared to open up about it.

It was really following the split with my ex-wife that I realised how powerful, in a negative, destructive way, emotions can be… and of such a variety.

After my separation, I was living and working entirely by myself.

The loneliness I experienced was intense.

Cabin fever

Following the separation from my ex-wife I was living and working all by myself; for the preceding 13 years I'd lived and worked with her… after the split I was all by myself.

Underneath the iceberg

My predicament post-separation saw me experience all sorts of negative feelings simultaneously: sadness, loneliness, worrying about money issues, guilt and feeling sorry for myself. I experienced overwhelming contradictory thoughts…

On the one hand I'd been abused by my ex-wife and on the other I still cared for her, worried about her.

I also wanted to move on with my own life!

There I was, my mind consumed with worries and emotions, challenges at work and I was living and working by myself.

In hindsight I let my problems get the better of me; there are so many people in the world in a far worse situation than the ones I have been in.

Nonetheless I felt lonely, I suffered from cabin fever, a proneness to being ratty and a loss of confidence.

I'd frequently be feeling sorry for myself and at times choose to shut myself away from the world.

This didn't get me anywhere and when I realised what I was choosing to do, I found a solution was to go out for a walk… I could do that several times a day, an instant fix. I'd also make more of an effort to reach out to people on the phone and to fix up to see people socially.

2020/2021, and in the Covid era there's lots of people saying that working from home is great, they feel liberated. However, I do believe in the fullness of time for many the novelty will wear off, and the feeling of isolation will kick in.

My own experience of working from home is that it's not for everyone. I've worked for myself for over 30 years now, I've had the choice of working from home or from an office, and I've done both.

My own preference is to work from an office.

For me, initially, there was a novelty factor working from home. However, as the months and then years went by, I felt that the loneliness was spectacular. Working from home can feel great but once you start encountering problems in your life it's far from ideal – at home, there's no escape from your husband or wife, no break from them, no interaction with others.

Working from home for a few weeks, or a few months, is like being on a

Underneath the iceberg

honeymoon. However, my own experience suggests that for many of you, after many months or years, it can be so lonely, sad, trying and can compromise your wellbeing.

It's fine when you have no problems but when you encounter major issues in your work or home life, the isolation and loneliness can become a demoralising and depressive issue.

I found that when working from home, getting out of the house at least twice a day kept cabin fever at bay; if you're working from home this is something you may wish to think about.

In the last 15 years, I've chosen to work from an office, in a business centre.

Ashamed

Do you know that one in five men is abused by their wife or girlfriend?

I do, because I was one of them.

If you think about five men whom you know who are in a relationship with a woman, one of those is likely to be abused.

Which one is it?

Here's another thought for you. Let's flip this…

Think about ten women who you know who are in relationships with a man, two of these ladies are likely to be abusers. Which two are they?

I'm now going to talk about domestic abuse.

This is so embarrassing… the experiences and words I am going to share do not do justice to what I experienced and how I felt.

I'm a man …

I'm supposed to be strong. I want people to see me as being manly, resilient, worthy, successful, confident, intelligent and indestructible.

And to have to admit to being bullied… and to being abused by a woman.

What a weak and pathetic specimen of a man am I?

One in five men is abused by their wives or girlfriends. I was one of them, one in five victims.

My ex-wife Caroline was highly intelligent, quick thinking, controlling and a

Underneath the iceberg

manipulative type. This manifested itself in her hitting me, kicking me, biting me and trying to pull my hair out.

You can't hit back at a woman.

What was actually worse was her verbal abuse – she'd get into mad states, and drunken states… I've never seen anyone in my life, nor on TV or at the movies, as aggressive as she was…

She'd get in such as state she would even froth at the mouth.

I suffered this abuse from her for 13 years.

Her abuse would typically be a temporary thing; she'd go into a rage for perhaps 5, 10 or 15 minutes, often it would take her a while to calm down and come to her senses.

It was generally something which would happen on a weekly basis.

Her manner was very controlling.

In the fullness of time her abuse and controlling manner resulted in me coming to dislike her, ruining our initial love, killing my self-confidence in my social/domestic life and in my work.

I came to feel nervous when I should have been proud; when I met clients, presented to clients and interviewed candidates I'd often be thinking "I hope they can't see that I'm nervous". I was a nervous personality before being with Caroline; her abusive behaviour made it worse.

Over the course of the years, her violent manner led to me flinching at the slightest of movements by her which might lead me to think she was going to hit me, and in the fullness of time led me to flinch whenever other people were around me and made sudden movements.

It wouldn't be until some 10 years after splitting up from her that my nervous reactions stopped.

She was a Jekyll and Hyde type character; one minute she'd be perfectly normal, loving, charming and the next, mad!

I felt trapped, how could I overcome the abuse from her? I felt stuck, what could I do to get out? And if I'm honest there were several aspects keeping me in the relationship…

Underneath the iceberg

A love or fondness for her was gradually diluted over the years by her abusive behaviour which came in mixed doses, sometimes extreme aggression, other times lighter, and it came in peaks and troughs.

She could be OK for a week or two and then snap.

There was the financial thing… because we had made so much money (I didn't know anyone else with an 11-bedroom house and parklike gardens) and an amazing lifestyle which compensated somewhat for the abuse.

Importantly we had our business together, the offices were in the house, we employed a small team and it worked well… if I left, I'd be leaving behind the business and with it, income.

Last but not least, our 'children' or more accurately described our dogs. People like Caroline and me who didn't have children but had dogs, felt about our dogs like other people feel about their children.

I felt locked into the relationship but in hindsight I should have done one of three things much sooner than I did:

1. Perhaps I should have spoken with a trusted friend about what to do but I didn't want to admit to being abused by my wife. Probably a better idea: I should have gone to see a counsellor either by myself or with her. If I had said, "let's go see a counsellor" she'd have denied having a problem, then kicked off into another abusive episode. It's possible that if I went to see a counsellor by myself then possibly a counsellor may have been able to help me to come to terms with leaving the relationship and being brave enough to get out sooner than I did.

2. When I look back on it all these years later it strikes me that I simply should have said, "Your behaviour is unacceptable, we need to separate for two weeks for you to think about your behaviour and when I come back if you revert to your abusive behaviour… then we separate again and if you can't sort yourself out, then we separate permanently".

3. The expression "a leopard doesn't change its spots" probably applied; I should have made the decision to leave many years earlier.

I don't consider myself a weak person, I'm above average in height, physically fit and I'm a very agile person, I turn my hand to most sports well.

Underneath the iceberg

I don't consider myself mentally weak either. I'm resilient, persistent and strong with a never-give-up attitude.

I don't consider myself stupid, I'm a very level-headed person, perceptive and balanced.

Sometimes you've just got to walk away from people.

I look back on it and don't understand how I allowed her to abuse and manipulate. Anyway, I'm stronger now, I get better every day.

There are men and women out there, around us, people we love and care about, and strangers we'd like to think that we'd care about… who are abused. Men and women.

They're in your friendship circles, they're at work, their happiness and lives compromised by bullies, men and women.

We're in a society in which it feels shameful to speak out; this applies to both men and women.

Alcohol abuse

Neither my ex-wife Caroline nor I took drugs but she had an alcohol problem which meant she was prone to mood swings and other consequences of drinking too much – you can Google them, they're not very pleasant!

When it comes to mental health most of us think about anxiety, stress, depression and psychiatric disorders.

Is being an alcoholic a mental health issue?

Technically not but there's big link.

But 37% of people with mental health issues are alcohol abusers, 50% of people with mental health issues are drug users.

There are probably more people with these addictions around you than you'd think, in your social network and your workplace!

However, because of how it changes your brain chemistry, alcohol can contribute to and worsen symptoms of depression, anxiety, stress, mood disorders, thoughts of suicide, self-harm and psychosis.

I think that middle and upper-class people think alcoholism is a working-class condition but it transcends all age groups. The middle and upper-class

Underneath the iceberg

alcoholics simply drink mainly behind closed doors.

As I've said in this book, Caroline's behaviour on nights out was embarrassing, she would progressively become more and more drunk until she reached a comatose state.

We'd often go out on big nights out, to balls and events, prestigious venues. For me they were difficult to enjoy as I'd be thinking she'll get drunk, she'll get comatose.

If I was lucky, she'd get tired and be ready to go home, and to do so voluntarily, and it would be easy for me to walk her out of the venue with my arm gently around her.

However, it seemed like there was this fine line which got crossed: too early and she wouldn't want to leave, too late and she'd be visibly drunk out of her head, unable to walk unassisted.

Unfortunately, she was ever frequently embarrassing.

Whenever I tried to confront her about it in the cold light of day she'd simply proceed to go into yet another rage.

Her personality was difficult, the alcohol made it worse.

In hindsight I was living with someone with a personality disorder and who was an alcoholic.

It ruined her life, her relationship with me and ruined my life with her, and affected my life for many years to come and, to an extent, to this very day.

I wouldn't wish this on anyone.

You would have been oblivious to the fact that she was an alcoholic.

To the outside world, it would not have been something people would have seen. Alcohol and drug abuse aren't always recognisable.

The reality is that alcoholism isn't something that you'd just apply to what you and I might mistakenly call homeless down-and-outs living underneath a bridge.

But also to people you'd call normal, intelligent or professional types, i.e. most of those individuals around us.

Mental health issues, disabilities, unemployment and so on don't just affect the person. They affect their partners too.

Underneath the iceberg

These issues are more prevalent than you would think.

Emotional intelligence…

We've all got abilities and hidden talents that give us scope to fully exploit our opportunities in life and be the best version of ourselves, and we have the capacity to create our own disasters.

When I reflect on my life thus far, I can see how sometimes I've made the right decisions and sometimes the wrong ones, and how they've affected my success and happiness.

We can learn from our mistakes, and I've made many.

The decisions we make are, to a lesser or greater extent, determined by our emotional intelligence. It's something with which I've become ever-increasingly aware, and so I'd like to share with you what I have come to learn about it.

If you were to choose one word to describe it, think of it as "judgement".

Or, to put it another way, it's all about making better decisions.

Which means making choices that are smart and acting on them.

Sometimes the best option is to do nothing!

Your emotional intelligence, aka EI, is shaped by five dimensions:

Self-awareness – understanding yourself, your behaviours and your emotions.

Self-management – how well you manage your own behaviour. You can also call this self-discipline.

Social awareness – understanding other people's issues and emotions.

Social management – how you interact with others.

Motivations – these being your preferences, achievement orientation, drive, commitment, initiative and optimism.

EI is responsible for 58% of performance in all job types and similarly impacts your success and happiness outside of work.

Let me tell you more about how I see it!

There are the things that you do at home and work, that only affect you…

They'll triangulate on three factors:

Your self-awareness, your self-management and your motivations.

Underneath the iceberg

And there are those things which you do which involve others.

These are dependent on your social awareness and social management.

However, it's not as simple as that!

Your interactions with other people can be dependent on all five dimensions.

And it's your people interactions that often carry the highest stakes, particularly for people in leadership and influencing roles and, of course, in all of your relationship issues at work and at home.

Some of my observations about EI include:

Your self-awareness

Self-awareness is the cornerstone of your emotional intelligence.

It is being aware of what you know and what you don't know.

I've found that the older I get, the more I realise what I don't know.

We need to be careful not to overestimate ourselves.

It's critical to your personal and professional development.

Increasingly leaders want to hire curious people. Increasingly they actively look for curiosity as an attribute when interviewing.

And it's an essential quality, with regards to our improvement.

A trap is jumping to conclusions and saying or acting on things without properly thinking them through, finding out the facts or properly asking others about a situation or their perspective.

Going hand in hand with self-awareness is the extent to which you are open to receiving feedback, i.e. how well you receive feedback.

Regardng this, most people I talk to lack clarity about their priorities and goals in life.

Career planning often takes a back seat to life's other demands. Over time goals get forgotten.

No goals equals no direction.

Your self-management

Don't you just hate it when you make the same mistake twice? I do.

Underneath the iceberg

Occasionally I repeat a previous mistake, and I kick myself. Why didn't I keep myself in check? This is one of the aspects of self-management.

You can also think of self-management as being self-discipline.

Another aspect of it is being too impulsive or too indecisive.

Wouldn't you love to get it right all the time? Me too.

When faced with more significant issues with broader ramifications, applying your emotional intelligence means thinking things through properly and making better decisions.

One of my observations of people is that they lose focus on what matters most. The big trap is doing what is in front of you vs what is most important. You've got to make time to do stuff that is most important but not urgent.

For XXXX's sake, schedule and ringfence things in your calendar that move your life forward.

I've noticed that one of the biggest self-discipline obstacles standing in the way of people performing at their best and fully realising their potential are distraction, being lazy or taking easy options and lacking energy.

We need to do what is most important to us vs what is in front of us.

Your social awareness

If you want to get on with people to develop good relationships, be influential and be a good leader, you'll need a good level of social awareness.

Understanding how people feel about things is part of it, as is empathy.

The temptation is to think that other people think in the same way as we do… wrong. We're all unique.

If you want to influence other people, you need to understand their objectives, interests, issues, concerns and feelings.

In life, everyone is on a different journey.

A trap is jumping to conclusions and saying or acting on things without properly thinking them through, finding out the facts or properly asking others about a situation or their perspective.

Everyone I've ever met wants to be popular, even the quiet, reserved folk.

Underneath the iceberg

Unless you connect with someone, they'll never be 100% on side.

Alienating yourself! At its worst, a lack of social awareness can mean people don't realise that they've been unreliable, disrespectful or selfish, and have the negative consequence that people don't want to work with you.

Perhaps in a work capacity, colleagues, customers and suppliers.

What they don't say.

You'll never make a great leader without having good social awareness. It's impossible to influence individuals without understanding how someone is feeling.

Every good manager has learned the importance of managing people individually, which means understanding their strengths and motivations, so it's essential to tune into people.

An integral part of social awareness is thinking about the implications of your actions on other people.

Your social management

Your people decisions will be your biggest ones. Invariably they're also the most time-consuming.

Our people interactions are ones with many dilemmas.

Sometimes we've got to accept there's no pleasing everyone.

Whenever I'm assessing leadership talent, I'm tuning into personality types, and I'm often taking up soundings on people.

Realising your full potential is dependent on you being able to get stuff done through other people, not as a solo operator.

There's a dynamic… too strong, too weak, and a middle line: assertive.

If we want to be successful in life, we've got to have an impact.

On the surface, we have a view that the better people are confident ones and good talkers.

But it's not as simple as that.

There's no point in being an impressive person who doesn't get stuff done through others if you're leading a team or project.

Underneath the iceberg

I've noticed some of the best people with the best ideas are the quiet types!

They're not always comfortable forcing a point home. For these types, their best approach in meeting situations may be writing up and submitting the agenda or creating a list of key points – then referencing those.

Don't be a wallflower… where and when appropriate, ask the key questions.

If it's not a meeting situation, you may wish to put down your requests for action or thoughts in an email, memo, report etc.

I speak with a lot of people, and I'm regularly asked about dilemmas people face. Sometimes the most important questions are the toughest ones.

For these, consider being clear about what you want and you can either say it or put it in writing.

I'm a very transparent person. However, I see many people coming unstuck because they weren't transparent.

Transparency builds trust.

Our effectiveness in getting things done via others as a leader or project manager is dependent on social management. It's not an easy line to tread.

Pleaser types and bullies.

Some people want to please. The danger here is being too weak. Some people are forceful types, the danger being seen as a bully.

Pleaser types sometimes please everyone except themselves, which can become counterproductive. If your needs are not met, you become resentful.

The bullies in the world are sometimes oblivious to their behaviour.

Your motivations

When we're motivated about something, we excel. This is because we're interested in it, we are therefore focused, we are confident and energised.

We need to be cognizant that the opposite can apply and therefore be aware of this.

While your motivations can be seen as personal to you, they influence your perception of others and how you see the world, leading to a bias.

You need to think about your motivations and the implications of them on

Underneath the iceberg

others. Sometimes your motivations will incorrectly shape your perception of situations in which other people are involved.

For me, reflection is the key to emotional intelligence.

I'm talking about your own reflections of yourself and for you to think about feedback from others, formal and informal.

Reflecting on past situations: when and how we've made mistakes. And reflecting on current issues we're facing now, to think them through.

❉ ❉ ❉

Appendix 2
Chronic stress

Do you know what chronic stress is?

You probably don't.

As I've said, I came to experience chronic stress.

Over a period of 10 years I experienced trauma and crises; sometimes they came along simultaneously, at others times one problem would follow another. My experiences included but were not limited to grief, guilt, loneliness, acute financial worries and betrayal.

I suffered sleep deprivation, lower energy levels and cognitive impairment... at times my judgement was poor, and often my focus and concentration span, my effectiveness and performance at work compromised.

I mentioned this before; there were times when I couldn't even read a book or a newspaper.

Stress at work created stress in my time outside of work.

And my stresses of life outside of work compromised my time at work!

If you look up "chronic stress" on Wikipedia, here is some of the information you'll find:

Chronic stress is the response to emotional pressure suffered for a prolonged period of time in which an individual perceives they have little or no control.

It involves an endocrine system response in which corticosteroids are released.

While the immediate effect of stress hormones are beneficial in a particular short-term situation, long-term exposure to stress creates a high level of these hormones.

This may lead to high blood pressure (and subsequently heart disease), damage to muscle tissue, inhibition of growth, and damage to mental health.

Anxiety is one of the phenomena associated with chronic stress...

It is closely related to fear, which is a response to a real or perceived

Chronic stress

immediate threat; anxiety involves the expectation of future threat, including dread.

People facing anxiety may withdraw from situations which have provoked anxiety in the past.

In addition to anxiety, other mental health problems associated with chronic stress include depression and personality disorders.

Chronic stress causes the body to stay in a constant state of alertness, despite being in no danger.

Other explanations which you'll find on Wikipedia include:

Prolonged stress can disturb the immune, digestive, cardiovascular, sleep, and reproductive systems. Other symptoms people may experience include anxiety, depression, sadness, anger, irritability, social isolation, headaches, skin problems, menstrual problems, abdominal pain, back pain and difficulty concentrating. Others include panic attacks or a panic disorder.

Chronic stress can increase an individual's risk of psychiatric disorders and some physical disorders such as cardiovascular diseases, high blood pressure and diabetes.

i.e. consequences can include increased exposure to having a heart attack, diabetes, a broad range of physiological problems and this will all affect performance at work…

Chronic stress suppresses neural pathways active in cognition and decision-making, speeding up ageing. Also, being chronically stressed worsens the damage caused by a stroke and can lead to sleep disorders.

Chronic stress results in your body releasing cortisol which causes wakefulness, so overexposure causes stress-induced insomnia.

The signs and symptoms of chronic stress can include:

- Irritability, which can be extreme
- Fatigue
- Headaches
- Difficulty concentrating, or an inability to do so
- Rapid, disorganized thoughts

Chronic stress

- Difficulty sleeping
- Digestive problems
- Changes in appetite
- Feeling helpless
- A perceived loss of control
- Low self-esteem
- Loss of sexual desire
- Nervousness
- Frequent infections or illnesses

I'd like to offer up four suggestions of things which may help you…

Firstly:

Exercising. It's a proven stress buster and elevates your mood.

For me this is my magic bullet, more about this later! Great for men and women.

Secondly:

Gratitude statements. This is a concept championed by counsellors and coaches. It's all about being grateful for what you've got, thinking about the good things in your life and kind of thanking the world or yourself for them.

Some people advocate that you write them down in a journal/diary at the end of the day before you go to sleep, otherwise you might play them through your mind. This isn't something I chose to do as I kind of felt this was more for people more in touch with their inner self than me!

However, when I reflect back on my hardest of times, I should have written down or played gratitude statements through my mind. In hindsight, if I were a fly on the wall observing my own behaviour and the way I chose to feel, I'd see myself like a spoilt brat…

I felt so sorry for myself, so stressed, like the world was on my shoulders, yet the problems I had were miniscule when you think about the broader problems across the world like starvation, sexual abuse, human rights and those caught up in war zones.

Chronic stress

Thirdly:

Taking time out on a regular basis, e.g. every 2-3 hours, to chill, to meditate.

You can do this with an app like Calm, Headspace or play a short clip on YouTube... I've noticed women are really positive about this while men are more reserved...

I only came across this concept myself recently. I try to take a break every 2 hours, I listen to something for 2 minutes; other people may prefer 5 or 10 mins but what I find is that it re-sets my brain.

It's kind of refreshing, works well, not only if you're stressed but at any time. Not only a stress buster but also it boosts your cognizant performance.

You should try it rather than looking at a screen all day!

Fourthly...

Learning to forgive yourself.

This can sound easier said than done. However, a lot of our stresses are when we've made mistakes or things we've done make us feel guilty about perhaps knock-on effects on others. Perhaps we've done bad things or made poor choices resulting in damaging actions... However, the reality of life is that we're going to make mistakes. Everyone makes mistakes and I believe it's important that we learn to forgive ourselves.

For me, it's taken many years to be able to do this, but now I can do so, this is really powerful, and I find it takes worrying weights of my shoulders.

If you are suffering chronic stress as I did, it's probably because you've suffered a series of traumas, i.e. crises or big problems over a prolonged period of time.

And given there is a physiological consequence of chronic stress, i.e. it has the effect of releasing cortisol, this means you're not going to escape from it overnight.

Which means that to get over it, it's probably going to take some time.

For me, I believe I experienced chronic stress for months and years, and that I did so on more than one occasion.

Chronic stress

I do believe the passage of time can be a healer.

And, of course, in some situations you may need to resolve whatever problem you are facing.

You may benefit from seeing a counsellor.

❋ ❋ ❋

Appendix 3
Counselling

I didn't want to open up to people I knew about the depth of my problems, my shortcomings nor my innermost feelings.

One of the merits of seeing a counsellor is that it is 100% confidential, it's private and you can tell them anything.

I'd like to put my experiences of seeing a counsellor in a context...

As I said before I'd suffered chronic stress...

In the worst chapters of my life, which were those immediately after my separation from my ex-wife, and through a series of crises that followed over a period of c.10 years, my chronic stress was at its worst.

There were times when I was sleeping when I would accidentally wake myself up, having randomly moved my leg, arm or head in a nervous state, more of a movement than simply a nervous twitch, in reaction to some worrying thought or memory.

When I was awake, there were times when my hands would be ever so slightly shaking; I was in a heightened state of anxiety.

My almost constant state of anxiety was such that if I became relaxed my thoughts would switch into an auto-pilot mode with me thinking:

"What should I be worried about?"

I suffered anxiety for years and even when I'd been temporarily stress-free, I'd quickly revert to thinking: "What issues am I facing? There must be something I've overlooked," and no doubt I'd find something.

Whenever I was taken by surprise or presented with the tiniest of problems my reaction was to think the worst and become worried about troubles which hadn't even happened. For example, the prospect of dropping a glass or having dropped one; I reacted to minor issues as you would major ones.

I reckon I got very close to having a nervous breakdown.

These were difficult times in my life, ones in which I felt so low, confused

Counselling

by what the world was throwing at me, and anxious, that I decided to see a counsellor.

As a guy you don't want to open up about feelings to others; it seems weak to do so, you don't want to share with people things which you're ashamed about. I didn't want to tell my mother, father, brother, friends…

I didn't want to open up to people I knew about the depth of my problems, my shortcomings nor my innermost feelings. One of the merits of seeing a counsellor is that it is 100% confidential, it's private and you can tell them anything.

Counsellors are not magicians – my own experience was that in having counselling I became more settled, less stressed and felt more comfortable in myself.

The counsellor would get me talking, she'd ask questions, what's going through my mind, what's happening kind of stuff… and then she'd ask how I felt.

The simple aspect of just being able to tell someone what's gone on, how you're truly feeling, felt like a weight lifted from my shoulders.

A good listener, a good nodder. She'd express sympathy and ask me what my options were, what could I do to handle things, cope etc.

The calming experience which the counsellor was able to give me at my worst points was spectacular… My first experience of seeing a counsellor was immediately following my split with my ex-wife (the worst point in my life).

At the time my guilt was overwhelming, and my state confused, with mixed and contradictory feelings, having been abused by her yet still having love and concern for her…

I was so stressed, I was worried about her and I remember something the counsellor said which was…

"Caroline is responsible for her happiness and you are responsible for your own".

This simple expression and the way in which she said it helped me so much… I was able to grab this thought, and when my mind returned to feeling worried, guilty and anxious, take some solace from the meaning of it.

Counselling

I saw the counsellor regularly over a period of perhaps 6 months. To start off with perhaps weekly, then fortnightly and subsequently monthly. She was so helpful; counselling is something I very much recommend.

✻ ✻ ✻

Appendix 4
The underlying financial cost

I'm going to try to explain how my mental state impacted my earnings and financial net worth, how it impacted my performance at work.

I do so in the hope it resonates with you if you are personally suffering, or perhaps in how you perceive the people around you, the people whom you love, care about or work with.

My own experience of mental healthcare, particularly for grief, sadness, loneliness and acute stress, is that it comes at a cost, in fact two costs!

Firstly, there is the productivity cost and secondly the decision-making one.

Let me tell you more.

Our work and home lives are intertwined.

My observations are both self-observations and observations of others, I'm in my fifties so have lived a lot, seen a lot, experienced a lot myself and of others. In my capacity as a headhunter, I've observed people in many situations over decades and seen how their lives have unfolded, personally and professionally. And I've got my own experiences.

When I felt good at home it was easier to feel good at work, and vice-versa.

The reality is that there are people around you who are being bullied at work, abused at home, experiencing grief over the loss of a loved one or a pet, suffering cancer, caring for or worried about parents with dementia, living in fear and carrying a burden of debts or financial problems. There are those who have been unfaithful and suffer guilt, and those who have been cheated on who feel betrayed.

Single mums and single dads. People trapped in unhappy marriages.

Juggling demands at home and work.

And one of most people's biggest worries is the welfare of their children.

These people are all likely to be distracted to a greater or lesser extent.

Embarrassed, private or not wanting to be seen to complain or draw attention

The underlying financial cost

to their issues, these people are hurting but don't speak up.

There's the emotional trauma which I have experienced, and which other people experience, which gets brought into the workplace. Not only is it sad but also there is a financial cost.

You need to kind of experience stress and anxiety to properly understand or appreciate its magnitude, its impact and cost.

In the two years following the split from my ex-wife my billings were just 30% of the norm…

My job is one which requires a lot of focus and what I accomplish is exclusively due to my own efforts. I'm not part of a team or a workflow; it's entirely about how well I apply myself. I guess I'm what you would call a knowledge worker.

This really goes to show how stress, at its worst, can massively impact cognizant performance… imagine people you work with, or who work for you, being 30% effective.

It's difficult to measure the effect of mental health on the cognizant performance of individuals or a workforce, particularly in a team-based environment. The impact would be largely a hidden one. However, if you apply my experiences the effects would be significant.

Imagine the performance and contribution of the people you work with or employ, collapsing!

And there's a knock-on effect, one person's mood affects another, and the team; the more senior the person who's affected, the greater the ripple effect.

A hidden cost to the business…

- The more senior the role/person experiencing it, the bigger the cost.
- The higher up the value chain the role (the more complex the work), the bigger the cost.
- The greater the team-based interaction of someone in a role with others, the bigger the ripple effect.

Counting the cost…

How do you calculate the cost to a business of mental health?

Assuming 1 in 5 people have a MH condition, that's 20% of the workforce.

The underlying financial cost

There's a productivity cost that mental health issues bring to business.

This then begs the question of incidence. Do this 20% of the workforce suffer throughout the year…? If we factor this down, based on the fact that not all cases of MH will be severe, perhaps 50%, and assuming people experience this for 6 months, then that would translate into 5% prevalence.

If we said that the impact on cognizant performance is 70%, then we have a 3.5% impact on the workforce's effectiveness.

There's another cost…

The decision-making cost can have much greater implications.

If the person making the decision is in a senior role, then the decision can have a ripple effect and the consequences can be wide reaching.

Of course, regardless as to whether the person is senior or junior, someone's mood can negatively affect the team.

If I hadn't been working for myself, I'd have been sacked a couple of times!

Obviously, I didn't sack myself.

There were two times when my billings crashed down that were not attributable to economic crisis or times of bad luck, and these were when I was suffering some depression and acute chronic stress.

I've always been an excitable personality and I'm an ideas person; my mind runs at 100 miles an hour, but this has always been something I could control.

But when suffering chronic stress, my mind didn't stay still for different reasons.

Thoughts would be racing through my brain because I was unsettled, worried, anxious, stressed, feeling guilty, indeed partly from a lack of gratitude and respect from clients…

In my job as a specialist recruiter and headhunter there's more work involved than people would ever imagine. Much of my work has been success only, i.e. working for free until such time that a hire is made and passes through any probation/guarantee type, periods I'm not always retained (paid part of the fee up front).

Sometimes you're working for free, invariably clients' hiring requirements (assignments) consume a lot of time and regularly lead to loss-making situations;

The underlying financial cost

sometimes this can include retained situations.

At times it can be like living on a knife edge, the financial worry and dynamics involved carry considerable pressure; dealing with a lot of variable dynamics.

The people issues are a daily challenge, dealing with egos, often unrealistic expectations client and candidate side, U-turns, changes of mind/circumstance.

The mental challenge of handling people issues in recruitment is huge; people let you down on a weekly, sometimes daily basis and often people are ungrateful, unreliable and rude.

Maintaining your calm, a positive mood and a balanced approach despite people being awkward and often disrespectful is a challenge.

There's an expression…

People will never forget how you made them feel.

We all crave for respect and are operating in a world in which the expression of gratitude and manners is very much diminishing.

For anyone managing others, leading others, heading up a business or a project, the easiest, lowest cost and most effective thing which you can do is show gratitude, acknowledgement, respect, and listen….

When my levels of stress were at their highest I'd be in an unsettled state which meant I'd forget things which should have been simple to remember.

In the professional side of my life, when meeting with or interviewing people I'd have to make a concerted effort to make sure I was listening to what people were saying and to remain focused on what they said rather than letting my mind wander off.

I wasn't at my best… at my best I'd have asked the smartest questions, my memory would be razor sharp but when I was stressed it was compromised.

It's not just stress which is a problem, stress induces sleep deprivation, creating a double whammy impact on our cognizant performance.

One of the things I like about myself is that I recognise and face up to problems, and I recognised I had concentration issues which led me to be more disciplined in my approach to work.

I made a point of writing down the most important questions in advance of

The underlying financial cost

my meetings, and making a conscientious effort to listen intently, stay focused on what someone was saying, and make a note of the most important answers.

Being stressed or suffering mental health issues carries a stigma: "men are weak and women are pathetic"!

Man up

Men don't want to open up about stress and stuff, we see it as being weak to do so, similarly women don't want to either because they're worried about being seen as pathetic.

There's a mass of people at work, stressed... some of the stress work induced.

There's the stress we bring into work, the stress people create at work and the stress we take home from work.

The more senior people are, the kinder they tend to be; older people have experienced more of life's ups and downs, they often have less to prove and play a long game. The bullying in the workplace isn't just in your immediate environment, it extends into the way in which people treat suppliers.

The reality is that lots of people around us have pressures and problems, and we need to be more respectful of one another in a workplace in which the intensity of work has moved up levels of magnitude, as the digital environment means people do more work in less time.

In the last 10 years the boundaries between home and work lives have been removed.

The intensity of work has been elevated, people are doing more in less time, more is demanded of people; standards and targets rise over time...

We're all using more channels of communications, more platforms and apps, more devices, an ever-increasing number of chat and calendar demands, and interruptions forced upon us.

Every year, our workloads increase, expectations are elevated, we've got to do more in less time and do it to a higher standard.

More is expected of people, performance is more precisely monitored!

If you sat in my shoes and heard some of the stories of bullying in the workplace, you'd be amazed... often driven by a Hitler at the top with people

The underlying financial cost

(often, most importantly, HR) scared to stand up to them for fear of being placed in the firing line… I can't say I blame them.

I've observed this in many of the biggest global brands, more of a male shortcoming than a female one, typically people on a power trip operating to a short-term agenda; everyone else sees them as an idiot – power used properly as a leader means being assertive, used incorrectly it's bullying.

Eventually the bully moves on, a new good man or woman takes over and the company starts to become a great place in which to work again.

The world of work is changing fast, it used to be primarily driven by profit; increasingly it's now about making the world a better place in which to live, how business can contribute towards society, and making the company a great place in which to work.

How I see it is that we need to make a wholesale change and make every business a great one to work for… Business is human, we connect on a human level. Everyone wants to be respected; make this a pervasive trait across the workplace and you've got a winning culture.

Of course, the opposite applies, resulting in a toxic culture.

❋ ❋ ❋

Appendix 5

My magic bullet

Exercising is my magic bullet...

What I find is that exercising guarantees me quality time each and every day... Yeah.

There are 7 ways in which it helps me to be the best I can be.

And I believe it will work well for you too.

1. Exercising releases endorphins...

- These give us the feel-good factor. Enabling you to lift yourself up if your life is on the floor and to come across more positively in your interactions with people.
- It's a stress buster, it'll help you fix your mood if you're stuck in a rut.
- If you're unemployed it'll help you to build positivity, self-confidence, and put you in a better place to enable your job search activity to be more productive and ultimately empower you to be able to find a better job faster.

2. Look good, feel better.

- We all know that exercising helps us to avoid putting on excess weight but what I notice is that too many people overlook the fact that it also enables us to maintain a good posture.
- When we're physically fit, we're toned, so we wear our clothes better and it's not just about keeping weight off our tummy. If you carry excess weight, it shows on your face and neck.
- We're living in a world where our personal and professional brand has an importance and value... There's the issue of how the outside world sees us! Fit and in good shape, or unfit and in bad shape... guess who people prefer to work with?
- And when we think we look good, this helps build our self-confidence.
- Several years ago I put on quite a bit of weight, I looked less sharp, I got

My magic bullet

tired more easily. and what I found worked well to get my weight down was walking. After around 6 weeks of walking for an hour 4 or more days a week, I was looking far better.

- If you're significantly overweight, you can start by just walking. And as the days or weeks go by, then mix it; walk, run, walk, run… a bit of walking, a bit of running, slowly build it up. It worked wonders for me.
- The older we become, the more vulnerable we are to our energy levels dropping, losing our posture and physical form, and becoming outdated in our image and manner. I'm no longer young but I exercise every day. I'm not claiming to look great but boy oh boy do I feel better for it. I make exercising a priority and believe you should too.

3. Energizing

- Exercising enables you to elevate your cognitive performance because by being energised you can perform better for longer.
- If you're in a leadership role, or one in which you're influencing other people, you need to be energised yourself in order to be able to energise others!
- My experience tells me that if you build and sustain your energy levels you build mental resilience. This is key to not only recovery but also sustaining your performance as a preventative measure to keep stress at bay.

4. It provides an escape from pressure…

- Allowing you to take your mind off the issues which are troubling you… if you're sat indoors it's easy to become fixated on problems. By getting out and about you'll see things which distract you in a positive way, helping you to take your mind off issues and enjoy being calm.
- Helping you to avoid loneliness… simply by being outside, we tend to notice people, animals, cars etc.
- Alleviate cabin fever… being stuck inside, stuck at a desk isn't good. By getting outside, having a change of environment, together with movement, is liberating and empowering.

My magic bullet

- I find exercising helps me to organise my thoughts, frame things in better context, to tidy problems away (compartmentalise them) and in doing so liberate my mind to think more holistically and productively.

5. Exercising by myself enables me to be more emotionally intelligent.

It's easy for us all to make some silly mistakes, that's one trap; on the other hand we can made good decisions. However, sometimes these can be even smarter ones.

Good choices, bad choices…. A matter of awareness and judgement.

Your emotional intelligence (EI), how you develop and apply it, shapes your success and happiness in your work and home life.

For me I can attribute most of my best and worst decisions to how well or badly I applied my emotional intelligence – which by the way, unlike IQ, is something which you can develop.

If you're not already familiar with EI, it's shaped by 5 dimensions:

- Your self-awareness
- Your self-management
- Your social awareness
- Your social management
- Your motivations

Your EI accounts for 58% of performance in all job types

If you're stressed or feeling down, you can do things which exacerbate your problems or mood by making bad decisions – I made some costly work and social ones.

Conversely, you can make some good ones, and I found that when I was self-aware of my emotions I'd be able to do something about it. I think many of the problems we have in life are because our expectations are often too high.

We live in a privileged era, our expectations of life and people are high, often unrealistic.

It's our expectations which are often our biggest problem, if we can recognise

My magic bullet

this (self-awareness) and consider if we need to adjust them, we can be more realistic.

I think it's possible for us to manage our mood!

Forming a platform on which you can approach your work and home life better, and be the best version of yourself.

Importantly, having time apart from the pressure of work and distraction of people and things, gives us time to reflect on what our goals and priorities are, what your goals and priorities are – both the big ones and the ones we need to act on, on a daily basis.

I find by exercising by myself, and without the distraction of headphones/audio, I can enjoy a relaxing environment to reflect on what's most important and how to best approach things.

6. Handle relationship issues better.

I do appreciate that I'm repetitious… it's only because I care.

Our people issues are unbelievably time consuming, distracting and worrying.

Stakes are often at their highest when it comes to people issues – it's easy to upset people.

Sometimes we've got to accept that…

You can't please all of the people all of the time.

However, I do find exercising gives me thinking time, enabling me to reflect on my own issues, those of other people, and doing so in a relaxed environment, allowing me to think about things I may have overlooked…

And to contemplate to what extent have I tuned into other people's situations, feelings etc, and in what ways might my own perspectives or preferences be biased or flawed.

When you exercise, you can chill out and contemplate the people issues you are facing with a calm head. Away from people and life you can think through the issues you are facing with people at work and at home, what choice of actions are available to you.

What are the implications of your various choices and what are the best ways in which you can interact with people?

My magic bullet

Of course, sometimes doing nothing is the best option.

Your people decisions in life will be your most important ones.

For me, I find exercising by myself gives me the big and frequent wins in this respect.

Exercising gives you an escape from people, and gives them a break from you! Sometimes we can be living and working with people, get upset with one another. Having a breathing space is liberating and relieving.

When you're under pressure and things are going against you, it's easy to obsess over your problem/s. Whilst people are happy to support one another, be a good listener and show encouragement; if you repeatedly talk about the same issue week after week people won't like you for it.

I remember one of my friends had been sympathetic, a great listener and support when I was facing a crisis; she'd listened to me talk about the same thing for days on end, it may have been weeks, she then said....

"Robert, you need to stop talking about the same issue all the time, it's not good for you and it's boring."

7. Out-of-the-box thinking.

Exercising gives you time to think, and to do so in an out-of-the-box manner.

This applies when your life is rocking and all things are good; it also applies when you feel crushed.

When you're anxious, stressed and depressed it's easy to become consumed by your problems – at least that's what I found. Which can mean that instead of you being able to think freely and creatively, your thoughts and approach can become insular.

Stress or no stress, if you sit in the same place when you're indoors, with other people and with devices to hand – your mind is consumed.

If you go out, exercise by yourself and without headphones/audio, you're better able to relax, and with exercising comes the release of endorphins, which create the feel-good factor. This I have found enables me to think in more of an energised way, to feel good, liberated and confident.

I do not believe you can be at your best nor think creatively if you're stressed; exercising is a stress buster.

My magic bullet

Exercising enables you to develop out-of-the-box thinking.

Importantly, one of the benefits I experience when exercising without headphones, is that my mind can wander more freely than with the distraction of audio; my creative thinking flows better, I think up smarter ideas, develop them in my mind and I can capture (remember) them more easily. I make a note of them on my phone when I get back.

For me, exercising is my magic bullet, enabling me to recover if I am down and to perform at my best when things are going well, enabling me to be the best version of myself.

It works for me, and it'll work for you.

❉ ❉ ❉

Appendix 6
What I've done to recover

I'm now going to share with you what I've done to recover when my life has crashed down around me.

These actions have helped me to regain my self-confidence, self-belief and return to my winning ways.

I've already talked extensively about my magic bullet, which is exercising, which has given me my platform for managing my mood and energy levels.

Exercising

So exercising every day is my first initiative to get back in a winning groove and a by-product of exercising, is that it energises you…

Re-energising.

There have been times in my life when I've experienced crises and my life has spiralled downwards over a period of months, making me feel tired, demoralised and exhausted.

It's obvious that you need to hydrate, eat and sleep, and exercise.

When you're feeling down for weeks or months on end it takes its toll.

What I've come to discover, appreciate and internalise is that energizing is fundamental to being the best version of yourself, enabling you to maximise your cognitive performance, to energise others and as a preventative measure to beat stress.

If your job is a leadership or high impact/influential one then you've got to be able to energise others, and to do that, you've got to be energised yourself.

I tend to think of energizing in my own way with exercising front of my mind.

I appreciate it's not just about exercising but also eating well, properly hydrating yourself and getting good, regular sleep.

For me, the eating and drinking bit is easy… I make sure I eat 3 times a day and drink regularly, I know my energy levels drop if I don't do so, which means

What I've done to recover

for me it's like a religion. I'm constantly meeting and talking with people in leadership and high-performance roles.

Last week I spoke with a business leader at 18.00; he said he hadn't had anything to eat nor drink all day since a single coffee in the morning. I've noticed Monday he's on it and by Friday he's tired, not as sharp nor as impressive.

Another client of mine worked for one of the top 10 tech companies; he was seen as the next UK boss, lined up for the big job. However, come the end of one year, the stress had got to him. Lacking in energy, everyone around him could see he was stressed and burned out.

He was unable to inspire others, his mind and ideas were cluttered, mixed up, messed up, his team lost faith in him, his peers and bosses could see he couldn't handle the pressure.

Within a period of 3 months he went from next in line for the CEO job to become the first in line to be moved on!

All work and no play. One of the senior female execs I know well would work flat out in the week but she failed to properly and consistently energise herself; come the weekend she'd be exhausted... she'd spend most of it catching up on lost sleep and by Monday she was ready to repeat it all over again.

In contrast, the best leader I've ever met was always immaculately presented, energised, sharp and on it; she set aside time for energizing and her chosen form of exercise is yoga.

I'm not a CEO, I run my own little micro not major business, but I'm in a high stress, high performance job. I'm quite good at making sure I go to bed early, eat and drink regularly.

I don't always sleep well, or perhaps to put it another way, I generally sleep badly. However, what I do is go to bed early to compensate.

For me it's exercising which has been my salvation.

There've been many times when my life has spiralled downwards. Sometimes it's because I've been unlucky and at other times through my own mistakes; at its worst it's been over a period of months, making me feel tired, demoralised

What I've done to recover

and exhausted. What I want to advocate is the merits of exercising; for me it's been my magic pill and salvation.

Exercising is a stress buster, boosts energy levels and enables you to maximise your cognitive performance, i.e. work smarter, longer…

I exercise religiously every day, which helps take my mind off my problems, to compartmentalise and marginalise them.

I exercise first thing in the morning because I found from my previous experiences that if I planned my exercise during working hours I'd feel bad about exercising when I should be working…

And that if I planned to exercise after work, I'd face one of two obstacles. Firstly, my day might run on beyond working hours which meant I came to realise that as each day takes hold, interruptions and demands can take priority, meaning exercising would get postponed, delayed, cancelled and put off till tomorrow… tomorrow being a day that never comes, the trap being it never happens.

And secondly, for me furthermore, by the end of the day I'd be tired and tempted to skip it.

So that's why each day, every day, I exercise first thing in the morning.

I find it sharpens me up so that as soon as I start work, I'm alert, focused and on it.

There are differences between exercising indoors and doing so outdoors; these are in my opinion physical, psychological and emotional intelligence ones… natural daylight is good for us, exercising by ourselves and without any distractions is liberating, gives you a break, gives you thinking time…

I have found since Covid and lockdown 1, that the benefits of exercising outside go above and beyond those of doing so inside.

If you can't run, walk.

Refresh.

Look good. Feel better.

When people are stressed and tired, they often stop making an effort.

Like a lot of people when faced with stress, I'd become complacent, and my

What I've done to recover

work and home space had become a mess.

I have come to recognise these situations and now act more quickly to head off the problems clutter creates by tidying up and re-organising.

Another quick fix which works well for me, is to buy myself some new clothes.

I believe heavily in investing in myself, and my mood; I find it's a pick-up and helps me take back my pride, to stand tall.

I buy quite a lot of new clothes. I think clothes look at their best for up to 12 months, after which they can begin to lose their shape, form, colour and look dated and tired. I find a wardrobe refresh raises my confidence level and helps me to feel more of a role model.

In my job I interact with a lot of people, and I need to be influential in my dealings with them; I make a concerted effort to present myself as professional and successful. I try to set an example myself in respect of how I present myself, my approach and my ideas, in the context that the people I deal with need to be impressive.

Combined with energising, I find a refresh helps me to re-establish and elevate my mood and self-belief.

If you can't splash the cash then make more of an effort with what you've got.

Think more about your choice of outfits, be more disciplined about what you wear and how you wear clothes… iron your shirts or blouses, dry clean your clothes, polish your shoes, get your hair cut… a refresh will help you to re-establish and elevate your mood and self-confidence.

Re-set goals and re-focus.

People lose sight of goals.

I've noticed this in others, and I've noticed it in myself.

Occasionally you need to re-frame your goals.

When you're stressed it's easy to do what's in front of you vs what's most important. Instead of doing the right things most of the time, I'd get distracted and sidetracked.

What I've done to recover

For me, what I have often found is that I have multiple to-do lists… in my writing/to do book, on-line in things like OneNote, in Notes on my phone!

To kick-start my return to my winning ways I re-set my goals and priorities.

I find that it sets me on a pathway to success.

I think about what I want to achieve, I visualise success and the benefits, break it down into the things I know I need to do to make it happen, these goals being both challenging and realistic.

I focus my mind on making this success happen and make a concerted effort to focus on doing more of the right things and stop doing the wrong ones.

What I'm talking about is developing and maintaining a high level of self-discipline. When I re-focus, I do so with an emphasis on the positive.

I have developed a habit of compartmentalising worries and stress…

When I've suffered anxiety and chronic stress, I've found I can become consumed by my worries, however strange as it may seem, not wanting to let them go!

You may be thinking this guy Robert Tearle is a right idiot, but I think if you've faced trauma, crisis and depression, what I am saying will resonate with you.

My own experience of anxiety, stress and depression was that I've felt that I wanted to spend some time reflecting on my problems and feeling sorry for myself.

Here is what I came to understand and what worked well for me… what I chose to do was to limit these moments to less than 5% of my time.

Enabling me to take control of my life and create for myself an environment with an emphasis on happiness and success.

Re-align.

For me re-alignment is more of a professional than a personal issue.

What I am about to say about re-alignment may not apply to you in the way in which it applies to me, but I believe it will do in some way.

My job is subject to various dynamics, in particular changes in my customer base; if my customer base is active I'm active, if its inactive then I'm in trouble.

What I've done to recover

Sometimes my sponsors, relationships/contacts move on… and I can lose influence. And at least once a year, candidate side things go wrong; for example, if it's a senior hire, the interview process may have been drawn out, perhaps there's a lot at stake and the person changes his or her mind…

I'm associated with the candidate!

Recovering from these failures is easier said than done.

Companies go through stages of high growth; if successful they reach a plateau and then evolve into different areas, i.e. they enjoy continued success like Apple and its phone, then tablet and then apps, music etc

Other companies may grow and get acquired, some go into decline.

Industries morph, like video to online, Blockbuster knocked to one side by Netflix.

What does this mean to me?

It means I enjoy periods of success when my clients are recruiting, I'm well connected, well respected, and conversely, they can stop recruiting or stop recruiting through me.

The industry I headhunt into, the tech/digital sector. is constantly evolving; what was new a few years ago can be old today… I've got to be ready to catch the next wave, to make changes in how I engage in the market, in which niches, with which companies and with whom.

This probably applies to you in your career; we need to constantly evolve.

Re-aligning is for me the most significant initiative I have taken to enable me to recover from a low point or when I've been failing.

This for me goes hand in glove with what I've just talked about… re-setting goals. I have sat back and thought about my goals, what I am trying to achieve and what I need to do next to be successful, i.e. re-establishing my priorities.

When things go wrong, we often need to make changes. I'd become aware that I needed to adjust my behaviour.

Different people will have different priorities, and mine was my approach to work.

The demands of most working environments, of work, the work itself and of

What I've done to recover

the people you work with, are subject to change. People's personal and home lives intermingle, they're inter-dependent and impact one another, and those we interact with.

With the passage of time, markets and the companies in those markets, and the strength of those companies in those markets, evolve. And likewise, the demands of employees, customers and suppliers, including people like me.

Sometimes what is expected of us changes, is elevated, or augmented, and what we do may become no longer valued or needed.

You've got to be ready to catch the next wave.

This changing landscape is particularly prevalent in the sector I work in, the tech sector, which is fast-paced and subject to constant change and disruption. New areas of growth emerge, and others reach a plateau or wither.

Therefore, I look to get involved in recruiting into the emerging and higher growth markets.

Which means identifying the next big thing, catching the next wave and identifying new companies to approach, new decision-makers and making new approaches. Re-aligning what I do with the market and trends.

Reconnect

I'm married again now but when I was single I found that when I was feeling down it was easy to shut myself away from the world. When I reflect on my low points, I can see that I kind of withdrew from being pro-active about networking in the work side of my life and socialising in the private side of it.

If I was feeling unhappy, I didn't really want to have to see people and make the effort.

This isn't unique to me; other people have told me similar things and I've also noticed it in folk.

I came to realise that when I was down, I would be less inclined to seek out meetings with people in my work and set up social arrangements in my personal life.

When you're down and things aren't going your own way, it's possible to get lost.

What I've done to recover

Both in a social and professional context, it's easy to become withdrawn.

Whatever job you do, you need to be engaged with your work and the people you work with.

When I've been at a low point it's often been when I've not been making money, not been getting results and when my client base has run dry. There have been times like this when I've taken my eye off the ball and made the mistake of speaking to the same people about the same things.

The easy way for me to reconnect and pick back up has been to reach out to people in my network with whom perhaps I may not have spoken for some time.

I switch on my positive self, talk about positive things, ask about positive situations… come across as being a winner, happy, and shut out negativity.

These interactions help me feel better about myself.

They make me feel positive and as though I have taken the initiative to be proactive, and from a practical perspective often these people are my best source of leads.

Giving me easier, quicker victories and boosting my confidence.

With a greater self-esteem and flow, it puts me back in a mode of reaching out to people; I find it easier to reach out to new contacts client side, people with whom I'm unfamiliar, which is fundamental to success in my job.

Whether you're selling something or simply wanting to reconnect with your work and elevate your mood and performance in your job, I believe making a conscious effort to interact with people with whom you are familiar, and vice versa, helps to rebuild your self-confidence.

For me, it's all about discipline, focus and rediscovering self-belief.

It's not about you, it's about them.

Here's a final thought I'd like to share with you about my own experiences of overcoming nerves and anxieties in a working situation.

I came to realise that when I was stressed, feeling down and depressed, I also suffered a loss of confidence, which was an issue when meeting people, interviewing candidates, when meeting with multiple people in client situations

What I've done to recover

and if I was presenting or at an event.

I found that the best way to address this issue of being nervous and lacking confidence was to focus my attention on other people and what mattered most to them. I came up with my own little mental pick-me-up phrase "It's not about me, it's about them".

Giving me something to think about allowed me to focus on something other than being self-conscious and being overwhelmed by nerves.

Thinking about what's of importance to other people, how I can help them or how can what I am talking about help them, enables me to channel my nervous or negative energy into a positive approach.

Taking my mind off my own nerves by focusing 100% on the interests of other people.

What are the issues they face?

I believe that if you genuinely want to help people, this can be part of your job even if you are selling something or giving someone bad news; you can switch off or reduce your nerves by focusing on others. What's most important to them?

I find that in tuning into what's of interest to other people enables me to avoid getting consumed with my own nervous thoughts.

A final work note for you… think before you share.

The whole world of social interaction is quite new; how we interact with it is something we're all becoming increasingly familiar with. However, at times we really need to keep ourselves in check.

Act in haste, repent at leisure…

We need to think twice before we tweet.

A lot of people are posting stuff about their success, mood, emotions, predicament etc.

It's important that we think about the underlying messages which we are sending out on social media which could be mood induced and perhaps counter-productive.

On LinkedIn too many people and companies are too often sending out

What I've done to recover

arrogant messages that directly or indirectly say, "Look at me, I'm brilliant" or "My company is the best". Do this too often and people will think you're showing off.

Similarly, some people are sending out a repetitive set of negative messages such as "I can't find a job, please help me".

Do things like this and you'll look too desperate, too sad, too weak.

It's easy to post on social media about something without thinking about the underlying message/s we're sending out.

We all need to be careful if we are on a high when it's possible to be big headed about us or our company; it can be interpreted as being arrogant. Some people need to show more humility.

At the other end of the spectrum, if we are down, we need to make sure any negative messages we're sending out are not too excessive nor too frequent.

I appreciate I've kind of put it out there here in my book!

❉ ❉ ❉

Appendix 7
Great expectations

I've been talking about the ups and downs of life, mental health issues and some of my self-observations and observations of others.

When I look around me at the common problems people face, with the exception of physical or mental healthcare, what I see is that most of our problems come down to expectations of life.

Here's something for you to think about, and that is expectations.

We watch TV, the movies, see stuff on our phones, and many of our impressions are that life is going to be like it is in the movies: big houses, fast cars, health and beauty, a life which is always entertaining, happy, permanent employment, no money issues…

But it's not like that.

Our expectations are unrealistic, many of us need to re-set them and be more grateful for what we have got, for whom we have in our lives, loved ones, family, friends, for the beauty of the world…

Over several years, as I reflected on my situation and the unfortunate events, trauma and crises which had happened in my life, I came to realise that often I was feeling sorry for myself, blaming circumstances, events and everybody else, anybody except me. Now, I blame myself.

I've been married to my wife Alex for 3 years now, we've been together for 7… I am pleased that my love for her is unparalleled. The love which she gives me and which I give to her is something I wish everyone could enjoy.

It has depth. However, I loved my ex-wife Caroline and for so many years I have felt guilt that I let her down; I have a fondness for her to this day.

She was a complex character, who had some fabulous qualities: funny, insightful, vibrant, quick witted, absolutely loved animals and was an avid supporter of animal welfare, in particular the Born Free Foundation and the Brooke Hospital for Sick Animals.

If you've read this story fully, you'll realise some of the contradictory feelings I

Great expectations

have for her, she was a remarkable person. This book is dedicated to Caroline, whom I miss dearly. Life can be very cruel, she died before her time. Even though I split up with her and she was a difficult personality, the grief which I have experienced has been spectacular.

In addition to Caroline being my wife, she was my partner in business and boy oh boy was she good.

In this book I've said quite a lot of things about her which are negative, but she had her good points.

Like each and every one of us, Caroline was imperfect.

If you have suffered the loss of a loved one or are facing serious problems, my heart goes out to you.

There is an expression, death is crushing to the ones it leaves behind.

Some of my issues may be similar to your own, and some of the techniques I've used to recover and return to my successful ways will also work for you.

My situation is somewhat unusual; I work for myself, my income is largely commission only, subject to high peaks and troughs, and getting paid can take three to six months. It's precarious, and there are a lot of moving parts.

I do believe that when you're facing crisis and emotional turmoil, it's not good to spend most of your time by yourself, and we live in an era when more and more people work from home.

I have chosen to work from an office in a business centre which places me in the company of others, and when I observe other people, I can relate to the isolation of working solo from home (having previously done it myself) and how this can manifest itself in suffering sadness, depression, anxiety and stress; it can be mentally crushing.

I think we need to be self-aware and socially aware of the loneliness we can experience but which we don't share.

If you're suffering stress, anxiety and depression you're not alone.

Grown men cry in the shower. We just don't want to talk about it.

I'm not the only guy who's had problems.

If you were in my shoes, you'd observe the lives of a lot of people with sad

Great expectations

stories. One man told me how his life had fallen apart. He was in his early fifties and had worked hard all his life to support his wife and children. He came home one day and found his wife in bed with another man.

He felt destroyed, emotionally and financially, but eventually brought his life back to a successful and happy chapter. He told me how his father had said how proud he was of him for keeping himself together mentally, to which he replied:

"You didn't see me crying in the shower".

It's unrealistic to think that you can travel through life without encountering some crisis in your work and/or home life.

As you look around you, you will see people who are like swans. On the surface, they seem calm, but underneath it all there's a lot going on.

I have thought long and hard about putting my mental healthcare issues down on paper before deciding to do so. The theme of this book covers the ups and downs of life, and the feelings of a man.

I'm not saying don't talk to people about your problems, but make sure you talk with the right people, ones with whom your conversation won't compromise your work interests.

You may wish to think twice before deciding who to talk to.

For example, talk to a friend if you have one whom you are comfortable to confide in, or talk with a counsellor or, if appropriate, someone in HR.

One of the merits of seeing a counsellor is that it is 100% confidential, it's private and you can tell them anything.

That's what I've done when I've been beaten down by life. I went to see a counsellor. Giving me someone to talk to, it's helped me to calm down and de-stress.

In general, guys don't want to talk to other men about their problems, anxieties or the state of their mental health. It's not seen as a masculine thing to do; it makes them feel weak. And they don't want to talk to women about it either as they think it emasculates them.

I feel as though I have encountered one trauma after another, but I have always recovered, I have always found a way through; and having financially hit rock

Great expectations

bottom several years ago, have since proceeded to have my best billings month ever, and I have come to find deeper personal happiness.

I have learned to better recognise difficulties in advance, in particular stress and anxiety, the circumstances in which these may arise, and how to make adjustments sooner to avoid problems.

The techniques which I have outlined have worked for me and I have been able to repeat them. I believe they'll work well for you too.

I sincerely hope you've enjoyed my story and these appendices, and perhaps in reading about me and my life so far it may help you directly or in your relationships with others.

Best wishes

Robert

✱✱✱✱✱✱

Printed in Great Britain
by Amazon